COPPER WORKERS, INTERNATIONAL BUSINESS, AND **DOMESTIC POLITICS** IN **COLD WAR CHILE**

ANGELA VERGARA

COPPER WORKERS,
INTERNATIONAL BUSINESS,
AND DOMESTIC POLITICS
IN COLD WAR CHILE

The Pennsylvania State University Press
University Park, Pennsylvania

Library of Congress Cataloging-in-Publication Data

Vergara, Angela, 1972– .
   Copper workers, international business, and domestic politics in
     Cold War Chile / Angela Vergara.
        p.   cm.
Summary: "Traces the history of the labor movement in Chile through the experiences of copper miners employed by the Anaconda Copper Company from 1945 to 1990. Covers the economic, political, and social history of the 45-year period when the Cold War dominated Chilean politics"—Provided by publisher.
Includes bibliographical references and index.
ISBN 978-0-271-03335-8 (pbk : alk. paper)
1. Chile—Politics and government—1920–1970.
2. Chile—Politics and government—1970–1973.
3. Copper miners—Chile—History—20th century.
4. Copper miners—Labor unions—Chile.
5. Cold War—Influence.
I. Title.

F3099.V38 2008
331.88′122343098309045—dc22
                        2007047238

Copyright © 2008 The Pennsylvania State University
All rights reserved
Printed in the United States of America
Published by The Pennsylvania State University Press,
University Park, PA 16802-1003

The Pennsylvania State University Press is a member of the Association of American University Presses.

It is the policy of The Pennsylvania State University Press to use acid-free paper. This book is printed on stock that meets the minimum requirements of American National Standard for Information Sciences—Permanence of Paper for Printed Library Material, ANSI Z39.48–1992.

ANGELA VERGARA

COPPER WORKERS,
INTERNATIONAL BUSINESS,
AND DOMESTIC POLITICS
IN COLD WAR CHILE

The Pennsylvania State University Press
University Park, Pennsylvania

Library of Congress Cataloging-in-Publication Data

Vergara, Angela, 1972– .
   Copper workers, international business, and domestic politics in
    Cold War Chile / Angela Vergara.
       p.   cm.
Summary: "Traces the history of the labor movement in Chile through the experiences of copper miners employed by the Anaconda Copper Company from 1945 to 1990. Covers the economic, political, and social history of the 45-year period when the Cold War dominated Chilean politics"—Provided by publisher.
Includes bibliographical references and index.
ISBN 978-0-271-03335-8 (pbk : alk. paper)
1. Chile—Politics and government—1920–1970.
2. Chile—Politics and government—1970–1973.
3. Copper miners—Chile—History—20th century.
4. Copper miners—Labor unions—Chile.
5. Cold War—Influence.
I. Title.

F3099.V38 2008
331.88′122343098309045—dc22
                               2007047238

Copyright © 2008 The Pennsylvania State University
All rights reserved
Printed in the United States of America
Published by The Pennsylvania State University Press,
University Park, PA 16802-1003

The Pennsylvania State University Press is a member of the Association of American University Presses.

It is the policy of The Pennsylvania State University Press to use acid-free paper. This book is printed on stock that meets the minimum requirements of American National Standard for Information Sciences—Permanence of Paper for Printed Library Material, ANSI Z39.48–1992.

TO CHILEAN COPPER WORKERS
AND THEIR FAMILIES

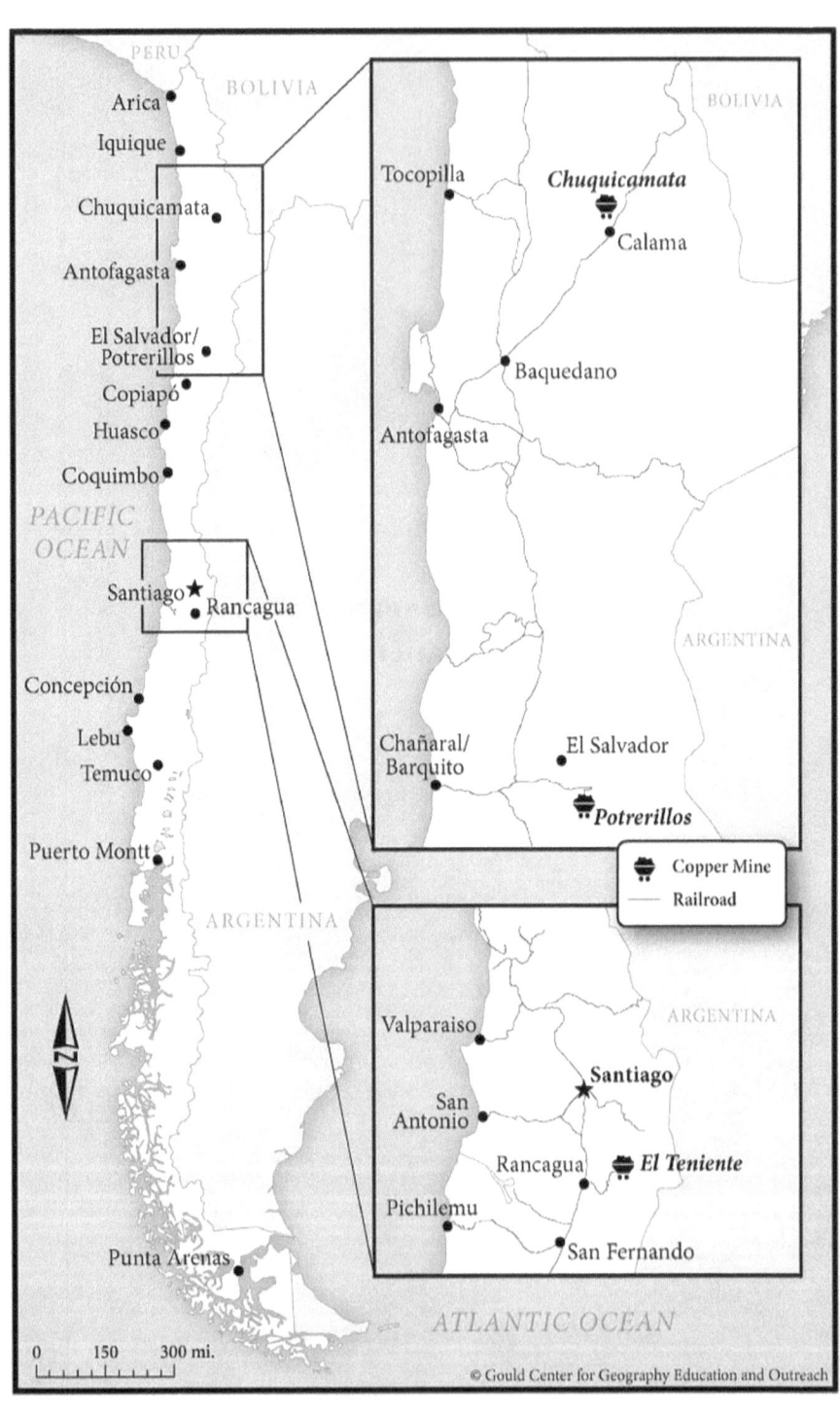

CONTENTS

ILLUSTRATIONS AND TABLES		ix
ACKNOWLEDGMENTS		xi
	Introduction	1
1	From Montana to Potrerillos	13
2	The World of Labor	37
3	Copper, Labor, and Political Repression, 1945–1952	65
4	Making a New Deal: Copper Laws, Modernization, and Workers' Rights, 1955–1958	93
5	Nationalism and Radicalization, 1958–1970	127
6	Experiencing Nationalization and Socialism, 1970–1973	155
	Epilogue: Repression, Economic Transformations, and the Struggle for Democracy, 1973–1990s	179
	Conclusion	195
BIBLIOGRAPHY		199
INDEX		213

ILLUSTRATIONS AND TABLES

Figures

1. Andes Copper advertisement, example 1	98
2. Andes Copper advertisement, example 2	99
3. Poster of lazy well-fed man versus hardworking man	115
4. Poster illustrating the consequences of lethargy versus hard work	116
5. Poster of broken machines resulting in wasted time	117
6. El Salvador's aeriel view	121

Tables

1. Average annual copper production per company (thousands of metric tons), 1925–1969	19
2. Andes Copper general managers, 1917–1971	28
3. Andes Copper's camps population, 1941	40
4. Population and housing availability in Andes Copper camps, late 1960s	43
5. Labor force at Andes Copper, 1941–1970	51
6. Labor unions in Andes Copper Company and Potrerillos Railway Company	59
7. Consumer price index, 1950–1963	90
8. Andes Copper wage increases, 1959–1970	130
9. Strikes at Andes Copper Company, 1960–1969	131
10. Proposed layoffs in Potrerillos, El Salvador, and Barquito, December 1961	134
11. Presidential election, 1964, Potrerillos and El Salvador	146
12. Electoral results for Salvador Allende in mining electoral districts, 1952–1970	157
13. Copper production, 1970–1972 (metric tons)	159
14. Nationalized companies, 1972	161
15. Board of directors of Cobresal, 1972	165

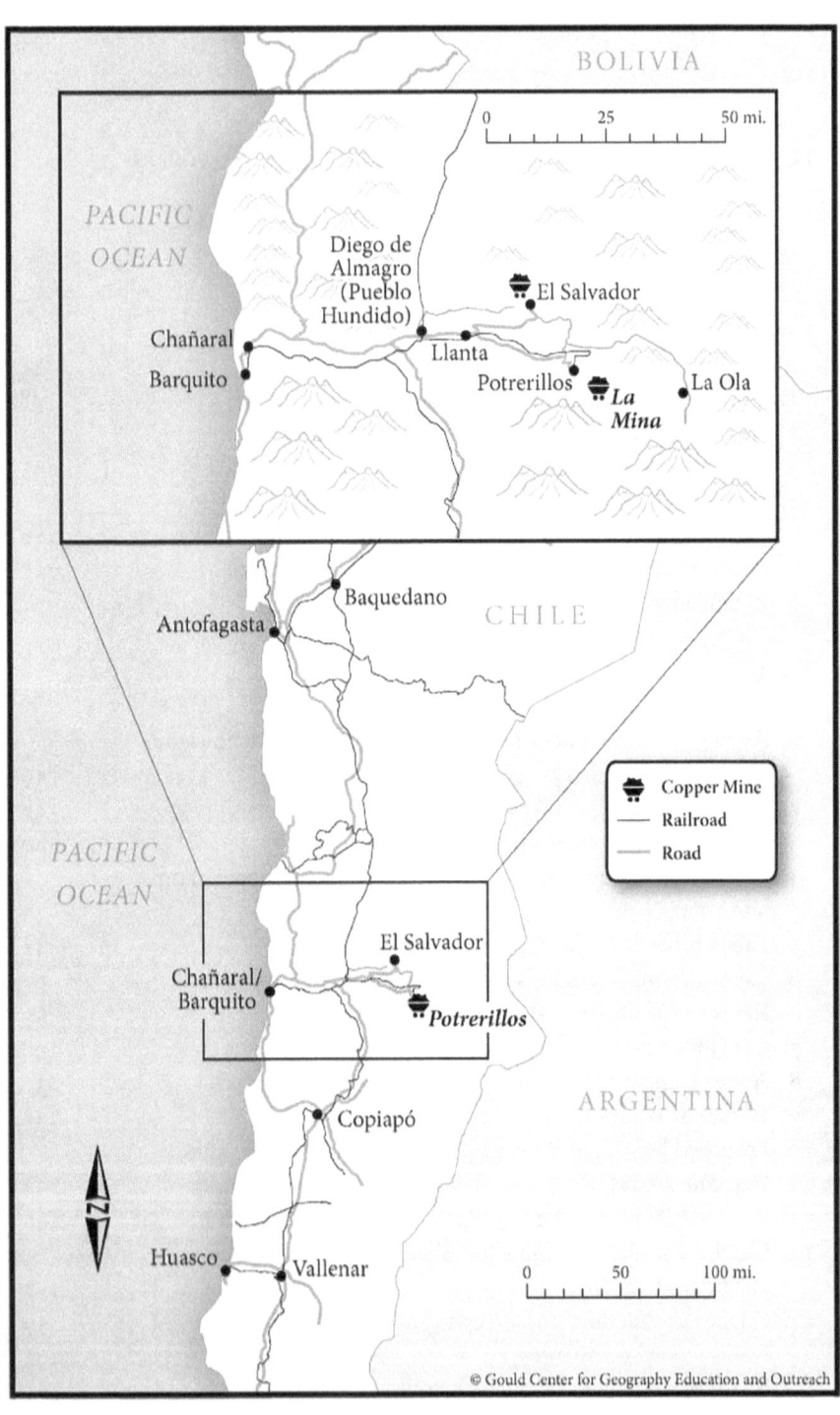

ACKNOWLEDGMENTS

Many people and institutions in Chile and in the United States helped make this project possible. While there are too many to recount them all here, I will mention a few. At the University of California, San Diego, I am especially grateful to Dain Borges for his questions, commentaries, support, and encouragement at all stages of this project. I also had the great opportunity to work with Paul Drake, who read several drafts and provided excellent commentaries. I would also like to thank Brian Loveman, Christine Hünefeldt, and Becky Nicolaides for their commentaries and encouragement. Brian Loveman read and edited several versions of this manuscript, and throughout the years I have continued learning from his extraordinary knowledge of Chilean history, politics, and law.

I am especially grateful for the financial support I received from the History Department and the Center for Latin American Studies and Iberian Studies at the University of California, San Diego. I also am grateful for the research grant I received from the University of Texas Pan American, the Bernard L. Majewski Research Fellowship at the American Heritage Center at the University of Wyoming, and a Summer Visiting Scholars Research Grant at the University of Chicago.

Librarians and archivists provided invaluable assistance: Ellie Arguimbaou from the Montana Historical Society; Patrizia Sione at the Kheel Center, Cornell; Oscar Monroy at the Biblioteca Pública Chañaral; the staff at the George Meany Memorial Archives; the staff at the Federación de Trabajadores del Cobre; and the always friendly staff at Archivo Siglo XX (Archivo Nacional de la Administración Central del Estado) and Salón Fundadores at the Biblioteca Nacional. Juan Beltrán from la Dirección del Trabajo facilitated access to the documents stored at the Inspección del Trabajo in Santiago, and Oscar Giraux from the Inspección del Trabajo in Copiapó contacted me with many of the union leaders at El Salvador. Eduardo Loyola from Codelco-Chile invited me to visit El Salvador and Chuquicamata, and Juan Guerra, José Borcosque, and Iván Ardiles from Codelco-División

El Salvador warmly received me in El Salvador, made sure I understood how copper was produced, and facilitated my research stay. Rodrigo Vargas from the División El Salvador facilitated the reproduction of images from *Andino*. My cousin, Rosa Vergara, collected the electoral data, and Francisco Carrasco, my research assistant in Chile, helped tie together numerous loose ends at the end of the project.

Several people read drafts and conference papers that later became chapters and answered many of my questions. The feedback, questions, commentaries, and conversations were always motivating and useful. I thank Trinidad Gonzales, Tom Klubock, Jody Pavilack, Julio Pinto, Rafael Sagredo, Joel Stillerman, Jeff Strickland, and Francisco Zapata. Peter Winn and Karin Rosemblatt provided very useful and clear commentaries and suggestions on how to improve my first draft. Thanks also to Sandy Thatcher and Kristin Peterson at Penn State University Press for their editorial assistance, to Romaine Perin for her copyediting, and to Erin Greb for drawing the maps. Figure illustrations appear courtesy of Codelco Chile División

Friends and family have made this book possible. My friends from graduate school have provided constant support and encouragement; special thanks to Fred Dick, Gabriela Soto-Laveaga, Ken Maffitt, Elena Songster, and Adam Warren. My mother, Teresa Marshall, taught me to "finish what you start"; gave me an excellent education; and, when I started my research, became enthusiastic about the history of El Salvador and Potrerillos. My father, Francisco Vergara, taught me how to read and later to love Chilean history and especially working people's history. Camilo arrived when I was printing the first entire draft of this manuscript. As he learned how to walk and talk, he took special care of my research files, rearranging and coloring them in original ways. I am especially in debt to Mike, to his love, good humor, encouragement, and support. He edited the entire manuscript more than once, and he never lost interest in it. He always enjoyed talking about the history of copper workers and the history of Chile, and his knowledge of the labor movement and experience with collective bargaining were always extremely useful. This book would have never been possible without all the people who shared their stories, memories, and knowledge. I thank, among many others, Adam Durton, Jaime Estévez, Jim Feeney, Cristián Gálvez, Francisco Lira, Ricardo Ponce, Guido Soriano, Ramón Silva Ulloa, William Thayer, Edwin Trench, Manuel Trigo, and Hugo Yánez.

Introduction

On July 11, 1971, Chile nationalized its large-scale copper industry.[1] President Salvador Allende celebrated this extraordinary event in the southern city of Rancagua, near the El Teniente mine, the largest underground copper mine in the world. In a speech he gave for the occasion, he restated the importance of copper for the country and the responsibility of copper workers in sustaining the national economy and the revolutionary process under way in the country. Until his tragic death in September 1973, he would constantly remark that copper was the "wage of Chile" (*el sueldo de Chile*) and that the nationalization of copper would lead the country toward its economic independence. "Fellow miners," he declared in Rancagua, "strong workers of the red metal: once again I have to remind you that copper is the wage of Chile like the land is its bread. With their revolutionary consciousness, peasants are going to supply the bread of Chile. The future of our homeland, the wage of Chile, is in your hands. To work more, to produce more, to defend the revolution from the political point of view of the Popular Unity [coalition] and to defend the revolution with the production that will support the government of the people."[2]

As Allende clearly understood, copper was twentieth-century Chile's most important commodity. In the 1960s, the material supplied nearly 80 percent of Chile's foreign exchange and more than 20 percent of the state's income.[3] However, until 1971, Chilean copper was controlled by

---

1. *Large-scale copper industry* was a legal term used in the second half of the twentieth century. It refers to foreign-owned copper mines producing more than twenty-five thousand tons of copper a year.
2. Salvador Allende, "En el día de la nacionalizacón del cobre," in *Su pensamiento político* (Santiago: Quimantú, 1972), 187.
3. Patricio Meller, *Un siglo de economía política chilena (1890–1990)* (Santiago: Editorial Andrés Bello, 1996), 32–36.

U.S. corporations and its marketing shaped by international forces beyond the control of the country. Many Chileans believed that their dependence on the international market and foreign capital was increasing the nation's economic instability and causing its endemic inflation. In 1958, in his influential book *En vez de la miseria*, Chilean economist Jorge Ahumada argued: "The Chilean economy tends to be very unstable because exports fluctuate greatly. Exports are unstable because they are made up of 60 percent of copper, a product for which demand changes violently and frequently."[4] The central role of copper in the national economy and the perception that there was a pervasive relationship between foreign ownership and economic instability made the production, taxation, and ownership of copper mines a highly political and contested issue in modern Chile.

In 1971, President Allende also recognized the critical economic and political influence of copper workers and made efforts to incorporate them into the nationalization process. As a senator and presidential candidate, he had visited the copper camps and was familiar with the activism and radicalism of copper workers. He met with copper workers in February 1971 during a meeting of the Copper Workers Confederation to discuss the implications and directions of the nationalization and the peaceful revolution that he had proclaimed on taking office. Accordingly, the slogan of the nationalization effort specifically recognized the importance of workers in making nationalization of copper a reality: "With the effort of its workers, the capacity of its technicians, and the support of all the people, the nationalization means that Chile comes of age" [se pone pantalones largos].[5]

Allende, however, underestimated or decided to ignore the copper workers' complex reality and demands, and he faced challenging labor conflicts in the mines. A strike in the El Teniente mine, from April to June 1973, shortly preceding the military coup that ousted Allende, on September 11, 1973, considerably weakened the government and aggravated Chile's internal political and economic crisis. By expecting copper workers to give up their demands for economic improvement, Allende ignored the role that high wages played in the copper industry. From within the leading sector of the national economy, copper workers organized one of the most powerful and successful union movements in the country. Through local and national strikes, their unions improved conditions for members and

---

4. Jorge Ahumada, *En vez de la miseria* (Santiago: Editorial del Pacífico, 1965), 68.
5. *Atacama* (Copiapó), 10 July 1971.

gained a voice in the debate about copper and nationalization. The workers earned some of the best salaries in the country. But behind good material conditions and political influence lay the harsh reality of mining copper in the Chilean Andes. Production of the element was a dangerous, difficult, and backbreaking job. The large-scale copper industry employed more than twelve thousand people, who lived and worked in isolated, high-altitude, foreign-owned camps. Workers were entitled to free housing and a wide range of social benefits, but most blue-collar miners' homes lacked private bathrooms and there was no high school in the towns. Copper workers suffered chronic occupational diseases and had a short life expectancy; moreover, accidents were frequent in the mines and plants. The extreme contrast between the prosperity of copper companies and workers' everyday lives and the gap between miners' salaries in Chile and in the United States encouraged and legitimated Chilean miners' demands for economic improvement.

In this book I explore the history of copper workers by looking at the living and working conditions of the workers and the sociopolitical aspects of copper production. The study focuses on one particular complex of mines and plants, Potrerillos and El Salvador, from the end of World War II to Chile's transition to democracy in the early 1990s. Potrerillos and El Salvador are located in the province of Chañaral, in the southern part of the Atacama Desert, on the western slope of the Andes. At an altitude of seven thousand feet, Potrerillos and El Salvador have few water resources, almost no vegetation, and a high-desert climate. After its copper was depleted, Potrerillos was replaced in 1959 by the El Salvador mine, thirty miles away. From 1917 to 1971, the mines were owned by the Andes Copper Company, a subsidiary of the Anaconda Copper Company, then among the three largest copper corporations in the world. Since the nationalization of copper in 1971, the mines have been owned by the Corporación del Cobre (CODELCO), a state-owned copper corporation.

The history of Potrerillos and El Salvador was shaped by complex negotiations and conflicts between labor, foreign capital, and the national state. At the local level, workers, management, and state authorities defined the organization of production and of living and working arrangements. At the national political level, copper labor unions demanded from the state and legislators changes in labor and social legislation. At the same time, U.S. copper corporations, the national state, and the Copper Workers Confederation discussed the directions of copper policies and the rights and obligations of foreign investors. These interactions were ultimately shaped by the international copper market and changes in world demand and supply of copper. By taking into account how these actors interacted at different levels, I seek to overcome the traditional division in copper historiography, between the local, labor history of copper workers and management and the political and economic history of the relationship between the state and copper companies.

The cases of Potrerillos and El Salvador demonstrate how the characteristics of a foreign-owned-company town created enormous tensions between workers and management and, eventually, the state. As in many mining and company towns around the world, management was responsible for providing basic services, among them housing, food, transportation, health care, and entertainment. Andes Copper segregated Chilean workers from foreign supervisors and established two separate payroll systems (dollars for U.S. managers and supervisors and local currency for Chilean workers). It also regarded the camp as private property, restricting the access of visitors and independent shopkeepers. The intersections of living and working spaces, the strong presence of the company in workers' daily lives, the company's efforts to control and shape the working community, the gap between foreign managers and Chilean workers, and urban segregation became the basis of a radical and nationalistic labor culture in these camps.

Oriented to the export market, life in Potrerillos and El Salvador was shaped by global economic changes and international conflicts. The world market suffered from chronic instability, affected by constant changes in demand and supply, the U.S. government's price ceilings during times of war, and competing commodities such as aluminum. Andes Copper reduced and increased production according to alterations in the international copper market, causing instability in jobs, social benefits, and state revenues. The company used the instability of copper prices to reject workers' demands for economic improvement and to contest the efforts of the Chilean state to increase taxation. However, the contradictions of Chilean democracy and limitations of the domestic economy influenced workers' lives and politics throughout the twentieth century. While inflation and stabilization programs threatened working people's income and economic security, shifts in national politics limited workers' political rights.

Copper workers adapted to and contested these forces, transforming their own realities, the companies' production strategies, and the history of the nation. Workers strived not only to improve their material conditions, but also to redefine the structure of copper production and Chile's social, economic, and political development. These two efforts—improvement of economic conditions and larger political and national claims—were entangled in such complex ways in workers' everyday lives, discourse, and ideology that they cannot be separated.

In this book I trace the history of copper workers through three distinctive periods in Chilean and copper mining history: Chilean traditional democracy and foreign ownership of the copper industry (1945–70), Popular Unity and nationalization of copper (1970–73), and military dictatorship and state ownership of the copper industry (1973–90). In doing so, I explore the changes, transformations, and continuities in workers' rights, identity, collective power, and material conditions throughout these five critical decades of the twentieth century. From a larger perspective, this local history of copper workers becomes a window into the modern transformation of Chile as it experimented with and lived through very different political, economic, and social models of development.

Between the end of World War II and 1970, copper camps were union towns, copper was the most important export commodity, and foreign companies produced 90 percent of the country's copper. At the local level, the intersections of the workplace and the community increased the legitimacy of labor unions and expanded unions' responsibilities in social and daily activities. In Potrerillos, for example, local unions financed summer camps for children in the area; sponsored Christmas parties; and maintained restaurants, barber shops, libraries, and radio stations. The strength of unionism was especially visible during strikes, when the entire community participated on the picket line and the few strikebreakers (called *krumiros*) were often left naked and covered with chicken feathers in the middle of town. The growing economic importance of copper in the Chilean economy consolidated the political influence and economic power of the copper workers' unions. Yet their power was constrained by the unsolved contradictions of Chilean democracy, specifically in the cycles of inflation and stabilization policies and in the tensions between the expansion of democracy and the periodic repression of popular and labor movements.

Between 1970 and 1973, workers attempted to overcome their traditional dependency on management and Chile's dependency on foreign copper companies. Following Salvador Allende's presidential election victory in September 1970, workers joined the ambitious project of nationalizing the copper industry, democratizing local social and urban services, and redefining labor relations. It was an extremely difficult and conflict-laden process, conditioned by embedded labor practices, a national economic crisis, political polarization, and U.S. sanctions against Chilean copper and the Chilean economy. The Popular Unity coalition challenged the image of copper workers as radicals and revolutionaries, exposing the tensions that existed in the copper industry and the social, political, and regional divisions within the copper workers' labor movement.

Following the military coup of 1973, this traditional industrial community began to disintegrate. Repression rapidly demobilized workers, facilitating the imposition of economic policies and laws that destroyed union influence and hard-won gains in the workplace. For the following seventeen years, an authoritarian state company replaced the socialist project of nationalization and reestablished many of the old labor practices. The traditional argument that workers' benefits were a heavy load for an industry trying to be competitive in the international market was the basis for the attack on workers' gains. In the 1980s, copper workers reorganized, but they were unable to overturn the dramatic transformation of their industry. Beginning in the 1990s, neoliberal-inspired economic policies and the effects of intensified globalization introduced new challenges, such as dismantling of mining towns, flexibilization of employment conditions, reorganization of working shifts (twelve-hour shifts), and the threat of privatization. Today (2006), the El Salvador mine is becoming too expensive to exploit and authorities have announced plans to the close it by 2010.

Copper Workers and Labor History

Despite the importance of copper and copper workers in Chilean history, their history remains incomplete. In the 1970s, Chilean scholars Jorge Barría, Manuel Barrera, and Francisco Zapata published the first serious studies on Chilean copper workers. Barría, a labor historian, carefully studied the institutional aspects of labor unions in the copper industry between 1956 and 1966, showing how copper labor unions successfully combined labor laws, direct action, political alliances, and trade solidarity to improve local conditions. Barrera and Zapata, by contrast, emphasized the unique characteristics and status of copper workers as an "isolated mass," an occupational community, and underlined workers' location in a strategic and export-oriented industry. They sought to explain the controversial political role and bargaining agenda of copper workers. Geographical isolation, harsh living and working conditions, and heavy dependence on the company created solidarity among workers, intensified labor conflicts and strikes, and inspired deep-rooted anti-imperialist ideas.[6] While Barrera emphasized the notion of an economic enclave and isolation to understand the activism of copper workers, Zapata focused on the relationship between local conditions and a pragmatic union agenda that prioritized immediate demands over larger political claims.

In the late 1990s, U.S. scholars began looking at copper workers through the lens of community and working-class formation. Thomas Klubock focused on the construction of a working-class community in the copper mine of El Teniente during the first half of the twentieth century. By looking at labor migration; the experience of work; the role of women; the characteristics of the community; and corporate labor, welfare, and gender discourse, Klubock explained the emergence of a distinctive collective identity and a militant union movement. By shifting the analysis from the union hall to the community, Klubock shows the complexity of gender relations and the emergence of a local community as it negotiated and adapted to the demands of capital and the state.[7] The work of anthropologist Janet Finn complements this study by showing the construction of a cohesive and vocal labor community in the open-pit Chuquicamata mine in connection with the unique characteristics of living conditions, the company's welfare and gender policies, and patterns of labor recruitment. Finn also demonstrates the interrelationship between events in Chuquicamata and Anaconda's most important mine in the United States, at Butte, Montana.[8]

The scholarship of the 1970s effectively explained some of the unique aspects of living and working conditions in the copper industry and the ways in which these shaped the agenda of the unions. It tended, however, to provide a picture of the copper mines and copper workers as isolated from the rest of the country and the world. It also gave a very homogenous view of the Chilean side of the copper camps, disregarding the divisions within the community and the distinctive experiences of men and women

---

6. Manuel Barrera, *El conflicto obrero en el enclave cuprífero* (Santiago: Universidad de Chile, 1973); Jorge Barría, *Los sindicatos de la Gran Minería del Cobre* (Santiago: INSORA, 1970); Francisco Zapata, *Los mineros de Chuquicamata ¿Productores o proletarios?* (Mexico City: Colegio de México, 1975).

7. Thomas M. Klubock, *Contested Communities: Class, Gender, and Politics in El Teniente's Copper Mine, 1904–1951* (Durham: Duke University Press, 1998).

8. Janet Leigh Finn, *Tracing the Veins: Of Copper, Culture, and Community from Butte to Chuquicamata* (Berkeley and Los Angeles: University of California Press, 1998).

and of blue-collar and white-collar workers. Thomas Klubock and Janet Finn filled many of these gaps, especially by acknowledging the role of women. Yet many questions remain unanswered. How did this community, formed in the first half of the twentieth century, evolve in the second half? How did changes in Chile's political, social, and economic structure shape life and politics in the copper mines? How did changes in the postwar international copper market affect local conditions? How did copper workers in the post–World War II decades influence the history of their industry and Chile?

Influenced by recent research and debates on the Latin American export sector, labor, and globalization, this book integrates the local history of workers in Potrerillos and El Salvador into the larger history of the global copper market and copper consumption, U.S. imperialism, and the Chilean national state.[9] This case study suggests a need to expand our analysis from the ways in which the international and national forces affected the lives of working people to how local communities shaped corporations' strategies. Mining families and union members in Potrerillos and El Salvador transformed the decisions and production strategies of Andes Copper, forcing it to incorporate workers' demands, throughout the second half of the twentieth century, a period usually disregarded by labor historians studying Chile. In addressing the events of this time, I shift the debate from the process of working-class formation to the identity, struggles, and politics of a mature proletarian labor force.[10] I returns to the union hall to understand the ways in which workers collectively undertook the

---

9. See, for example, Steve Striffler, ed., *Banana Wars: Power, Production, and History in the Americas* (Durham: Duke University Press, 2003); Steven Topik, Carlos Marichal, and Zephyr Frank eds., *From Silver to Cocaine: Latin American Commodity Chains and the Building of the World Economy* (Durham: Duke University Press, 2006).

10. Among the labor historians who have addressed the second half of the twentieth century are Franck Gaudichaud, *Poder popular y cordones industriales: Testimonios sobre el movimiento popular urbano, 1970–1973* (Santiago: LOM, 2004); Brian Loveman, *Struggle in the Countryside: Politics and Rural Labor in Chile, 1919–1973* (Bloomington: Indiana University Press, 1976); Joann C. Pavilack, "Black Gold in the Red Zone: Repression and Contention in Chilean Coal Mining Communities from the Popular Front to the Advent of the Cold War" (Ph.D. diss., Duke University 2003); Heidi Tinsman, *Partners in Conflict: The Politics of Gender, Sexuality, and Labor in the Chilean Agrarian Reform, 1950–1973* (Durham: Duke University Press, 2002); Joel Stillerman, "From Solidarity to Survival: Transformations in the Culture and Style of Mobilization of Chilean Metalworkers Under Democratic and Authoritarian Regimes, 1945–1995" (Ph.D. diss., New School for Social Research, 1998); Peter Winn, *Weavers of the Revolution: The Yarur Workers and Chile's Road to Socialism* (New York: Oxford University Press, 1986).

challenge of improving local conditions, shaping the national debate, and overcoming the impact of international forces.

The identity and history of copper workers were especially complex because these workers negotiated three unique experiences: participating in the export and foreign-owned sector of the economy, identifying collectively as Chilean blue-collar workers, and being male as well as mine workers. These three experiences became the basis of a collective identity that emphasized economic nationalism, an aggressive collective bargaining tradition, a pragmatic and independent political agenda, a demand for the incorporation of the "working class" in the national political and economic debate, and strong trade union solidarity.

Chilean copper miners worked in an export-oriented, foreign-owned company. As historian Charles Bergquist argues, workers in the Latin American export sector had a tremendous impact on the political and economic history of their countries. Their influence, he explains, was conditioned by the particular characteristics of each export industry, such as the nationality of the company (foreign or national capital), capital investment, use of technology, and the impact of the cycles of boom and bust.[11] In the case of Chilean copper workers, the foreign ownership of the industry and a dual pay system (dollar and local currency) helped to consolidate a discourse in which the demand for labor rights intertwined with calls for economic nationalism and an anti-imperialist ideology, this nationalism reinforced by the development of a (politically and economically) dependent relationship between Chile and the United States. Their special status as export workers also led them to develop unique relationships with international labor organizations.

But copper workers' identity and politics were also conditioned by their experiences as Chilean workers. Three important characteristics of modern Chilean democracy had an especially strong impact on copper workers: embedded inflation, institutionalization of labor relations, and the state's ineffectual enforcement of labor rights. Inflation, a result of combined structural forces (for example, dependence on the export market, stagnation of national agriculture), government spending habits, monetary policy and emissions, and wage policies, was a constant threat to working people's income. The institutionalization of labor relations, the high participation of

---

11. Charles Bergquist, *Labor in Latin America: Comparative Essays on Chile, Argentina, Venezuela, and Colombia* (Stanford: Stanford University Press, 1986).

the state in regulating labor conditions and mediating labor conflicts, and the relative independence of labor unions from the state and political parties shaped the ways in which labor unions approached collective bargaining and solved local conflicts. Yet the state's commitment to guaranteeing workers' rights was inconsistent, and through special legislation and force, the state attempted to control, repress, and co-opt the labor movement.[12]

In the mines, Potrerillanos and Salvadoreños experienced the daily risks of mining copper at an altitude of seven thousand feet. Large-scale mining is unique because it combines a heavily industrial mode of work, a system of life and work isolated from major urban centers, and a strong dependency on unpredictable natural forces. Copper miners worked in dusty underground tunnels, crushing plants, and hot smelters, constantly exposed to toxic fumes and the risk of accidents. The characteristics of the industry forced them to live in isolated company towns, under geographical and extreme weather conditions, and dependent on the company's services. Geologists could only guess at the life expectancy of the mine and the quality of the ore, and miners speculated about when and how the future depletion of the mine would eventually destroy their way of life. Like many miners around the world, Chilean miners were proud of their work, physical strength, and manhood.[13] They challenged the unpredictable character of nature and tested their own lungs by entering the mountain and digging its ore. Inside the mine, they joked, teased one another, and challenged traditional job hierarchies. They were superstitious and respectful of nature and resisted—until the late twentieth century—the entrance of

---

12. Alan Angell, *Politics and the Labour Movement in Chile* (London: Oxford University Press, 1972); Ruth Berins Collier and David Collier, *Shaping the Political Arena: Critical Junctures, the Labor Movement, and Regime Dynamics in Latin America* (Princeton: Princeton University Press, 1991).

13. On mining and miners' culture in the Americas, see Heraclio Bonilla, *El minero de los Andes: Una aproximación a su estudio* (Lima: Instituto de Estudios Peruanos, 1974); Carlos Contreras, *Mineros y campesinos en los Andes* (Lima: Instituto de Estudios Peruanos, 1987); Adrian DeWind, *Peasants Become Miners: The Evolution of Industrial Mining Systems in Peru, 1902–1974* (New York: Garland, 1987); David Emmons, *The Butte Irish: Class and Ethnicity in an American Mining Town, 1875–1925* (Urbana: University of Illinois Press, 1989); Alberto Flores Galindo, *Los mineros de la Cerro de Pasco, 1900–1930: Un intento de caracterización social* (Lima: Universidad Católica de Lima, 1974); Thomas Greaves and William Culver, eds., *Miners and Mining in the Americas* (London: Manchester University Press, 1985); Mary Murphy, *Mining Cultures: Men, Women, and Leisure in Butte, 1914–1941* (Urbana: University of Illinois Press, 1997); June Nash, *We Eat the Mines and the Mines Eat Us: Dependency and Exploitation in Bolivian Tin Mines* (New York: Columbia University Press, 1979); Juan Luis Sariego, *Enclaves y minerales en el norte de México. Historia social de los mineros de Cananea y Nueva Rosita, 1900–1970* (Mexico City: CIESAS, 1988).

women into the mine. Outside, a mining culture characterized by heavy drinking, promiscuity, gambling, and consumerism mixed with strong solidarity, union activities, and political commitments.

This book tells the story of Chilean miners in Potrerillos and El Salvador, their struggles at the local and national level as they made efforts to improve their living and working conditions and expand their rights. In Chapter 1, I describe the Anaconda Copper Company's decision to invest in Chile, the construction of the Potrerillos mine, and the formation of a foreign community in the Chilean Andes. Arguing that the transnational dimension of capital shaped production and marketing decisions at the local level, I address the structure of capital and the relationship between Anaconda and its subsidiary Andes Copper. The focus of Chapter 2 is the working community in Potrerillos, specifically how the structure of that company town and unionization shaped the living, working, and political experiences of its copper workers.

The subsequent chapters are organized chronologically. Chapter 3 covers 1945–53, a time of crisis in the Potrerillos mine and of political repression directed against the Communist Party and the wider Left in the country. The instability of the international copper market, the crisis of Chilean copper, the depletion of Potrerillos, and state repression restricted workers' resources and opportunities for economic improvement. Potrerillos workers experienced intense labor conflicts, economic hardship, and both political and labor repression. They adapted to these forces of change by distancing themselves from the Communist Party, establishing a relationship with the U.S. labor movement, and negotiating with state authorities.

In Chapter 4, I analyze the beginnings of a new era, in the relationship between workers, foreign capital, and the state. In 1955, the Chilean government offered copper companies tax breaks in exchange for increased production and investment. Taking advantage of this favorable investment climate, Andes Copper launched the El Salvador Project. It built a new mine to replace the depleted Potrerillos mine and a modern camp to house the labor force. The following year, in an attempt to reduce conflict in the copper mines and control the militant working class, President Carlos Ibáñez approved the Statute of Copper Workers of 1956.

The impact of economic nationalism, high labor costs, persistent labor tensions, and an unstable national economy on the company's production scheme are the subject of Chapter 5. Responding to the challenges of the 1960s, Andes Copper increased investment, modernized its facilities, and introduced new technological advances. An important component of this wave of modernization was mechanization and automation. In an attempt to gain flexibility and reduce labor costs, the company hired large numbers of private contractors for construction and maintenance. Similarly, national pressures and labor costs provoked copper companies to reduce their foreign staff members. The social and labor consequences of management schemes led to intense confrontation with labor unions, eventually undermining the company's position in the country.

Chapter 6 concentrates on the period of the Popular Unity coalition (1970–73). I analyzes the process of nationalization by looking at workers' participation in the industry, labor relations, and living conditions. Although nationalization of the copper industry was a long-standing workers' demand, and workers in Potrerillos were highly committed to its success, there were serious conflicts. I explore the tensions in the copper mines resulting from conflicts born of the legacies of the social and labor system constructed by foreign corporations; the problematic transition from a private to a state, socialist company; national problems such as economic crisis and the violent politicization and polarization of Chilean society; and international pressures. A description of developments in the copper mines since the military coup of 1973 is presented in the epilogue.

Copper workers have been influential in the modern history of Chile. They not only produced the "wage of Chile," they also strove for the expansion of labor rights, the nationalization of copper, and the return of democracy. Their story is key to understanding the ways in which labor has shaped the history of Chile; they played a part not only as victims of models of economic growth, undemocratic political institutions, and imperialism, but also as active participants in contesting, negotiating, and making their own history and that of Chile.

1 ★ From Montana to Potrerillos

Copper was one of the most important mining commodities in the international market of the twentieth century. Produced in remote geographical areas, from the Sonoran Desert to the Chilean Andes, it rapidly became a valuable raw material for the burgeoning electrical and war industries. In the first two decades of the century, U.S. corporations dominated the market, displacing small-scale producers throughout the world and concentrating production in a few hands. By 1945, the "Big Three" (Anaconda, Phelps Dodge, and Kennecott) were producing 80 percent of U.S. copper and struggling to monopolize production, control the market from "mine to consumer"—using an old phrase of Anaconda's—and manipulate world supply and price. Despite their efforts, the international market suffered from chronic instability, affected by constant shifts in demand and supply, U.S. government price ceilings during wartime, and pressures from competing commodities such as aluminum. In this context, Chile, as one of the world's most important sources of copper throughout the twentieth century, played a central role in the corporations' investment and production strategies.

The history of Anaconda and its relationship with Chile were emblematic of the expansion, internationalization, and industrialization of copper mining early in the century. Through heavy investment in capital and sophisticated technology, Anaconda transformed Chilean copper mining into a large-scale industry. Oriented to the international industrial market and shaped by the transnational dimension of capital, Anaconda's properties in Chile accommodated the needs and demands of the company's New York office. In the aftermath of the Great Depression, copper was the leading export sector in Chile. The industrialization and growth of production had serious consequences for the Chilean economy, aggravating the country's dependence on the export market and foreign capital. As Chile's reliance on copper consolidated, copper policies became a central concern. Different sectors of society, including workers, offered alternative solutions for the so-called copper question, from laissez-faire to nationalization, politicizing the copper debate. Copper also became an issue in diplomatic relations between the United States and Chile. Its role in the national and international economy, its function as source of raw material for the war industry, and its foreign ownership made Chilean copper an important issue for the U.S. government.

In the following sixty years, the histories of Chile, Anaconda, and the United States became intertwined. While Chile was central to Anaconda and the lives of many of its managers, the company became dependent on Chilean ore for maintaining its fabrication and elaboration plants in the United States. In the end, Anaconda's dependence on copper and on Chile turned fatal. In 1977, six years after Chile had nationalized Anaconda's properties, the company faced acute financial problems and was bought by the Atlantic Richfield Company (ARCO). In 1982, ARCO—a company that did not believe in the economic future of copper—closed down Butte, the first and most important of Anaconda's mines in the United States. In 1986, ARCO sold off all of what had been Anaconda's properties, ending more than one hundred years of the company's history.[1]

In this chapter we focus on the characteristics of Anaconda as a multinational corporation investing in Chile. The transnational dimension of capital and the instability of the international market influenced the construction process, the local organization of production, and the company's marketing and investment decisions, shaping the daily life of the company in Chile. Foreign employees and their families became a crucial element of Anaconda in Chile, coloring the everyday life of a U.S. company and U.S. society in a remote South American region. Their foreign origin reinforced the traditional class segregation of the company town, sparking the flame of nationalism among Chilean workers.

Anaconda in Chile

In 1954, historian K. Ross Toole described the Anaconda Company as

> a $600,000,000 corporate empire. It is a monstrous and complex organization which operates mines, smelters, fabricating plants,

---

1. For a general history of Anaconda, see Isaac Marcosson, *Anaconda* (New York: Dodd, Mead, 1976).

and subsidiary companies all over the world. The lines of its commerce extend from Chuquicamata, Chile, to Pawtucket, Rhode Island; from Green Cananea, Sonora, to Perth, New Jersey. . . . It owns plants of one kind or another in Muskegon and Kenosha, Perth Amboy and Potrerillos. It mines copper in Butte, makes wire in Oakland, cuts timber in the wilderness of Montana to make stulls for its mines in the Chilean Andes.[2]

How did this colossal corporation decide to invest in Chile? Following a period of combination in the late nineteenth century, Anaconda consolidated itself as a both vertically and horizontally integrated company during the first two decades of the twentieth century. In 1906, it purchased its first foreign property, the Cananea mine, in northern Mexico, and in the 1910s started investing in Chile. In 1922, it acquired the American Brass Company, the largest copper fabricating company in the United States at the time. By the eve of World War II, through its twenty-six subsidiaries and its investments in Canada, Chile, Mexico, and the United States, Anaconda was a successful producer and fabricator of copper and owned large copper deposits, smelters, and refineries throughout the United States and the world, controlling the copper market from mine to consumer.

Anaconda had many reasons to invest in Chile in the 1920s. Copper was abundant and, like many Latin American commodities at the time, virtually tax free. The Chilean Parliamentary Republic (1891–1924) welcomed foreign investors; promoted the growth of the export sector; and regarded the booming nitrate fields, not copper, as the engine of the national economy. There were few regulations affecting the copper industry. Between 1904 and 1925, foreign copper companies paid only a 6 percent tax on profits and after 1925 an additional 6 percent. Labor was cheaper and more accessible than in other mining regions. Despite the isolation of the mines, Andes Copper noted in 1916, there was "abundant labor" in Potrerillos and "Chileans make first class miners."[3] By 1924, the wage for a Chilean miner was a third of that earned by unskilled North American workers.[4]

2. K. Ross Toole, "A History of the Anaconda Copper Mining Company: A Study in the Relationships Between a State and Its People and a Corporation, 1880–1950" (Ph.D. diss., University of California, Los Angeles, 1954), i.
3. Andes Copper to Thayer, April 25, 1916, American Heritage Center, University of Wyoming (hereafter AHC), Anaconda Geological Document Collection (hereafter AGDC), box 70406, folder 17.
4. Thomas O'Brien, "'Rich Beyond the Dreams of Avarice': The Guggenheims in Chile," *Business History Review* 63 (1989): 122–59.

Above all, Anaconda sought in Chile a steady supply of copper ore for its fabrication plants.

The successful arrival of foreign copper companies in Chile made evident the limitation and crisis of the Chilean-owned copper industry. In the mid-nineteenth century, Chile had been the leading producer of copper in the world. With rich vein deposits, miners held small mining claims, used traditional techniques, and needed few capital resources. By late in the century, the rich deposit had vanished and the industry collapsed. Further, international prices fell as world production increased. Chilean entrepreneurs, like many other small mining operators in the world, lacked the capital, technology, financial expertise, and support of the state to exploit low-grade deposits of porphyry copper, opening the door to large-scale foreign companies such as Anaconda and Kennecott.[5] This transition was a traumatic experience for many Chileans who believed in the importance of a national industry and compared the denationalization of the copper industry to the loss of nitrate resources to British investors in the late nineteenth century.[6]

Events in the first years of Anaconda in Chile were emblematic of the resources possessed by large-scale corporations and the ways in which these entities entered, and eventually dominated, the local mining industry. In 1913, William Braden, the famous North American miner who had initiated the works at El Teniente at the beginning of the century, bought the Compañía Minera Potrerillos, located in the northern province of Chañaral, and acquired several mining claims in the region, totaling 3,532 acres.[7] Like many Chilean and small copper mining companies, the Compañía Minera Potrerillos was practically abandoned by 1910 because of high transportation costs and lack of appropriate technology.[8] In January 1916, Braden transferred his mining rights to the Andes Copper Mining Company.

Anaconda's investments in Chile expanded in the following years. In 1917, it organized a second operating subsidiary, the Santiago Mining

5. Joanne F. Przeworski, *The Decline of the Copper Industry in Chile and the Entrance of North American Capital, 1870–1916* (New York: Arno Press, 1980).
6. Santiago Macchiavello, *El problema de la industria del cobre en Chile y sus proyecciones económicas y sociales* (Santiago: Imprenta Fiscal de la Penitenciaría, 1923).
7. Marcosson, *Anaconda*, 211–12.
8. Enrique Kaempffer, "El mineral de Potrerillos: Breves apuntes para una memoria," *Boletín Minero* 81 (1903); Santiago Marín Vicuña, "La industria del cobre en Chile," *Anales del Instituto de Ingenieros de Chile* 20 (1920); "Reseña histórica y descriptiva del mineral de Potrerillos de la Andes Mining Company," *Boletín Minero* 408 (1934).

Company, to exploit two small mines located near Santiago: La Africana and Lo Aguirre. Unlike other copper mines, these were located in an agricultural valley; to stave off complications should mining activity affect farming in the area, the company purchased the agricultural land adjacent to the mines.[9] The Santiago Mining Company remained a small enterprise over the years—it only employed 373 blue-collar workers and produced about fourteen thousand tons of copper concentrate a year by 1958—and never played an influential role in the company's productive structure.[10] In 1923, Anaconda purchased from the Guggenheim brothers its largest mine in Chile, Chuquicamata (called the Chile Exploration Company). By 1930, Chuquicamata was producing 136,000 tons of copper and was the largest open-pit mine in the world.[11]

Anaconda was not alone in the copper business in Chile. The Guggenheim brothers had purchased from William Braden the El Teniente mine, located in the southern province of Rancagua, in 1908. In 1915, they formed the Kennecott Copper Company to control its copper deposits in Chile and the United States.[12] As U.S. companies investing abroad, Anaconda and Kennecott resembled each other. Besides being foreign owned and export oriented, both introduced modern technology, invested a large amount of capital, and implemented similar labor and social policies to shape the work force.[13]

These two companies monopolized the Chilean large-scale copper industry until the nationalization of copper in 1971, producing in 1960 about 80 percent of the copper in Chile and 20 percent of state revenues.[14] Before nationalization, Anaconda and Kennecott were subject to special legislation and taxation rules, with taxation the main link between copper

---

9. Anaconda Copper Mining Company, *Annual Report* (1917).

10. Sylvester to Director General del Trabajo, May 12, 1958, Archivo Nacional de la Administración Central del Estado (hereafter ARNAD), Dirección del Trabajo (hereafter DT), Providencias, 1958, vol. 17.

11. For a history of Chuquicamata, see Finn, *Tracing the Veins*; Eulogio Gutiérrez and Marcial Figueroa, *Chuquicamata: Su grandeza y sus dolores* (Santiago: Imprenta Cervantes, 1920); Ricardo Latcham, *Chuquicamata: Estado Yankee* (Santiago: Editorial Nascimento, 1926).

12. On the history of El Teniente, see María Celia Baros, *El Teniente: Los hombres del mineral, 1905–1945* (Rancagua, Chile: CODELCO-Chile, Mineral El Teniente, 1995); Luis Hiriart, *Braden: Historia de una mina* (Santiago: Editorial Andes, 1964); Klubock, *Contested Communities*.

13. Clark W. Reynolds, "Development Problems of an Export Economy: The Case of Chile and Copper," in *Essays on the Chilean Economy*, ed. Markos Mamalakis and Clark W. Reynolds (Homewood, Ill.: Richard D. Irwin, 1965), 205–6.

14. Meller, *Un siglo de economía política chilena*, 32–36.

producers, the Chilean economy, and the state. Taxation and state's regulations consistently increased throughout the twentieth century. In addition to an income tax, the Chilean state developed several mechanisms to increase revenues and link the copper industry to the Chilean economy. From 1932 to 1955, the state enforced a discriminatory exchange rate for foreign copper producers and in 1950–55 controlled part of the commercialization of copper. Chile's growing dependence on copper and the limitations of copper policies paved the road for nationalization in 1971.

Despite Kennecott and Anaconda's similarities, they differed in their dependency on Chilean copper, their internal structure, and their relationship with national political authorities and labor. Their differences shaped their relationships with the Chilean state, their production strategies, and their approach to labor relations. Unlike Kennecott, Anaconda largely depended on Chilean copper to supply its fabrication plants and made constant efforts to expand its production capacity in the country.[15] By 1964, 70 percent of Anaconda's production and 80 percent of its profits came from Chile.[16] It had a distinct internal structure, both personalized and centralized, with the company's president and the chief executives of its subsidiaries meeting every Friday at Anaconda headquarters in New York. The company closely supervised the operations of its subsidiaries, maintaining close control over them through its ownership of between 96 and 99 percent of their stocks. In New York, the presidents and vice presidents of Latin American operations were also Anaconda's officers and directors, blurring the boundaries between the parent and the subsidiary companies. Anaconda intervened in most of the decision and hiring processes of each of its subsidiaries. Indeed, despite its legal arguments, the company and its foreign subsidiaries behaved as a "unitary business."[17]

The Potrerillos Mine

The magnitude of Anaconda's investment, its capitalist organization, its enormous resources, and its extraordinary management capacity shaped

---

15. Theodore H. Moran, *Multinational Corporations and the Politics of Dependence: Copper in Chile* (Princeton: Princeton University Press, 1977), 129.

16. "Anaconda Announces Shifts in Its Top Leadership," *New York Times*, May 29, 1964.

17. "Before the State Board of Equalization of the State of California. In the Matters of Appeal of the Anaconda Company, Anaconda Wire and Cable Company, and the Anaconda American Brass Company," Sacramento, May 11, 1972, http://www.boe.ca.gov.

Table 1   Average annual copper production per company in thousands of metric tons, 1925–1969

Year	Andes Copper (Anaconda)	Chile Exploration (Anaconda)	Braden (Kennecott)	Total
1925–29	49	111	85	245
1930–34	26	70	82	178
1935–39	44	140	116	300
1940–44	84	214	139	437
1945–49	64	210	128	402
1950–54	43	164	139	346
1955–59	41	236	160	437
1960–64	80	264	158	502
1965–69	316	279	165	760

SOURCE: Norman Girvan, "Las corporaciones multinacionales del cobre en Chile," in *El cobre en el desarrollo nacional*, ed. Ricardo Ffrench-Davis and Ernesto Tironi (Santiago: Ediciones Nueva Universidad, 1974), 115.

the development of work at Potrerillos. Andes Copper built the mine, the plants, and the camps according to modern ideas of mining exploitation and industrial management, and it successfully introduced new technology to make a low-grade deposit a profitable enterprise. Transportation and communication improved with the construction of a company railway and port facilities, and this isolated Chilean region became part of the world economic system. To shape the labor force, Andes Copper built company towns and provided workers with basic urban and social services (see Chapter 2). Since then, copper has greatly shaped the history of the province of Chañaral and that of Chile, influencing regional flows of migration, economic resources, labor activism, and local politics.

Anaconda combined enormous capital investment with extraordinary human and technological resources. Participating in the project was a team of experienced, highly competent mining engineers and geologists, whose careers were emblematic of the paths followed by many professional miners and geologists at the time. Louis D. Ricketts was the first director of Andes Copper. He had previously worked for Calcumet and the Arizona Mining Company in Ajo, Arizona, where he had developed a successful method for treating low-grade porphyry ore. Since the characteristics of the Arizonan copper districts were similar to those found in the Chilean Andes, his experience was extremely valuable.[18] Louis R. Wallace, who

18. James McBride, *The Mission, Means, and Memories of Arizona Miners: A History of Mining in Arizona from Pre-history to Present* (Phoenix: Arizona Mining Association, n.d.), 22.

moved to Potrerillos in 1917 to supervise the construction process, had also worked in Arizona. William Wraith, a mining engineer who had graduated from the Michigan College of Mines, designed the mine at Potrerillos and the transportation system from Anaconda's headquarters in New York.[19] Wilbur Jurden, head of the company's Engineering Department and "Anaconda's master builder," designed the smelter and refinery.[20]

The construction of Potrerillos was lengthy, expensive, and uneven. Although the company had initially estimated spending 7 million dollars on building the mine and necessary facilities, the process took longer—from 1917 to 1926—and proved more difficult than expected, costing the company more than 45 million dollars.[21] Geological characteristics, geographical location, and lack of water posed endless technical challenges and increased costs. During its first two years, Andes Copper developed the necessary services for plant operation: water supply, energy plant, transportation system, and repair shops. In the process, the company received generous, long-term concessions from the Chilean state, including water and land rights.[22] In the bay of Barquito, Andes Copper constructed port facilities, a steel pier with three mechanical cranes, and a power station that had a steam power plant with a capacity of thirty thousand kilowatts. In 1919, the company inaugurated three private railway lines, overcoming one of the most serious obstacles faced by previous mining adventures in the area: lack of efficient transportation. The lines connected Pueblo Hundido and the mill site in Potrerillos (56 miles), the mill site and the mine (5.5 miles), and the port of Barquito to the intersection with the state railway in Chañaral (2.85 miles). To run the railway, Anaconda created a new subsidiary, the Potrerillos Railway Company.[23]

Despite these initial achievements, work was delayed at Potrerillos because of technical problems, effects of altitude, problems with the labor force, material shortages, and the instability of the copper market. Problems of supply affected work during World War I, and adverse market conditions forced management to reduce construction projects in 1921–23 and to completely suspend them in 1924.[24] These crises evidenced the vulnerability of

---

19. William Wraith, "Leaching, Flotation, Smelting Included in Andes' Operations at Potrerillos, Chile," *Engineering and Mining Journal* 128 (1929).
20. Marcosson, *Anaconda*, 213.
21. Marcosson, *Anaconda*, 213.
22. Anaconda Company, *Prospectus* (1935), 20–21, Museo El Salvador, Salvador, Chile.
23. Anaconda Copper Mining Company, *Annual Report* (1917).
24. Anaconda Copper Mining Company, *Annual Report* (1923).

copper to fluctuations in the international market and to the strategies of multinational corporations. As part of a large, powerful entity, Andes Copper was able to reduce production and survive through times of depression, passing on the costs of economic downturns to the regional economy, the labor force, and an increasingly copper-dependent Chilean state. In the following decades, the impact of bearing the costs of recessions was exacerbated by the fact that U.S. price ceilings for copper during World War II and the Korean War would prevent Chile from enjoying the boom cycles.

After two uncertain years, work resumed in 1924 under the supervision of Oscar M. Kuchs, who had worked in Potrerillos in the early 1920s. Driven by its dramatic dependence on mining production, the local community warmly welcomed the return of Kuchs, who, as a Chañaral newspaper noted, had always found "the sincere affection of authorities, elites, and people in general."[25] The expectations were high, and people in Chañaral strongly believed that the reopening of mining operations in Potrerillos would "bring prosperity to industries and trade in the province."[26] Yet the city of Chañaral had little to offer. Its desert landscape did not sustain agriculture or cattle ranches and the city had never developed any local industry besides mining. Andes Copper established sophisticated supply networks, bringing construction materials from Europe and the United States, cattle from northern Argentina, food from the Chilean central valley, and workers from the south and north of Chile. Moreover, the company's decision to build a private port in Barquito, only 2.85 miles from Chañaral Bay, and a company town in Potrerillos meant no direct investment in the city of Chañaral.

The following two years were a time of intense activity and optimism in Potrerillos. In 1925, Andes Copper started working on the construction of the metallurgical plant, on the La Ola pipeline, and on the preparation of the mine for ore extraction. The construction of the pipeline, a remarkable work of engineering, overcame geological difficulties, high altitude, and water scarcity. The La Ola River, the only reasonable source of water, was about twenty-five miles east of Potrerillos, but only flowed for about nine miles on the surface. To deliver water resources, a group of engineers led by William B. Saunders created plans for a diversion dam, a formed of a twenty-eight-mile-long pipeline and seven tunnels. Following a long, zigzag trail, mule carts transported the pipe material from the assembly

---

25. *El Progreso* (Chañaral), February 10, 1925.
26. *El Progreso* (Chañaral), January 27, 1925.

plant to the intake at La Ola Dam, where crews assembled the pipe.[27] Saunders summarized the difficulties of the construction process in an article published by the American Society of Civil Engineers: "The difficulties attending this construction make a story in themselves. The organization of the necessary supervising staff, the selection and training of a large number of men in all departments of work, the effect of climate conditions at high altitude, the difficulties in getting together and organizing the transportation facilities, and last, but not least, the delay in receiving necessary materials were the disturbing factors encountered on this work. To appreciate the task, it is necessary to the see the country traversed."[28]

There is little information about working conditions during the construction phase. The first labor stoppages stemmed from unsafe working conditions and poor salaries that were largely the result of management's negligence. In December 1919, construction laborers in the tunnels at Las Vegas addressed a list of demands to general manager Louis Wallace; these included basic things: shelter, health care, hygienic conditions, and a wage increase.[29] Working conditions were especially harsh and dangerous in Las Vegas. The tunnel under construction was about three-quarters of a mile long; inside it, ventilation was insufficient, machinery was limited, and water reached the knees. Construction workers lived in a provisional camp next to the tunnel, where sanitary conditions were poor. As in the rest of the country, the company severely repressed most efforts at labor organizing and, in 1919, fired the about five hundred workers who had participated in the Las Vegas strike actions.

Protests continued in the following years, usually supported by the Federation of Chilean Workers (FOCH). Founded by Luis Emilio Recabarren in 1909, the FOCH was one of the most influential labor organizations in early twentieth-century Chile, especially in the northern part of the country. Chañaral, like many other Chilean cities, had a local chapter of the FOCH and several labor activists eager to organize the regional labor force. Recabarren himself was a charismatic political and labor leader and journalist. A typographic worker, he had started his political career as a member of the Democratic Party. After breaking with it in 1906, he founded the Partido Obrero Socialista in 1912 (it became the Chilean Communist Party in 1922).

27. William B. Saunders, "The Construction of La Ola Pipe Line in Chile," *Transactions* (American Society of Civil Engineers) 1795 (1930).
28. Saunders, "Construction of La Ola Pipe Line."
29. *El Progreso* (Chañaral), December 9, 1919.

In July 1925, mining engineer Wraith reported that Andes Copper employed twenty-four thousand people and that workers were "coming in at the rate of 150 men a week."[30] Only La Ola employed more than a thousand people, at its peak of activity in 1926.[31] For the most part, Andes Copper preferred the contract system. In La Ola, Saunders, the leader of the engineers, explained, "Much of the work was done on a strictly piece work basis. Often a 'capataz,' or foreman, would be given a contract and he, in turn, would divide his profits with the laborers."[32] The company also hired workers directly. Salaries varied little throughout the construction years. In 1920, unskilled laborers earned an average of $1.50 a day and skilled workers $1.60 to $1.80. Salaries for supervisors (called foremen) ranged between $2.00 and $5.00 a day. The daily wage for foreign skilled labor was $5.00 to $6.00 plus benefits. In describing the costs of labor, Andes Copper noted that workers were cheaper than in the United States, but high altitudes decreased their efficiency.[33]

Construction work was dangerous, accidents frequent, and emergency care limited. In October 1925, nine workers suffered severe injures from an explosion in the energy plant.[34] Three workers were injured in Barquito on January 4 and 5, 1926, and "were taken to the hospital after being abandoned at the beach without any aid."[35] On the eleventh, another worker was taken to the hospital from Barquito.[36] Two days later, a worker lost a finger in the sawmill at Barquito.[37] In October 1926, ten workers died and five were injured in an accident in Sifón Bajo while building the pipeline.[38] Authorities reported two other serious accidents in Potrerillos that year. The national government responded to the dramatic increase in accidents and workers' complaints by sending an official commission to inspect the mine.[39] The commission, however, found little evidence of employers' responsibility or negligence and eventually sided with management.

---

30. Wraith to Laist, July 1, 1925, Montana Historical Society Archives (hereafter MHSA), Helena, Anaconda Company Records (hereafter ACR), box 78, folder 6.
31. Saunders, "Construction of La Ola Pipe Line."
32. Saunders, "Construction of La Ola Pipe Line."
33. Andes Copper, c. 1920, MHSA, ACR, box 76, folder 1.
34. *El Progreso* (Chañaral), October 3, 1926.
35. *El Progreso* (Chañaral), January 5, 1926.
36. *El Progreso* (Chañaral), January 12, 1926.
37. *El Progreso* (Chañaral), January 14, 1926.
38. *El Progreso* (Chañaral), October 14, 1926.
39. *El Progreso* (Chañaral), November 6, 1926.

In December 1926, the mine delivered its ore to the primary crushing plant. The deposit was in the form of sulfide and oxide ores; the two types were clearly separated, making their extraction easier. Each was submitted to a different process. To produce blister copper, the sulfide ore was treated through a complex system of crushing, concentrating, calcining, smelting, and converting. Until 1965, Andes Copper shipped blister copper from Barquito to the United States (to Raritan Copper Works at Perth Amboy, New Jersey) for electrolytic refining. The oxide ore passed through a process of leaching, in which sulfuric acid solutions dissolved the copper minerals. From the leaching plant, the solution passed through a process of purification and precipitation (electrolysis) before it was finally taken to the furnace, where it took its final shape. Since Anaconda was a vertically integrated corporation, an important part of the copper produced in Chile went to the Anaconda fabricating plants in the United States (made into wire, cable, and brass).

The mine's prosperity was short lived. Andes Copper reduced production during 1930–37 as the international price of copper reached its lowest point in the twentieth century. To confront the impact of the Great Depression, Andes Copper laid off workers, established a four-day weekly work schedule, and reduced wages and salaries by 10 percent.[40] There was a strong feeling of depression and crisis among management, workers, and the local community. "The outlook here is very gloomy," wrote geologist William March in 1932; "everyone thinks that it is only a question of time before they shut down Andes."[41] That same year, the company only produced about 10,540 metric tons (a seventh of the total production of 1929).[42] By 1933, the smelter and mine were working at minimum capacity, kept going only to prevent a complete and costly shutdown of operations.

Local conditions were worsened by Chile's political and social instability. A concerned March described a dangerous political conjuncture: "Things don't look any too cheerful for the country is broke, taxes are going up, and communism seems to be gaining ground."[43] March was witnessing one of the most unstable political and economic years in Chilean modern history.[44]

40. *El Progreso* (Chañaral), December 31, 1931.
41. March to Sales, June 14, 1932, AHC, AGDC, box 317.
42. Marcosson, *Anaconda,* 214.
43. March to Sales, January 20, 1932, AHC, AGDC, box 315, folder 1.
44. On the Great Depression and its political implications, see Michael Monteon, *Chile and the Great Depression: The Politics of Underdevelopment, 1927–1948* (Tempe: Arizona State

In July 1931, General Carlos Ibáñez, who had assumed power after a military intervention in 1924, was forced to flee the country, driven out by massive popular protests. In the following months, Chile suffered the dramatic social and economic consequences of the Great Depression and the collapse of the nitrate industry, and popular unrest soared, as did the number of political conspiracies. The country experimented with different political solutions, among them the one-hundred-day Socialist Republic, all of which failed, opening the door to the victory of Arturo Alessandri in the presidential election of 1932. Holding the presidency until 1938, Alessandri enforced strict economic measures.

In 1932, William Braden described Chile as a "mining country" where "the mining laws are liberal, the workmen are strong and the more intelligent Chilians [sic] are cognizant of the advantages of foreign capital and experience." He also noted that these favorable conditions were changing: a "heavy tax was imposed upon the large copper companies" and "the labor and 'social' laws are burdensome, costly, and sometimes abusive."[45] As Braden acknowledged, the global depression had altered Chile's economy, the role of the state, and workers' legal rights. Chile emerged from the depression with a copper industry as its most important source of foreign income, a collapsed nitrate industry, a growing industrial sector, an interventionist state, and a new labor code (see Chapter 2). These changes reframed the relationship between U.S. copper companies and the Chilean state and workers. In 1932, Chile enacted new legislation to regulate foreign investment and the exploitation of natural resources. Laws 5.107 and 5.185 established special taxes and regulations for the copper, nitrate, and iron industries. In addition to increasing taxation, the new laws imposed a differential and higher exchange rate on foreign copper producers. According to law 5.185, copper companies had to pay in dollars the "legal costs of production" at the differential exchange rate determined by the Chilean state.[46] The tax rate on copper profits increased an additional 6 percent in 1934, 15 percent in 1939, 50 percent in 1942, and 60 percent in 1952.[47]

University, 1998); J. Gabriel Palma, "Chile, 1914–1935: De economía exportadora a sustitutiva de importaciones," *Estudios CIEPLAN* 12 (1984).

45. William Braden, "Exploring for Gold in South America," c.1932, AHC, Blair Stewart Papers, box 20.

46. Reynolds, "Development Problems," 232–36.

47. Norman Girvan, *Copper in Chile: A Study in Conflict Between Corporate and National Economy* (Kingston: Institute of Social and Economic Research, University of West Indies, 1972), 8.

Managing Andes Copper

Andes Copper's history in Chile was determined in part by the company's internal organization and the characteristics of its management and staff. The employment of foreign managers and professionals was a distinctive element of the large-scale copper industry, shaping labor and social relations in the mining camps. It is unclear exactly how many U.S. nationals and Europeans worked in Potrerillos in the early days. In 1925, Wilbur Jurden, a mechanical engineer in Montana, reported three hundred United States nationals working in Chuquicamata, the largest of Anaconda's properties in Chile, but he also noted that numbers in Potrerillos were smaller.[48] In 1941, the Chilean Ministry of Public Heath reported ninety-nine foreign employees, seventy-four of whom were married, in Potrerillos.[49] The numbers declined in the following decades. On the eve of nationalization there were fewer than twenty foreign employees. While most management positions were filled by foreigners, some Chileans, especially lawyers, built successful careers in Anaconda. One example was conservative Chilean politician Rodolfo Michels, who had been senator from 1932 to 1940 and in 1940–44 Chile's ambassador to the United States. Michels joined Anaconda in 1944 as the company's representative in Santiago, and in 1962 he was elected vice president and moved to New York.[50] Chilean lawyer Guillermo Carey followed a similar path. As an expert in corporation law in Santiago, he had worked closely with Anaconda's subsidiaries throughout the 1940s and 1950s. In 1964, he was appointed vice president and director of Anaconda's subsidiaries in Chile.[51]

The company had a traditional hierarchical structure. At the top was a general manager, usually with a long trajectory in the company; below, superintendents were in charge of the different divisions (mine, plants, power plant, services). "Managers at the Chilean copper operations had long reins," remembered Alan Dutton, and "wielded a lot of power over a

---

48. Jurden to Laist, Anaconda, July 6, 1925, MHSA, ACR, box 78, folder 6.
49. Manuel de Viado, "Informe sobre la Comisión Oficial al Mineral de Cobre de Potrerillos" (ARNAD, Ministerio de Salubridad, Previsión y Asistencia Social, Providencias, August–September 1941, vol. 2079-2248).
50. *Diccionario biográfico*, 11th ed. (Santiago: Empresa Periodística, 1959–61), s.v. "Rodolfo Michels"; "New Vice President Elected by the Anaconda Company," *New York Times*, October 28, 1962.
51. "Anaconda Names Chile Units' Head," *New York Times*, September 26, 1964.

vast operation."[52] Their power and long experience in the company made them, as Chilean sociologist Pablo Huneeus notes, authoritarian and personalistic figures.[53] For example, William J. Bennett, general manager in the 1960s, arrived in Potrerillos in 1926. A native of Butte, Bennett had earned a degree in chemical engineering from Montana State College. After working at Anaconda for three years, he moved to Chile to become supervisor of the leaching plant in 1926.[54] Described by Frederick Laist as one of "our more experienced young research men," Bennett built a long and successful career in Potrerillos: plant superintendent in 1946, assistant manager in 1954, and general manager in 1955.[55] He stayed so long in Potrerillos that local people called him "the Last of the Mohicans," and rumor had it that he knew every person in the camps and taped all phone conversations.[56] Bennett moved back to the United States only after retiring in 1967.

After their time in South America, some general managers went on to have a successful career in the United States. Charles Brinckerhoff arrived in Potrerillos in 1935 as assistant mine superintendent and remained in Chile for twenty-three years. He ascended rapidly: general manager of Potrerillos in 1944, general manager of Chuquicamata in 1948, president of Anaconda in 1958, and chief executive officer in 1964.[57] Similarly, Norbert Koepel arrived in Potrerillos in 1919, became general manager in 1948, and then became vice president of Andes Copper at Anaconda headquarters in New York in the 1950s.

The personal stories of the men and women who moved from the United States to build a mine and a community in this remote mining region usually started in mining communities in the United States. Many had already worked for Anaconda or other mining companies and were living in cities such as Butte, Great Falls, or Anaconda, Montana; or Salt Lake City, Utah. Once hired, they traveled by train to New York, where they obtained a passport and visa and waited for the next steamship to

---

52. Adam Dutton, e-mail message to the author, November 23, 2003.
53. Pablo Huneeus, *Estructura y dinámica social en los trabajadores del cobre* (Santiago: Instituto de Sociología Universidad Católica de Chile, 1974), 64.
54. *Diccionario biográfico*, 6th ed. (Santiago: Empresa Periodística, 1946–47), s.v. "William Bennett."
55. Laist to Wraith, July 8, 1926, MHSA, ACR, box 78, folder 6.
56. Héctor Maldonado, *El alegre y legendario Potrerillos del ayer* (Copiapó, Chile: Talleres Gráficos de la Universidad de Atacama, 1983); Huneeus, *Estructura y dinámica social*, 64.
57. National Academy of Engineering, "Charles M. Brinckerhoff," *Memorial Tributes: National Academy of Engineering* 4 (1991), 29–34.

Table 2 Andes Copper general managers, 1917–1971

Name	Year of Birth	Arrived in Potrerillos	Previous Positions, with Years, in Andes Copper	Period as General Manager
Oscar M. Kuch		c. 1920		1925–41
Irl L. Greninger	1878	1917	Assistant manager (1931–41) Mine superintendent (1925–31)	1941–44
Charles M. Brinckerhoff	1901	1935	Mine superintendent (1937–44)	1944–48
Norbert F. Koepel	1919		Assistant manager (1946–48) Plant superintendent (1941–46)	1948–55
William Bennet	1900	1926	Assistant manager (1954–55) Plant superintendent (1946–54)	1955–67
L. O. Fines			Assistant manager (1958–67) Plant superintendent (1954–58)	1967–71

SOURCE: Frank Trask III, "Senior Staff Andes Copper Mining Company 1925 to 1971," http://www.losandinos.com/.

South America. In the 1920s, the journey from New York to the Chilean port of Antofagasta took about twenty days. From Antofagasta, one took a boat to the port of Chañaral or a train to Pueblo Hundido.[58]

Andes Copper developed a strict hiring process to fill management and staff positions in Potrerillos. Isolation and the difficulties involved in hiring local professionals, or an initial reluctance to do so, motivated the company to look in its U.S. properties for the most "suitable" men for the jobs in South America. (Women came only as wives and daughters, and some of them worked as teachers in the American school.) Because of the unique characteristics of a foreign operation in an isolated place and the distance between Chile and the United States, the definition of a good employee went beyond technical or professional expertise to include personal and family aspects. Andes Copper hired people who had experience in copper mining in the United States or abroad, were "acquainted with the Anaconda way of doing things," had the "proper personality," had outstanding personal and family records, and were in good health.[59] In other words, as Andes

---

58. Andes Copper, "Information for Employees," Potrerillos 1918, MHSA, ACR, box 451, folder 2.

59. Roberts to Sidley, June 30, 1921, MHSA, ACR, box 119, folder 6; Roberts to Cole, December 17, 1918, MHSA, ACR, box 119, folder 6.

Copper stated, "men should be chosen who are vigorous and healthy; are of mature judgment; possess tact; and caution; but at the same time energy, progressiveness, and the ability to think and act quickly."[60] The company also preferred young men, under forty years old, "unless they are technical men or specialists, especially necessary to us."[61]

Hiring decisions clearly show the company's preferences. In January 1925, Frederick Laist, the metallurgical chief at Anaconda, Montana, hired Thomas Z. Humphrey to be the smelter superintendent of Andes Copper. According to a letter of recommendation, Humphrey had a college degree, had served in the army during World War I, and had many years of experience in Anaconda's plants. He was "unusually good at handling men" and had excellent personal qualifications.[62] Humphrey's positive characteristics were more important and decisive than his lack of practical experience with smelters. The company also valued his wife, who Laist described as "a woman of unusually sterling character and pleasing personality." Mrs. Humphrey had worked as a domestic science teacher in Montana, and Laist considered her "quite a point in Humphrey's favor."[63]

Anaconda subsidiaries preferred hiring people within the extended "Anaconda family," and many employees moved around the company's different properties. Similarly, until the late 1950s, Anaconda made no efforts to hire Chilean professionals. In the 1920s, Martin Martin, from the Employment Department at Anaconda, recruited staff members and skilled workers in Butte to work in Chile. Frederick Laist remarked on the importance of cooperation between Butte and the subsidiaries operating in Chile and believed that it was easier to hire people in the United States than in Chile.[64] Once in Chile, North American skilled workers and management staff usually moved around Potrerillos, Chuquicamata, and La Africana. L. A. Callaway, who became the reduction works superintendent of Andes Copper, worked in Chuquicamata before moving to Potrerillos in 1925.[65] He was plant superintendent in 1925–41 and assistant manager in 1942–46. This policy persisted in the following decades. In 1937, Walter March, chief geologist in Chuquicamata and Potrerillos, especially favored

---

60. Anaconda Copper Company, October 23, 1915, MHSA, ACR, box 75, folder 13.
61. Dickson to Cole, December 5, 1928, MHSA, ACR, box 119, folder 6.
62. Laist to Wraith, January 7, 1925, MHSA, ACR, box 78, folder 6.
63. Laist to Wraith.
64. Laist to Moran, January 27, 1925, MHSA, ACR, box 78, folder 6.
65. Laist to Wraith, December 30, 1924, MHSA, ACR, box 111, folder 6.

this idea, because he was "tired of training green men."[66] Although the number of Chilean professionals increased in the 1950s and 1960s, the company still showed a preference for Anaconda's men. In 1951, for instance, Anaconda hired John Hilsinger to work as a diamond drill supervisor in Potrerillos. Vincent Perry, chief geologist of Anaconda, described Hilsinger as "a very quiet, modest person, but this does not mean that he will not insist on good results from his native labor." Hilsinger's experience in Anaconda was especially valuable: "he did excellent work for the Company handling natives in Brazil and British Guiana, and proved himself a conscientious, loyal employee with outstanding skill as diamond drill operator and supervisor."[67]

European and U.S. nationals joined the staff of Anaconda's foreign subsidiaries, attracted by good salaries; benefits; professional growth potential; and, probably, opportunities for adventure. "There is nothing romantic about life in South America," explained the chief accountant of the Santiago Mining Company in 1920, but there were plenty of opportunities for the man who wanted to "better himself, gain a wide experience and make a reputation."[68] As Adam Dutton remembers, "Most professionals were attracted by the money and steady employment, both scarce commodities during the late '20's and '30's."[69]

The economic benefits were clear in the first years of employment. Superintendents initially received a salary of $350–400 a month, and supervisors were hired at $200.[70] Some people received even higher salaries, as did H. F. Forsyth, who moved to Potrerillos in 1925. While in Anaconda, he had worked in the Engineering Department, earning with a monthly salary of $450. In Potrerillos, he became chief engineer at $625 a month and received free housing in the American camp. Although the cost of living in Potrerillos was higher than in Butte, the former locale offered social benefits, such as free housing, education, and long vacations.[71] A 1920s contract of employment stipulated that Andes Copper would pay first-class transportation and traveling expenses for the employee and his family if he stayed at least one year; the company also provided a furnished

66. March to Sales, December 23, 1937, MHSA, AGDC, box 319, folder 1.
67. Perry to Swenson, April 25, 1951, AHC, AGDC, box 70406, folder 10.
68. Jenks to Roberts, June 21, 1920, MHSA, ACR, box 119, folder 6.
69. Adam Dutton, e-mail to the author, November 23, 2003.
70. Laist to Wraith, July 8, 1926, MHSA, ACR, box 78, folder 6.
71. Sales to Bellinger, June 20, 1930, AHC, AGDC, box 313, folder 1.

house, or a room in the case of single employees, and light and water. Every three years, foreign employees were entitled to a three-month vacation in the United States or, in the case of European employees, their country of origin.[72]

Following the Great Depression, economic benefits shrank, and foreign employees complained about low salaries. In 1936, Walter March, the chief geologist in Chuquicamata, complained that inadequate wages were affecting the quality of work: "[I cannot] keep my men turning out good work when I cannot get them raises which they deserve."[73] Salaries had not improved by 1942, when March wrote to Reno Sales in New York expressing his disappointment with the small raise he had received. Also that year, an employee in Chuquicamata named Weissenborn decided to quit, as his salary was "not sufficient to warrant his staying." Weissenborn, March related, feared being laid off "should another depression develop," and Weissenborn's economic burdens had increased with "his wife no longer able to teach school and the coming expense of sending his children to school in the States."[74]

Despite the meager economic benefits of the 1930s and 1940s, many young geologists and engineers took jobs in Chile as a way to gain experience in the field. In 1930, Víctor López arrived in Chuquicamata to work for Anaconda. López was a Venezuelan citizen living in the United States who had recently graduated from Columbia University. His initial salary in Chile was $150 dollars a month. In 1935, he returned to the United States, to begin postgraduate work at the Massachusetts Institute of Technology. In writing his final thesis, he drew on his geological experience in Chile.[75] Similarly, there was a belief within the company that prospects were better there than elsewhere. March explained why he rebuffed an offer from the Hochschild Company: "Although they offered me considerably more than I am making at present, I turned down their offer on account of both the possible effect of the high altitude on my wife and the feeling that I will be better off in the long run by remaining with the Anaconda organization."[76] March remained as chief geologist of Andes Copper from

---

72. Andes Copper Company, "Contract of Employment," c. 1920, MHSA, ACR, box 76, folder 1.
73. March to Sales, March 25, 1936, AHC, AGDC, box 319, folder 2.
74. March to Sales, August 6, 1942, AHC, AGDC, box 405.
75. Taylor to Sales, June 24, 1930, AHC, AGDC, box 313, folder 1; March to Sales, 16 August 1935, AGDC, box 316.
76. March to Sales, November 11, 1935, AHC, AGDC, box 318.

1925 to 1946, when he moved to Butte to become director of the Montana Bureau of Mines and Geology.

The characteristics and outlook of foreign employees working in Potrerillos changed over time. During construction, 1916–30, the company recruited staff and professionals as well as a large crew of skilled workers, among them bricklayers, electricians, machinists, ironworkers, carpenters, and pipe fitters. When construction gave way to production, foreigners were more likely to be found in professional jobs than in skilled jobs. Similarly, as scholars have pointed out for other North American companies operating in Latin America, once work became stable and standardized, professionals and bureaucrats replaced pioneers and adventurers.[77] In the mid-1950s, the construction of the El Salvador mine, located less than thirty miles from Potrerillos, attracted a new wave of trailblazers, many of whom had worked in other mining projects around the world. Ted Clements clearly represents this phase. An electrician, Clements arrived in Potrerillos in 1926. Originally from New York, he moved first to Bolivia in 1919 to work at the Patiño mines; then to Cerro Pasco, in Peru; and finally to Chile. He married a Chilean woman and retired in 1950, moving to the Chilean city of Vallenar. In 1958, he returned to El Salvador to supervise the work of electrical contractors.[78]

A Foreign Community

Foreign employees and their families became a crucial component of the camp's social fabric. To guarantee a stable community and satisfy the demands of foreign employees, Andes Copper built an "American camp," an exclusive sector of the town for foreign employees. The American camp maintained a middle-class and "American" standard of living. Considering the isolated location of Potrerillos, material living conditions for foreign employers were outstanding. As J. T. Roberts explained in 1918, improved living conditions for North American workers had been a critical preoccupation for the company, as they could be used to attract and keep "capable, trustworthy men who are familiar with Anaconda traditions and methods."[79]

---

77. Thomas O'Brien, *The Revolutionary Mission: American Enterprise in Latin America, 1900–1945* (Cambridge: Cambridge University Press, 1999).
78. Frank Trask III, "Ted Clements," http://www.losandinos.com.
79. Roberts to Cole, May 15, 1918, MHSA, ACR, box 117, folder 10.

Housing at the American camp was carefully arranged, from the general manager's residence to the collective foreign single-men's quarters, located next to the few houses used by Chilean staff. The company offered foreign staff three types of arrangements: family houses, staff houses for single men, and dormitories for single men. Family houses were of the California-bungalow type. They were made of concrete and had a living room, a dining room, two or three bedrooms, a house cleaner's or laundry room, hall, and vestibule. Staff houses for single men had a living room, two bedrooms, a bathroom, and a storeroom in the basement. Only single men earning a minimum salary of two hundred dollars a month were eligible to live in staff houses, which were designed for two people. All other foreign single men boarded at the dormitories, for thirty dollars a month.[80] The camp had a wide range of well-equipped institutions and exclusive services: elementary school, a social club called the Copper Club (with billiard tables and a library), tennis courts, and a golf course.

In personal memories, the good conditions at the American camp were stressed. T. Z. Humphrey, the superintendent of the smelter, moved to Potrerillos with his wife, older son, and mother-in-law in 1926. His youngest son, William, was born and raised in Potrerillos during the late 1920s and early 1930s. William described the American camp as "an American enclave," where he and other foreigners had no "association with Chilean people." The Humphreys lived in a house that was "almost an exact replica of the houses in Miami, Arizona, that they built in Inspiration. The floor plan was the same except the houses were built of adobe." The houses had wooden floors and "plenty of electricity." Despite the isolation, William Humphrey recalled having access to a wide variety of food, including meat, chicken, canned salmon, and tins of butter from Holland.[81]

The American camp became an English-language camp. North American teachers taught in the elementary school; nurses consoled their patients in their mother tongue; and North American women were able to buy corn-flakes, St. Charles condensed milk, and beauty magazines at the exclusive North American store. The community observed traditional North American holidays, including Thanksgiving, the Fourth of July, and Halloween, and played such sports as golf, bowling, and baseball. The result was a protected

80. Andes Copper, "Information for Employees."
81. William Humphrey, "Mining Operations and Engineering Executive for Anaconda, Newmont, Homestake, 1950 to 1995," an oral history conducted by Eleanor Swent in 1994 and 1995, Regional Oral History Office, Bankroft Library, University of California, Berkeley, 1996, 7–17.

environment, a North American island in foreign territory. Small children attended a special grade school, the American School. Most teachers came from the United States, but under the regulations of the Chilean government, the school had to have "a qualified Spanish teacher to teach Spanish language and the history of the country."[82] The town did not have a high school and, as Ruth Bates, who grew up in Potrerillos in the 1920s and 1930s, remembers, the "company paid for tuition and board for the foreigners' children to go to boarding school in their country of origin."[83]

Life for families, especially the women, was not easy, as they were forced to adapt to the isolation and remoteness of the natural environment. Although many believed that conditions in the camps were not suitable for families, women and small children were among its first residents and created the basis of a foreign community.[84] Many foreign employees arrived as single men and subsequently married the daughters of other foreign employees. In 1939 James Feeney's father arrived in Potrerillos, where he met James's mother. James's maternal grandparents had arrived in Potrerillos in 1927, when his mother was seven years old.[85] Since many families stayed a long time in Chile, they often built strong bonds that lasted a lifetime.

Social life and entertainment was limited to the small community. Beside playing golf and tennis, people organized bridge and formal dinner parties. William Humphrey recalled the existence of some "wild" people, heavy drinking, and "wife-trading."[86] During the summers, families spent time in Barquito, where the company maintained a guesthouse and a swimming pool.

The experiences at this camp are similar to those of such camps in other mining towns. Helen Henshaw, the wife of a Cerro de Pasco's employee, lived in La Oroya, Peru, in the 1940s. Describing social life at her mining camp, Henshaw recalled, "We played bridge, and golf . . . [and] learned a little Spanish . . . and we had luncheons. . . . The women did a lot of reading, but there wasn't a lot for women to do except bridge."[87]

82. Ruth Bates, e-mail to the author, November 18, 2003.
83. Bates, e-mail.
84. Taylor to Sales, March 21, 1933, AHC, AGDC, box 318.
85. Jim Feeney, e-mail to the author, October 13, 2003.
86. Humphrey, "Mining Operations," 39–40.
87. Helen Henshaw, "Recollection of Life with Paul C. Henshaw: Latin American, Hometake Mining Company," an oral history conducted by Eleanor Swent, Regional Oral History Office, Bankroft Library, University of California, Berkeley, 1987, 26–27.

The relationship between Chileans and U.S. nationals was complex, shaped by both racial and class prejudices. In 1941, Manuel de Viado noted that class, language, race, and a "different conception of life" widened the gap between management and workers in Potrerillos.[88] However, many U.S. nationals expressed admiration for the country; some of them married Chilean women and raised children who considered themselves *chilenos*, while others settled in Chile after retiring.

Conclusions

The economic and political power of Anaconda, the international dimension of its capital, and its successful vertical and horizontal integration shaped the production of copper in modern Chile. In the 1910s, Anaconda's decision to invest in the country was motivated by the company's need to find a reliable supply of copper for its fabrication plants and its desire to control the supply of copper worldwide. In Chile, it found ideal conditions: abundant copper, political stability, and low taxes. Conditions started changing in the 1930s. Chile's growing dependence on copper, new economic ideas, and the demands of the state-led industrialization process inspired changes in taxation and challenged the previously uncontested privileges of foreign capital. Until the nationalization of copper in 1971, the Anaconda Company and the Kennecott Corporation controlled the production, transportation, and marketing of Chilean copper.

Anaconda brought to Chile more than machines; it also brought a team of foreign experts who eventually created a community in the Chilean Andes. With the arrival of foreign managers and professionals, the company built an exclusive camp, segregated from the vast majority of local blue- and white-collar workers. The so-called American camp became an isolated enclave, where U.S. culture was reproduced and maintained by means of the English language and through education, social festivities, and consumption. In the following years, the presence of foreigners and their exclusive privileges created tensions among native workers, managers, and the state. The copper camps soon were viewed as constituting a foreign state, and the Chilean workforce articulated a very nationalistic discourse.

---

88. Manuel de Viado, "Morfología social de Potrerillos," *Previsión Social*, May–June 1941.

2 The World of Labor

Until the nationalization of copper in 1971, Potrerillos was a foreign-owned company town, a mining community, and a strong union city. At this geographically isolated mine, in the southern part of Chile's Atacama Desert, work was the major force organizing social relations, leisure time, and other aspects of life. Mine work was extremely hard, accidents and occupational diseases were frequent, unemployment was a constant threat, and labor relations were tense. The copper industry adopted modern technology and enforced a disciplined, impersonal mode of work. The characteristics of copper exploitation created a unique working environment: a large, male, young, migrant labor force living and working in isolated camps.

Beginning in the 1920s, Andes Copper offered a wide range of welfare programs to create a stable labor community and used repression to break down miners' traditional work habits. By the early 1940s, and despite the company's control, copper workers built a militant labor community and a distinctive collective identity. Based on the use of the Labor Code, the establishment of political alliances, and the relatively high cohesion of the community, copper workers improved their living conditions and achieved high salaries and fringe benefits throughout the second half of the twentieth century.

A Company Town

In 1918, Potrerillos, remarked Chilean journalist F. Muñoz Herrera, was one of the most thriving mines in the region. At this mine, Muñoz enthused, "buildings are very original. The little houses are for a single family only and have 3 rooms, kitchen, and bathroom. When you see them [the houses] for the first time, you may think you are in a completely

European city because they resembled houses built in Switzerland. . . . In other words, Potrerillos is improving. Alcohol is prohibited and everybody lives happily and joyfully without the damned vices that have destroyed and killed the race."[1]

Muñoz Herrera was witnessing the construction of a company town: an urban labor institution that shaped the living, working, and political experiences of copper workers in Potrerillos until the nationalization of copper in 1971. Defined as a working, planned community owned by a company and built exclusively to house its employees, the company town was a popular urban solution designed by employers across many industries and countries to control workers and develop successful businesses in isolated areas. Its urban structure and its morphology, layout, and internal regulations were the result of conscious intention. Despite regional and historical differences, company towns around the world shared important similarities. Companies provided their employees with social and urban services, implemented extensive welfare programs, and enforced a strict segregation between workers and management. In doing so, they sought to control the labor force, create an efficient working environment, and achieve higher levels of profit and economic success.[2]

In the 1920s, Andes Copper conceived of company towns as a solution to their production needs and to the challenge of developing a modern industry in northern Chile. They believed that good working and living conditions, a controlled environment, and a traditional family life would have a positive effect on production, reduce labor unrest, and improve worker efficiency. A decent living and working environment, noted Andes Copper assistant general manager Alvin Hoffman in 1927, would make "the men proud of the place where they work, and helps to make them clean and orderly, and anxious to hold their jobs, and this of course reduces the labor turnover."[3]

By building a company town, Andes Copper was also responding to the characteristics of the Chilean working class at the beginning of the twentieth century. By the turn of the century, Chilean peons had already become proletarians. In the nitrate fields, ports, and cities, workers had, since the late nineteenth century, participated in the wage economy and had experience

---

1. *La Verdad* (Chañaral), February 18, 1918.
2. For an overview of company towns in the United States, see Margaret Crawford, *Building the Workingman's Paradise: The Design of American Company Towns* (New York: Verso, 1995).
3. Hoffman to Kuchs, March 17, 1928, MHSA, ACR, box 76, folder 5.

with work discipline, mechanization, and impersonal labor relations. But the Chilean labor force remained highly unstable; industries and mines suffered from chronic worker turnover and high rates of absenteeism. Indeed, labor turnover hit Andes Copper hard during the construction of the mine and the plants, reaching 40 percent in the early 1920s.[4] Adding to this was a highly politicized and militant working class that, under the leadership of the Chilean Workers' Federation (Federación Obrera de Chile, or FOCH), the Partido Obrero Socialista (POS), and anarchist groups, was challenging the limits of employers' authority over the workforce as an aspect of its questioning the legitimacy of the Chilean aristocratic republic.[5]

Influenced by the model of the company town, geographical conditions, and its perception of the local working class, Andes Copper built highly regulated mining camps. Between 1917 and 1927, parallel with the construction of the mine and the plants, it planned and built an interconnected system of five mining camps for its labor force and staff members. Distributed from coast to mine (west to east), the camps were Barquito (port facilities and electric power station), Llanta (machine shops and railway station), Potrerillos (main camp, management office, and plants), Las Vegas (repair shops and sawmill), and La Mina. In 1959, when El Salvador replaced the mine at La Mina, the population of La Mina moved into a new town, El Salvador.

Like most employers around the world who created company towns, Andes Copper strictly segregated the workers in the camps by national origin, class, and marital status. The characteristics and distribution of housing were emblematic of the segregation and inequality that existed in the camps. The camps offered six types of housing: U.S. single-men's houses, U.S. family houses, staff bachelors' houses, Chilean single-men's barracks (*camarotes*), Chilean boarding houses, and Chilean family houses.

---

4. Saunders, "Construction of La Ola Pipe Line."
5. There is an extremely rich labor historiography about this period. See, for instance, Jorge Barría, *El movimiento obrero en Chile* (Santiago: Universidad Técnica del Estado, 1971); Peter De Shazo, *Urban Workers and Labor Unions in Chile, 1902–1927* (Madison: University of Wisconsin Press, 1984); Sergio González, *Hombres y mujeres de la pampa: Tarapacá en el ciclo del salitre* (Santiago: LOM, 2002); Elizabeth Q. Hutchison, *Labors Appropriate to Their Sex: Gender, Labor, and Politics in Urban Chile, 1900–1930* (Durham: Duke University Press, 2001); Fernando Ortiz, *El movimiento obrero en Chile (1891–1919)* (Madrid: Michay, 1985); Julio Pinto, *Trabajos y rebeldías en la pampa salitrera: El ciclo del salitre y la reconfiguración de las identidades populares (1850–1900)* (Santiago: Editorial de la Universidad de Santiago, 1998); Crisóstomo Pizarro, *La huelga obrera en Chile, 1890–1970* (Santiago: Ediciones SUR, 1986); Hernán Ramírez Necochea, *Historia del movimiento obrero en Chile, siglo XIX* (Santiago: Ediciones LAR, 1956); Julio Samuel Valenzuela, "Labor Formation and Politics: The Chilean and French Cases in Comparative Perspective, 1850–1950" (Ph.D. diss., Columbia University, 1979).

Table 3 Andes Copper's camps population, 1941

Camp	Total Population
Barquito	849
Llanta	362
Potrerillos	7,04
Las Vegas	592
Mina	3,89
La Ola	56

SOURCE: Manuel de Viado, "Informe sobre la Comisión Oficial al Mineral de Cobre de Potrerillos," Archivo Nacional de la Administración Central del Estado, Ministerio de Salubridad, Previsión, y Asistencia Social, Providencias, August–September 1941.

While housing for foreign employees was of outstanding quality and built according to the California-bungalow type, Chilean houses were small, were made of calamine or adobe, and lacked private bathrooms. Chilean family houses had three or four rooms (one or two bedrooms, a living room, and a kitchen) arranged as blocks of twelve houses with collective toilets in the center. Some family residences were attached houses, each row containing four to seven houses with collective bathrooms at the end. The *camarotes*, where the majority of blue-collar workers lived, accommodated around fourteen workers in seven rooms and had collective bathroom facilities.

Houses were company owned, rent free, and exclusively for company employees. Unlike some companies in the United States, Andes Copper never considered the possibility of encouraging home ownership. Residents were responsible for maintaining their houses and had to follow community regulations. Housing rules prohibited renovations or changes to the buildings, construction of any kind inside or outside the house, the running of businesses or shops, and the keeping of animals without company authorization. Houses were for residence purposes only; although residents could not use company property to generate extra income, families could rent rooms to single workers as a way to supplement their incomes. People who neglected the company houses would lose the right to have a house in the camps, or the Welfare Department would transfer them to a lower-quality house. A special crew of house inspectors from the Welfare Department spent two hours every day inspecting houses and buildings, making mandatory recommendations for required maintenance to the residents.[6]

6. Andes Copper Mining Company, "Reglamento Interno de la Andes Copper Mining Co. y Potrerillos Railway Co.," c. 1933, Biblioteca Nacional de Chile.

The quality of housing and urban services was a topic of much debate and conflict. In 1927, Chilean engineer Rodolfo Jaramillo described Potrerillos as "a real city, with streets and good roads, with churches and schools for the spiritual and intellectual welfare of the community."[7] That same year, *El Progreso*, the newspaper of the Radical Party in Chañaral, denounced the misery that existed in Potrerillos: "The buildings are sheets of zinc put on the ground, and the rooms would be better suited for pigs than for the human race. It is a thousand times worse than any prison cell."[8] These contradictory views were emblematic of the ways in which Chileans perceived conditions in Potrerillos and the foreign-owned copper industry in general. Like Jaramillo, many saw in Potrerillos a model company town and a real improvement on the crowded, unsanitary working-class neighborhoods of Chile. Others, however, criticized the outrageous segregation and inequality that existed in Potrerillos, conditions aggravated by the foreign nature of the company.[9]

The quality of housing declined in the late 1940s. Alleging economic difficulties caused by the international copper crisis and by the depletion of the mine, management disregarded living conditions. In the early 1950s, houses in Potrerillos and Barquito were often described as small and old and many still lacked private bathrooms.[10] In 1952, labor inspector José Luis Sepúlveda noted that it was common to see four to five single workers sharing a room and that sanitary conditions were deficient. Despite these limitations, as the Central Joint Salaries Board (Comisión Mixta de Sueldos) concluded in late 1953, living conditions in the copper camps remained better than in many other parts of the country. Unlike most Chilean workers, the commission explained, copper workers were entitled to free housing, water, and electricity, and prices at the company store were cheaper than in the open market.[11]

In the late 1950s, Andes Copper built a mine and a camp in El Salvador (see Chapter 4) and began a program of housing renovation and eradication of collective bathrooms.[12] While El Salvador represented a major

7. Rodolfo Jaramillo, "Mineral de Potrerillos de la Andes Copper Mining Co.," *Anales del Instituto de Ingenieros de Chile*, January 1927.
8. *El Progreso* (Chañaral), October 29, 1927.
9. See, for instance, Latcham, *Chuquicamata*.
10. Griffith and Illanes to Director General del Trabajo, December 17, 1953, ARNAD, DT, Providencias, 1954, vol. 5.
11. Griffith and Illanes to Director General, December 17, 1953.
12. *Andino* (Potrerillos), October 13, 1956.

improvement in living standards, conditions in the other camps improved slowly. In 1957, for example, the company started the construction of a new airport in Potrerillos, remodeled houses, paved several streets, started the construction of a new theater in Potrerillos, inaugurated a theater in the small camp of Las Vegas, finished the children's hospital, and constructed bunkhouses for single male employees in Barquito. In 1960, it modernized Barquito by building two-room attached houses with private bathrooms for white- and blue-collar married employees, eliminating some collective bathrooms, and repaired the old bunkhouses.[13] Regardless of these improvements, in 1969, Chilean sociologist Pablo Huneeus noted, 70 percent of Potrerillos households still lacked private bathrooms.[14] As a result, reported a 1968 government study, workers perceived that their most urgent need was not higher salaries but improved housing.[15]

In the 1960s, working families continued to denounce acute housing shortages, collective bathrooms, and unhygienic living conditions.[16] In the late 1960s, the Ministry of Public Housing described houses in Potrerillos and Barquito as old and reconfirmed the existence of a housing shortage. In El Salvador, the ministry calculated a housing deficit of about seven hundred units (Table 4).[17] The housing shortage and lack of opportunities for home ownership in the camps pushed some company workers to live in Pueblo Hundido and Chañaral. In 1969, 536 people (workers and their families) lived in Pueblo Hundido, fifty-two miles west of Potrerillos.[18] While the company gave a housing allowance to people residing outside the camps, living conditions and the quality of social services in Pueblo Hundido were extremely poor.

Isolation was a major element in the lives of copper workers. Their conditions—living at high altitudes, at long distances from urban centers, and with few transportation alternatives—limited their mobility and social and educational opportunities. During the first half of the twentieth century, the company-owned passenger train between Potrerillos and Pueblo Hundido ran twice a week and took about four hours. Pueblo Hundido was connected

13. *Andino* (Potrerillos), February 6, 1960.
14. Huneeus, *Estructura y dinámica social*, 52.
15. Consejería Nacional de Promoción Popular, "Valores y actitudes en los obreros de la gran minería en Chile" (Santiago: Universidad Católica de Chile, Instituto de Economía, 1968).
16. *Cobre* (Santiago), November–December, 1968.
17. Ministerio de Vivienda y Urbanismo, *Chañaral: Estudio pre-inversional* (Santiago: n.p., n.d.), 41–47.
18. Ministerio de Vivienda y Urbanismo, *Chañaral*, 41–47.

Table 4 Population and housing availability in Andes Copper camps, late 1960s

Camp	Population	Housing Units
El Salvador	8,300	1,084
Potrerillos	6,490	1,020
Llanta	535	102
Barquito	880	176
Total	16,205	3,965

SOURCE: Ministerio de Vivienda y Urbanismo, *Chañaral: Estudio pre-inversional* (Santiago: n.p., n.d.), 41–45.

by railway to Chañaral (capital of the department), to the south of the country (the Red Central Norte line ran from La Calera, northeast of Valparaíso, to Pueblo Hundido), and to the north (the Longitudinal Norte line ran from Pueblo Hundido to Pintados, in the northern nitrate district). To lower the costs of transportation, labor unions struggled to obtain free tickets for laid-off workers and their families and for workers attending special events such as sport competitions and bargaining meetings. In the 1960s, the expansion of ground transportation offered new opportunities for mobility, at least at the regional level. Andes Copper reinforced the isolation of the towns by creating a clear distinction between the "inside" and the "outside." Company guards and police officers enforced strict internal regulations and limited the entrance of visitors, who had to obtain special authorization from the Welfare Department.[19] Company officers screened job candidates in the employment office located next to the railway station in Pueblo Hundido and rapidly dispatched laid-off workers to other cities. These activities resulted from strict company policies, based on the private status of the camp, and generated great controversy over the extent of the company's control and the limits to citizenship rights. Reminiscent of large landowners who exerted total control over the people who lived and worked on their lands, mining companies argued that mining camps constituted private property. Labor leaders and left-wing politicians accused Andes Copper—and other foreign companies operating in the country—of creating a "state within the state," where the jurisdiction of Chilean laws and authorities was limited by the presence of a foreign company.[20]

---

19. Andes Copper Mining Company, "Reglamento Interno."
20. *La Verdad* (Chañaral), June 12, 1926.

Despite geographical constraints, people still traveled and participated in the political life of the country. Throughout the second half of the twentieth century, high school students, especially those whose parents were white-collar workers, moved out of the town to attend public and Catholic schools in La Serena, Copiapó, Antofagasta, and even Santiago. They spent their summers in the camps, arriving sometime before Christmas and staying until the first days of March, and thus became an important link between the camp and the rest of the country.[21] During the year, the arrival of theater companies, circuses, and popular artists broke up the monotony of life. Given the demographic weight of Potrerillos in the province of Chañaral, political candidates frequently stopped at the camps during times of congressional and presidential elections.

The intersection of social benefits and company regulations and control was a distinctive element of life in the copper camps. The influence of the company town model, geographical isolation, and legal obligations inclined Andes Copper toward implementing welfare services and maintaining basic social services and infrastructure in the camps. Looking to transform the Chilean mining laborer into a responsible and loyal industrial worker and to increase productivity, the company used social programs and urban services to exert control over workers and their families. The results were ambiguous. Although company welfare gave Andes Copper an enormous amount of power over the community and created a strong dependency of working people on their employers, it guaranteed neither workers' acquiescence nor stability. To the contrary, as workers perceived social services to be the company's obligation, protests and conflicts erupted throughout the camps against those services' poor quality and low availability.

In the 1920s, Andes Copper organized an entity, the Welfare Department, to oversee social and welfare programs such as housing, education, and company stores. In compliance with the law Educación Primaria Obligatoria (Compulsory Elementary Education law, 1920), which declared elementary education compulsory and ruled that industrialists in isolated places must build schools in their properties, Andes Copper built and maintained elementary schools in all the camps; funded part of the schools' expenses, including supplies and maintenance; and provided housing for the teachers. Aiming to create a stable community, Andes Copper used the schools to

---

21. See, for instance, *Las Noticias de Chañaral* (Chañaral), March 3, 1966 and January 25, 1967.

organize activities such as physical education classes, Boy and Girl Scouts' meetings, and vocational courses for women.[22] Until nationalization, the camps had only elementary schools and some high school classes at night, but mining families remembered and admired the educational opportunities provided by the foreign administration. The access to elementary education stood out in a country where, although literacy rates were high (80 percent in 1952), most rural, poor, and isolated areas had few schools and the majority of Chilean children dropped out of school before sixth grade.[23]

Although Andes Copper allowed private businesses to operate in the camp, and representatives sent by commercial houses from Chañaral and Copiapó usually visited the town, the company-owned store was the most important place to shop in the camp and a unique feature of living in a company town. It was not only a place to buy goods, but also a gathering place and a permanent source of conflict between the Chilean community and management. Isolation, the impossibility of growing anything on the desert land, and an initial hostility toward outsiders led Andes Copper to maintain company stores in each camp. According to Manuel de Viado, a physician from the Ministry of Public Health who visited Potrerillos in 1941, the company store was a mechanism "to control family expenses, prevent excessive shopping that could unbalance a budget, and obtain a more intimate knowledge of employees' conditions."[24] Over time, as William French explained for the case of the mining industry in northern Mexico, the company-owned store became more a workers' benefit than a company's instrument of control.[25] A newspaper article from 1946 suggests the ways in which the local community perceived the so-called company's benefits: "Miss Andes Copper, I have to tell you something . . . when shopping at the Caserón de las Colas [the big house of the lines], which you call the company store, one has to be as patient as a donkey to be in line forever, one has to withstand the bad mood of some of the girls [who work there] and look at the sour faces of the bosses. And it is better not to talk about the Malestar Department—(which you call Welfare), because everything is wrong there."[26]

22. *El Progreso* (Chañaral), April 5, 1932.
23. United States Department of Labor, Bureau of Labor Statistics, *Labor in Chile* (n.p.: U.S. Department of Labor, 1962), 4.
24. De Viado, "Informe."
25. William E. French, *A Peaceful and Working People: Manners, Morals, and Class Formation in Northern Mexico* (Albuquerque: University of New Mexico Press, 1996), 47–51.
26. *La Usina* (Potrerillos), December 21, 1946.

Until 1958, the company store operated on a complex system of ration cards and frozen prices and distinguished between essential products and a wide variety of imported and nonessential products. It sold essential products at the fixed prices of 1932, known as "frozen prices" (*precios congelados*), and each worker held a ration card determined by family size and salary; nonessential products, in contrast, were at market price plus the cost of transportation. The company rationed products such as meat, sugar, milk (canned), oil, tea, wine, and beer. During labor conflicts, it manipulated frozen prices and rations, to exert pressure over the unions and break down workers' solidarity. During the fifty-two-day strike of 1953, the company stores in Chuquicamata and Potrerillos increased prices for essential products, among them milk, arguing that "it would be ridiculous" for the companies "to subsidize the strike with low prices." As a result, the price of milk increased about 10 percent.[27] Moreover, company managers repeatedly argued that they were losing money with company stores and rejected workers' demands for better wages and benefits.

Problems in the company stores provoked furious reactions, including spontaneous daily protests from people waiting in line (these actions were usually led by women), formal labor union complaints, and wildcat strikes. The events that took place in August 1946 and August 1954 are emblematic of the ways in which the community protested the limitations of the company store in Potrerillos.

In the last week of August 1946, the store announced the arrival of several bags of sugar, a scarce product since the outbreak of World War II. After hearing the news, women ran to the store with their ration cards. Unfortunately, the demand exceeded the supply, and loud complaints and disorder followed the store employees' announcement that once again they were out of sugar. The police came to calm the situation and reestablish public order, but did so "through pushing and beating."[28] Similarly, in August 1954, problems with the supply of meat motivated 2,200 blue-collar workers and 450 white-collar workers to call an illegal strike. After long negotiations that involved local labor leaders, national labor organizations, management, and state authorities, the strike ended on September 23, after twenty-six days. In the settlement, management agreed to guarantee

---

27. *El Día* (Copiapó), November 20, 1953.
28. *La Usina* (Potrerillos), August 24, 1946.

the supply of 60 percent fresh meat and 40 percent Argentinean frozen meat and to give workers eight days to return to work.[29]

In 1958, after a long debate and worker dissatisfaction with the company store system, a union contract stipulated replacing rations with a system of compensations (*compensaciones*) for family dependents. Instead of ration cards and inexpensive products, workers received cash and were free to shop wherever they wanted. Management calculated the *compensaciones* according to the market prices of products and determined family allocations by the age of each family member. The company considered family dependents to be wives; children or stepchildren under eighteen years old; widows or abandoned mothers; and disabled fathers, all of whom had to live in the camp.[30] The *compensación* was paid monthly, but absenteeism was punished with a proportional discount, a practice that suggests that the company intended to use the system to discipline the labor force. Since the company paid part of the *compensaciones* directly to the spouse or the workers' dependent parents, women achieved some control over household economies. For male workers, as many old-time workers remembered, the *compensaciones* challenged traditional gender roles. In this context, many male workers perceived it as a "disaster" leading to a "breakdown of relationships" and marital disputes.[31] By giving economic power and financial independence to homemakers, the company both challenged the traditional patriarchal authority of male miners and reinforced the family unit as a viable and stable institution in the camps.

Throughout the first half of the twentieth century, the company put considerable energy into repressing certain individual behaviors, such as drinking, gambling, and fighting. Identifying these social practices as threats to production that caused high rates of absenteeism, labor turnover, and unnecessary violence, Andes Copper used private guards, police officers, and special regulations in efforts to change workers' habits. Between 1918 and 1932 and again during World War II, the company forbade the consumption of alcohol within the camps and, in the following years, restricted its consumption and sale. Similarly, it attempted to control prostitution, encouraged marriage and families, and fired workers identified as chronic gamblers.

---

29. Cabrera to Inspector Provincial del Trabajo, September 2, 1954, ARNAD, DT, Providencias, 1954, vol. 20.
30. "Convenio," Potrerillos, August 28, 1958, ARNAD, DT, Providencias, 1958, vol. 25.
31. Guido Soriano, conversation with the author, July 26, 2000.

Workers challenged the company's policies in the camps or decided to go to Pueblo Hundido for some entertainment, and heavy drinking, gambling, and prostitution continued to be serious problems in the community.[32]

The Labor Force

Potrerillos was a migrant-labor community, and Andes Copper recruited its labor force from other Chilean regions. As in the rest of the mining industry during the first half of the twentieth century, an important means of providing the company with unskilled laborers was the *enganche* system.[33] The *enganche* was a traditional vehicle for recruiting workers in nineteenth-century Chile and became popular in the Chilean nitrate boom (1880–1920). Labor recruiters traveled around the country, especially to small towns in rural areas, offering "good" jobs and salaries in the nitrate plants. Although they usually paid for transportation to the nitrate fields, their description of working conditions and salaries greatly differed from the reality in northern Chile and led to enormous abuses on the part of employers and recruitment companies.[34]

The Labor Code formally abolished the *enganche* system in 1931, but it remained as an informal recruitment practice. As late as 1951, El Día, a regional newspaper from Copiapó, accused Andes Copper of maintaining agents in the cities of Copiapó and Caldera. These agents offered potential workers a well-paid job in Potrerillos without providing formal written documentation. Agents visited northern cities in their big trucks and drove people to Potrerillos, but the company only hired a few workers, as third-class laborers. Those who were not hired, explained the El Día reporter, were simply returned to Pueblo Hundido, "where they are left on their own, because the train ticket from this town back to their places of origin is not paid."[35]

Most of the time, workers moved to Potrerillos because they knew someone or because of the industry's reputation for paying good salaries.

---

32. Angela Vergara, "Company Towns and Peripheral Cities in the Chilean Copper Industry: Potrerillos and Pueblo Hundido, 1917–1940," *Urban History* 3 (2003).
33. *El Progreso* (Chañaral), May 30, 1925.
34. González, *Hombres y mujeres*, 141–51; Michael Monteon, "The Enganche in the Chilean Nitrate Sector," *Latin American Perspectives* 3 (1979).
35. *El Día* (Copiapó), May 10, 1951.

Like Mexican workers migrating to the Midwest in the United States, Chilean workers followed the migratory routes opened by labor recruiters in the previous decades and developed their own networks of migration based on personal contacts and kinship.[36] In 1969, a miner in El Salvador explained that he left his town when he was eighteen years old and moved to the mine because he had a relative working there already.[37] Because of the inhospitable location and the character of the work, many workers initially regarded employment in the mining industry as a temporary job and an opportunity to "make money."

Whether through company recruitment or means of their own devices, workers came from widely divergent origins. Since the 1880s, when the nitrate industry started booming, northern Chile had been a common destination for rural people from the south and the Central Valley. The long Chilean agricultural crisis caused by the lack of modernization and technology and the monopolization of land by large estates forced many peasants to migrate. In addition, the crisis of the nitrate industry following World War I, the traditional mobility of nitrate workers, and high rates of unemployment in the far north provoked a current of migration from the north. Potrerillos and El Salvador have also attracted large numbers of migrants from the Norte Chico. An overview of one thousand personnel records of blue-collar workers who entered the company in 1925–73 reveals that about 40 percent of them listed as place of origin a town located in what today is the region of Coquimbo.[38]

Once in Potrerillos, employees were hierarchically organized in a complex pyramid from the unskilled laborer to the general manager. It was also almost exclusively a male and relatively young labor force. Divisions along occupational lines were reproduced in the scale of wages and benefits, the structure of the union movement, and the layout of the camps. Job hierarchies, urban segregation, and daily life experience and social interaction together created a clear distinction between Chilean workers and foreign employees. As in many other foreign-owned industries, a strong nationalism within the labor force stemmed from workers' daily experience of racial segregation.[39] Unlike in the

---

36. Zaragosa Vargas, *Proletarians of the North: A History of Mexican Industrial Workers in Detroit and the Midwest, 1917–1933* (Berkeley and Los Angeles: University of California Press, 1993), 13–53.
37. Huneeus, *Estructura y dinámica social*, 58.
38. Archivos de Personal, División El Salvador, Salvador, Chile.
39. Thomas M. Klubock, "Nationalism, Race, and the Politics of Imperialism: Workers and North American Capital in the Chilean Copper Industry," in *Reclaiming the Political in Latin*

case of the Venezuelan oil industry in the first half of the twentieth century, in which skilled workers were usually foreigners, in Chile both unskilled and skilled workers were Chileans.[40] Geographical isolation, the small size of the community, and common experience as company employees or dependents tended to blur differences between Chilean workers. Despite a common Chilean background, however, social, occupational, and gender distinctions existed and shaped people's lives and ideas. These differences were especially important for white-collar families, who perceived and struggled to establish themselves as a distinctive social class in the camps.

In the early 1940s, at its peak of activity, Andes Copper employed about 5,364 people, including both white- and blue-collar workers, and about one hundred staff employees. The labor force declined in the following years, and in the 1950s and 1960s, the size of the labor force ranged between twenty-five hundred and thirty-five hundred (Table 5).

In the mine, smelter, and plants, blue-collar workers worked daily shifts of eight hours, six days a week, but the normal hours were usually increased by overtime—limited to two hours a day, according to the Labor Code. Labor turnover among blue-collar workers was relatively high, and there was a great diversity of skills, salaries, and working conditions. In 1941, an average of 1,151 people worked in the mine, 798 underground and 353 on the surface, organized in three shifts. The first shift, with the most workers, began at eight o'clock in the morning and went until four in the afternoon, the second shift started at four and finished at midnight, and the night shift—with only about forty people underground—lasted from seven o'clock in the evening to three in the morning.[41] Mining underground was a world apart. Below ground, the three most important functions were extraction, loading, and maintenance. The mine had high rates of absenteeism, 9.4 percent in the 1940s.[42] The plants, shops, transportation, and services employed the rest of the workforce.

Small accidents were frequent and part of workers' everyday lives, but they never reached the tragic dimensions of those in the coal industry or at El Teniente. Silicosis, especially among those employed in extraction and

---

American History: Essays from the North, edited by Gilbert M. Joseph (Durham: Duke University Press, 2001).

40. Jaime R. Olivares, "The Creation of a Labor Aristocracy: The History of the Oil Workers in Maracaibo, Venezuela, 1925–1948" (Ph.D. diss., University of Houston, 2003), 112–20, 148–50.

41. De Viado, "Informe."

42. De Viado, "Informe."

Table 5 Labor force at Andes Copper, 1941–1970

Year	Average Production Workers	Average White-Collar workers	Average Staff-Employees	Total Andes Copper	Total Large-Scale Copper Industry
1941	4,517	748	99	5,364	
1950	1,736	426	98	2,260	15,613
1951	1,955	427	99	2,481	15,866
1952	1,990	413	98	2,501	15,938
1953	1,951	439	102	2,492	16,427
1954	1,995	407	106	2,508	14,551
1955	2,183	425	120	2,728	15,063
1956	2,402	510	159	3,071	16,647
1957	2,860	662	253	3,775	17,594
1958	2,443	691	337	3,471	17,274
1959	2,392	734	318	3,444	17,315
1960	2,316	774	257	3,347	17,084
1961	3,227				
1962	2,767				15,864
1963	2,888				16,131
1964	2,902				18,064
1965	3,001				17,198
1966	2,794	1,004			16,389
1967					19,000
1968					19,931
1969					19,201
1970	3,184	1,486	261	4,931	20,766

SOURCES: Manuel Barrera, *El conflicto obrero en el enclave cuprífero* (Santiago: Universidad de Chile, 1973); Manuel de Viado, "Informe sobre la Comisión Oficial al Mineral de Cobre de Potrerillos," Archivo Nacional de la Administración Central del Estado, Ministerio de Salubridad, Previsión, y Asistencia Social, Providencias, August–September 1941; Ministerio de Minería, *Anuario de la Minería de Chile, 1962–1975* (Santiago); Liliana Muñoz, *Estudio ocupacional de la minería del cobre* (Santiago: Servicio Nacional del Empleo, 1971); Clark W. Reynolds, "Development Problems of an Export Economy: The Case of Chile and Copper," in *Essays on the Chilean Economy*, ed. Markos Mamalakis and Clark W. Reynolds (Homewood, Ill.: Richard D. Irwin, 1965); Andes Copper Mining Company, "Informaciones para los sindicatos de Andes Copper Mining Company," Potrerillos, 27 June 1966, Archivo de la Dirección del Trabajo; Cobresal, "Primer encuentro de producción y participación de los trabajadores de Cobresal," El Salvador, August 1973.

crushing plants, was the gravest threat to workers' lives. During the second half of the twentieth century, people who worked the nigh shift (shift C) and who worked underground were entitl ed to special economic compensation.

Empleados (white-collar workers) and their families were a distinctive group. From a material perspective, they were better off than the majority of blue-collar workers in the camps, lived in separate houses, and had exclusive social clubs. Unlike blue-collar workers, they were more likely to be married and living with their families. In 1941, about 65 percent of white-collar employees were married, compared with 38 percent of blue-collar workers.[43] The number of married workers increased over time, and in 1966, Andes Copper reported that about 82 percent of white-collar employees and about 62 percent of blue-collar workers were married.[44] White-collar employees constituted about one-fourth of the total labor force and were concentrated in clerical positions, supervisory positions, and services such as the company store, schools, housing office, and hospital. With changes in legislation in the late 1950s, skilled workers such as machinists and electricians joined the ranks of white-collar employees. By 1966, they were almost a third of the labor force.[45] Like blue-collar workers, white-collar employees were divided according to their skills, experiences, and seniority, divisions that were reflected in a complex pay scale.

As in the case of Peruvian empleados described by historian David Parker, the social life, ideology, demands, and organizations of the copper empleado showed the development of a distinctive class identity during the first half of the twentieth century.[46] White-collar workers articulated a discourse through specific political and labor claims and a national view of class. The legal distinctions between blue- and white-collar workers established by the Labor Code of 1931 reinforced their self-identity as a class separate from blue-collar workers. Despite geographical isolation, copper empleados considered themselves part of a larger social group and claimed rights according to their status. For example, in 1940, when negotiating a union contract, empleados demanded a general improvement in salaries, rations at the company store, health care, and housing conditions. Both increases in the cost of living and the circumstances specific to the mine made economic demands urgent. Harsh working, living, and weather conditions forced empleados, the union argued, to spend more money on food and clothes. They also felt entitled to an increase in wages and social benefits to match conditions enjoyed by other empleados around the country.[47] In this context, they were part of a growing national movement of white-collar

---

43. De Viado, "Informe."

44. Andes Copper Mining Company, "Informaciones para los sindicatos de Andes Copper Mining Company," June 27, 1966, Archivo de la Dirección del Trabajo (hereafter ADT).

45. Andes Copper Mining Company, "Informaciones."

46. David S. Parker, *The Idea of the Middle Class: White-Collar Workers and Peruvian Society, 1900–1950* (University Park: Pennsylvania State University Press, 1998), 9–13.

47. Sindicato Profesional de Empleados to Andes Copper, October 31, 1940, ARNAD, DT, Providencias, 1940, vol. 35.

workers.[48] While their economic demands were not that different from the demands of blue-collar workers, they emphasized the difficulties with the aim of maintaining a white-collar status in the mine.

The urban and demographic characteristics of Potrerillos created unique opportunities for interactions, conflict, and cooperation between white- and blue-collar workers. White- and blue-collar employees shared such services and public spaces as schools, stores, hospitals, and theaters. Although they interacted in sport competitions, political meetings, and demonstrations, they had separate social clubs and union halls. In this unique environment, white-collar employees developed a dual identity. On the one hand, they were middle-class empleados who struggled to build social boundaries. On the other hand, they were Chilean workers in a foreign-owned industry. As these two identities coexisted, empleados simultaneously discriminated against working-class people in social events and established cross-class labor and political alliances. Political parties reinforced this dual identity. Most empleados supported the Radical and Socialist Parties and in the 1960s the Christian Democratic Party; blue-collar workers joined the Communist and Socialist Parties.

Social anxiety shaped the experience of the local empleados in the copper camps. The Potrerillos newspaper *La Usina* recounted in an ironic tone the class tensions existing in the community. In 1945, the reporter from *La Usina* described an incident during a party at the local white-collar social club. While "chic people" were dancing, many "*verdejos* were hanging out around the windows." Facing these unexpected spectators, "a flamboyant blonde-haired woman, from a very prestigious store downtown, closed the curtains and exclaimed: 'Let's close these, and then these indecent *rotos* cannot see us.'"[49] This was not an isolated incident. White-collar families usually described blue-collar workers, especially unmarried ones, as *verdejos* or *rotos*, terms with a strong class and cultural content.[50]

---

48. On *empleados*, see J. Pablo Silva, "White-Collar Revolutionaries: Middle-Class Unions and the Rise of the Chilean Left, 1918–1938" (Ph.D. diss., University of Chicago, 2000); J. Pablo Silva, "The Origins of White-Collar Privilege in Chile: Arturo Alessandri, Law 6,020, and the Pursuit of a Corporatist Consensus, 1933–1938," *Labor* 3 (2006): 87–112.

49. *La Usina* (Potrerillos), August 10, 1945.

50. Jorge Délano (Coke), caricaturist at the popular magazine *Topaze*, created the character of Juan Verdejo in the 1930s. Verdejo was a caricature of the common people of Chile, portrayed as "simple" and funny. To some extent, a *roto* was an older version of Verdejo. Born in the growth of Chilean cities and the massive migration from the countryside into urban areas and the nitrate fields, a *roto* represented the archetype of the rough, independent, migrant male. As

Gender ideas and roles reinforced class distinctions. White-collar families perceived the social and sexual behavior of single, male blue-collar workers as incompatible with the presence of "serious" women (wives, daughters) and young children. In May 1942, a group of women, wives of white-collar employees, denounced blue-collar workers who consumed alcohol outside the company store: "As they drink they start losing their manners and respect for the people and especially for women."[51] A couple of months later, *La Usina* mentioned that in the main street of Potrerillos, men "uttered insults and obscenities to the women who, at sunset, go shopping."[52] In the frequent parties organized by single workers in the camps, *La Usina* explained in September 1944, blue-collar workers fought "for any frivolous pretext, showing knives or throwing bottles everywhere."[53] As these incidents illustrate, white-collar families perceived the behavior of working-class men as a threat to their efforts to build a respectable community and protect women.

Despite social tensions, empleados allied themselves with working-class organizations. Their common experience as workers subjected to discrimination and segregation in a foreign-owned enterprise created a strong bond. This was also consistent with general national trends and the politicization and radicalization of white-collar labor unions in the 1930s and during the Popular Front (1936–41). In the 1940s, the tensions between the Radical Party and the Left; the divisions within the Left; and after 1948, anti-Communist legislation created some political tensions between blue- and white-collar unions in Potrerillos. In the 1950s, the contradictions of the Chilean economy and its inability to offer economic security to the middle class, the reorganization of the national labor movement and the founding of the Central Única de Trabajadores (1953), and the enactment of the Statute of Copper Workers (1956) reinforced a labor alliance between blue- and white-collar organizations in the copper camps.

While the labor force in the copper camps was almost exclusively composed of men, a growing minority of women also held formal positions. Women first worked in the hospitals, company stores, schools, and laundry

---

Verdejo, he was also comical, uneducated, and irreverent. See, for instance, Joaquín Edwards Bello, *El roto* (Santiago: Editorial Universitaria, 1994).
  51. *La Usina* (Potrerillos), May 7, 1942.
  52. *La Usina* (Potrerillos), December 3, 1942.
  53. *La Usina* (Potrerillos), September 7, 1944.

services and in a wide range of white-collar positions such as secretaries, clerks, and telephone operators. There were also professional women, primarily teachers, social workers, nurses, and midwives. In 1941, according to Manuel de Viado, the company employed 157 female workers: 3 foreign staff employees, 139 white-collar employees, and 25 blue-collar workers. While it is likely that many were wives and daughters of company employees, the existence of special housing facilities for single women suggests that some of them came by themselves. In 1941, the company maintained a nine-room house in Potrerillos and a one with four rooms in La Mina for female single employees.[54] In 1957, the company was finishing a new building to house thirty-two female blue-collar workers, fourteen of whom worked in the hospital.[55] Like other companies employing female workers at the time, Andes Copper preferred young, single women and enforced rules to protect the "morality" of single-women employees.[56] Under no circumstances could male workers enter female quarters, and the company imposed a rigorous curfew. Despite the restrictions, Cristián Gálvez, a former schoolteacher from Potrerillos, remembered that in the 1950s, "there were always women in the male quarters and men in the female quarters."[57]

Over time, economic conditions for copper workers improved. By the 1960s, salaries in the large-scale copper industry were above the national average, comparable to those of blue-collar workers in the steel plant at Huachipato and the oil industry in Magallanes. As shown in Markos Mamalakis's national wage statistics for the early 1960s, copper salaries were twice the average of those in the coal industry or in construction.[58] Copper workers were also entitled to a wide range of fringe benefits and wage supplements, in the form of cash, such as bonuses, and in kind, as in housing. Although such supplements and payments were common in Chile, they were more extensive and varied in the large-scale copper mines than in other industries.[59] In the 1960s, bonuses in Potrerillos and

54. De Viado, "Informe."
55. *Andino* (El Salvador), December 28, 1957.
56. *El Siglo* (Santiago), February 16, 1964.
57. Cristián Gálvez, conversation with the author, March 2, 2000.
58. Markos Mamalakis, *Historical Statistics of Chile: Demography and Labor Force* (Westport, Conn.: Greenwood Press, 1980), 318.
59. Peter Gregory, *Industrial Wages in Chile* (Ithaca: Cornell University Press, 1967), 12–33; United States Department of Labor, Bureau of Labor Statistics, *Labor Law and Practice in Chile* (n.p.: U.S. Department of Labor, 1969), 56.

El Salvador made up about a third of blue-collar wages and less than half of white-collar salaries.[60]

Bonuses varied depending on job classification, levels of productivity, and family situation and included overtime, sick pay, vacation payments, profit sharing, and Sunday pay (*semana corrida*). Further, the copper industry supplemented wages with a range of "technological bonuses" related to production and specific working conditions, examples being the shift C (late shift) bonus and the production bonus. There were also so-called lump-sum payments, among them Christmas, New Year, and national holiday bonuses. Extensive social benefits included family, schooling, housing, transportation, death, and birth allowances.

A Union Town

The copper camps were union towns. Labor unions played a critical labor, political, and social role and were the major force behind improvements in working and living conditions. The origins, organization, and role of the labor movement in Potrerillos derived from the formal requirements and subsequent modifications of the Labor Code of 1931, the political experience during the first years of the Popular Front (1936–41), and the intersections between the miners' working and the living spaces. Although the unions were post–Labor Code, they were also influenced by the labor experiences of the early twentieth century, which saw the struggles and politicization of nitrate workers in northern Chile and urban workers in cities and ports. As discussed in following chapters, the growing importance of the copper industry for the national economy and the Chilean state gave the labor movement in the copper mines unique bargaining and political power. However, the instability of both the national economy and the international copper market, changes in government coalitions and policies with electoral cycles, the uneven commitment of the state to enforce labor rights, and the antilabor attitude of the company prevented the consolidation of a permanently benign system of labor relations in Potrerillos and the copper mines more generally.

60. U.S. Embassy, 15 May 1961, U.S. National Archives and Records Administration (hereafter NARA), Department of State, General Records (hereafter GR), Chile 1960–63, box 2397.

The institutional basis of union power was the Labor Code, which regulated labor relations and employment conditions in the copper industry until the enactment of the Copper Workers' Statute in 1956. Enacted in 1931, the Labor Code gave Chilean workers the rights to unionize, engage in collective bargaining, and strike. It divided blue- and white-collar workers into two labor unions: the *sindicato industrial* (plant or industrial union) and the *sindicato profesional* (professional or craft union).[61]

Workers in industrial plants with more than twenty-five blue-collar workers had the right to form a union. After 55 percent of the labor force on the local shop floor approved the formation of a union, the union automatically regarded all workers as members and membership became compulsory. In contrast, white-collar workers organized along craft lines, also with a minimum of twenty-five members. All unionized workers elected the union leadership, regularly participated in assemblies, and paid monthly dues. The code stipulated procedures for collective bargaining and enforced arbitration through tripartite conciliation boards (*juntas de conciliación*) integrated by workers, employers, and state authorities. In a nationwide system, labor courts and Labor Department (Dirección del Trabajo) regional offices were charged with making labor and social laws a reality across Chile. The unions could call a strike when all phases of legal bargaining had failed. The strike had to be approved by an absolute majority in a secret election, which required a quorum of two-thirds of union members. The code required labor inspectors to oversee the elections and certify the results. It also prohibited general strikes and made local unions responsible for damages occurring during illegal work stoppages.

The Labor Code defined the internal structure, finances, and scope of action of the unions. The unions were democratic institutions. Active union members participated in a general assembly and elected the five members of the executive leadership: president, secretary, accountant, and two directors. The members of the directorate had to be literate, and they enjoyed trade union immunity (*fuero sindical*). Elected for a year, they could

---

61. For a detailed description of the Labor Code and the system of industrial relations in Chile, see Robert J. Alexander, *Labor Relations in Argentina, Brazil, and Chile* (New York: McGraw-Hill, 1962), 266–326; Angell, *Politics and the Labour Movement*, 57–81; Alfredo Gaete, *Código del Trabajo (concordado y anotado)* (Santiago: Ediciones Ercilla, 1945); Moisés Poblete, *El derecho del trabajo y la seguridad social en Chile: Sus realizaciones, panomara americano XXV años de legislación social* (Santiago: Editorial Jurídica, 1949).

be reelected. Under the Labor Code, union leadership was not remunerated, and directors continued to be full-time employees in their company. The primary goals of labor unions were to represent workers during labor conflicts and collective bargaining and to protect workers' individual rights. They were also supposed to improve conditions for their members, empowering workers to solve social and community problems.[62]

An important contribution of the Labor Code was the regulation of working conditions and rules of employment. In codifying these, it incorporated many of the social laws enacted during the first two decades of the twentieth century. It established the eight-hour workday, limiting overtime to two hours a day, and the six-day workweek and gave blue-collar workers paid vacations of seven to fifteen days a year. It abolished some of the most dreadful abuses that had been widespread in the nitrate industry, outlawing *enganches*, salaries paid in company tokens (*fichas*) rather than cash, and the exclusiveness of the company store, among other things. The code abolished child labor and gave white-collar employees an annual one-month service indemnity upon dismissal. It also reinforced employers' responsibility regarding conditions of safety and hygiene in the plants and in housing. Female workers were entitled to equal pay for equal work; twelve-week maternity leave; and in establishments with more than twenty employees, use of a nursing room (*sala cuna*), for children under one year old. The enforcement of these rights, as historian Peter Winn clearly demonstrates in his study of textile workers in Santiago, depended on the balance of power between local unions, employers, and state labor officers.[63]

The Labor Code, however, had several limitations. It denied public-sector workers the right to unionize and limited the formation of labor confederations. While the code initially allowed the unionization of rural workers, their rights were later severely limited. There were also problems with the scope of the jurisdiction of labor courts, and especially in the 1930s, lack of resources considerably restricted the code's effectiveness. These limitations forced workers to step out of the legal framework and they organized illegal strikes. Starting in 1936, internal security laws severely limited the independence of labor unions and the right to strike. Although it legalized, legitimated, and institutionalized the labor movement, the code also atomized working-class organizations and limited workers' action to the

62. Sindicato Industrial Obrero Andes Copper Mining Company y Potrerillos Railway Company Sección Potrerillos, "Estatutos," 1933, Biblioteca Nacional de Chile.
63. Winn, *Weavers of the Revolution*.

Table 6 Labor unions in Andes Copper Company and Potrerillos Railway Company

Union	Place	Members by 1973	Foundation
Andes Copper			
Plant	Potrerillos	840	December, 1932
Plant	Mina		1933
Plant	Barquito	204	March, 1939
Plant	El Salvador	2,068	January, 1959
Professional	Andes Copper	1,171	February, 1939
Potrerillos Railway			
Plant	Llanta	236	June, 1940
Professional	Llanta	104	June, 1940

SOURCE: Jorge Barría, "Organización y políticas laborales en la Gran Minería del Cobre," in *El cobre en el desarrollo nacional*, ed. Ricardo Ffrench-Davis and Ernesto Tironi (Santiago: Ediciones Nueva Universidad, 1974), 200.

shop floor. It was paternalistic and authoritarian, a top-down solution to the labor crisis and an attempt to incorporate workers into a controlled system of labor relations.

The enactment of the Labor Code had an immediate impact on the Potrerillos labor movement as workers accepted and adapted to the new laws. Although we should not disregard past organizational experiences, it was under the jurisdiction of the Labor Code, as Chilean historian Jorge Barría noted, that copper workers in Chile built solid institutions.[64] Between 1932 and 1940, workers organized four plant unions and two professional unions at Potrerillos, and these remained the backbone of the labor struggle in this mine (Table 6). Despite the limitations of the code, copper workers successfully used the labor legislation to improve their working, living, and economic conditions.[65]

Political developments in the late 1930s, including the organization of the Popular Front in 1936 and the presidential election of Pedro Aguirre Cerda in 1938, were instrumental in accelerating the incorporation of Chilean workers, and among them copper workers, into a structured system

64. Jorge Barría, "Organización y políticas laborales en la Gran Minería del Cobre," in *El cobre en el desarrollo nacional*, ed. Ricardo Ffrench-Davis and Ernesto Tironi (Santiago: Ediciones Nueva Universidad, 1974), 193–96.
65. For a comparison on the impact of labor legislation and politics on the labor movement, see John D. French, *The Brazilian Workers' ABC: Class Conflict and Alliances in Modern São Paulo* (Chapel Hill: University of North Carolina Press, 1992); John D. French, *Drowning in Laws: Labor Law and Brazilian Political Culture* (Chapel Hill: University of North Carolina Press, 2004).

of collective bargaining. Above all, the election of the Popular Front and the incorporation of progressive policy makers in the social ministries meant the enforcement of the labor legislation and the government's support for union and bargaining rights.[66]

Elected by a heterogeneous political coalition led by the Radical Party, Aguirre Cerda promised Chilean citizens "bread, roof, and shelter" and substantial economic and social reforms. His popular campaigns and discourse as well as the incorporation of the Chilean Workers Confederation (Confederación de Trabajadores de Chile, or CTCH) favored workers' activism. Under his short government (1938–41), public officers strove to enforce workers' rights and made legal strategies more accessible and useful to unionized workers. Public authorities authorized political meetings and respected the organized-labor movement. Not all Chilean workers enjoyed the benefits of these new political times: in a political compromise with the Right, the government heavily repressed and eventually delegalized rural unions, and the traditional landlord class retained its political, social, and economic power there for the following three decades.[67]

The limitations of the Labor Code and the historical politicization of the labor movement created a strong bond between leftist political parties and labor unions, encouraging unions to engage in politics. Alan Angell, in his classic study of politics and unions in twentieth-century Chile, has argued that economic weakness and legal atomization led local unions to seek an alliance with political parties. Chilean labor unions had to rely on friendly politicians to voice their concerns in the legislature, and Socialists, Communists, and Radicals contributed to union efforts through political mediation, economic resources, lawyers, newspapers, and leaders. The characteristics of the Chilean political system also implied that no single political party dominated the labor movement.[68] In addition, as Chilean historian Julio Pinto writes, workers in Chile had a long political tradition dating back to the late nineteenth century.[69]

In the copper mines, political parties were important actors. The political militancy of union leaders, the close relationship between unions and legislators, and popular activism during election times were clear signs of the influence that political parties had on the local labor movement and the

66. Klubock, *Contested Communities*, 103–12.
67. Loveman, *Struggle in the Countryside*, 113–88.
68. Angell, *Politics and the Labour Movement*, 58–59, 210–43.
69. Pinto, *Trabajos y rebeldías*, 251–312.

local population. As it did in many mining sectors, the Communist Party had an important and growing influence among copper workers, especially in El Teniente and Potrerillos. Similarly, on the eve of the Popular Front's election victory, the Socialist Party was quite strong in Potrerillos and La Mina, where there were several socialist union activists. The Radical Party, because of its strong presence in the regions of Coquimbo and Atacama, was also very influential, especially among white-collar workers.[70] In the late 1960s, the Christian Democratic Party started gaining some support among white-collar labor unions in the copper industry.

The relationship between labor unions and political parties was maintained in the personal and charismatic careers of certain legislators and in the political careers of some union leaders. Legislators representing mining and northern districts, among them Salvador Allende (Socialist Party), Raúl Ampuero (Socialist Party), Juan de Dios Carmona (Falange Nacional, later Christian Democratic Party), Roberto Flores (Socialist Party), Víctor Galleguillos (Communist Party), and Ramón Silva (Radical Party), built strong connections with the copper workers' labor movement. Among the most influential legislators in Potrerillos were Alejandro Chelén and Manuel Magalhaes, both born in Chañaral in 1911. Chelén worked in the nitrate industry in the late 1920s and in several small copper mines in Tarapacá and Inca de Oro from 1936 to 1948.[71] He joined the Socialist Party in 1934 and organized the presidential campaign of Pedro Aguirre Cerda in the province of Chañaral in the late 1930s.[72] In 1939, he founded *Avance*, the only socialist newspaper in the port of Chañaral. He was deputy for the Fourth District, which encompassed La Serena, Coquimbo, Elqui, Ovalle, and Combarbalá, in 1949–57 and senator for the district comprising Atacama and Coquimbo in 1957–65. As a legislator, he participated in numerous debates about copper policies and copper workers, defending the workers and describing their plight at the national level.

Known as the *diputado del cobre* (copper deputy) for his long-standing commitment to the copper workers, Manuel Magalhaes was an influential political figure in the region during the 1950s and 1960s. He attended high school in Copiapó and studied at the state university in Santiago, where he got his degree in dentistry in 1936. After graduating, he moved to Vallenar

---

70. Angell, *Politics and the Labour Movement*, 161.
71. Armando de Ramón et al., *Biografía de Chilenos*, vol. 1 (Santiago: Ediciones Universidad Católica, 1999), 266.
72. *El Progreso* (Chañaral), August 30, 1938.

and in 1938–49 worked as a dentist at the local hospital. While still at the hospital, he was elected to the municipal council (*regidor*) and then as mayor (*alcalde*) of the city of Vallenar. In 1949, he became deputy in the Third District, which included Chañaral. He was reelected four times, serving as deputy during five periods: 1949–53, 1953–57, 1957–61, 1961–65, and 1969–73. It is unclear when he joined the Radical Party, but he was already a party militant when elected to represent his college class on the student board in the early 1930s. He belonged to several social organizations (Sociedad de Odontológica, Rotary Club, Club Social Vallenar, and Liga de Estudiantes Pobres, among others) and was the founder and first director of Chañaral's fire department. Magalhaes died in Copiapó in 1996. His influence speaks to that of the Radical Party in the area, going back to the 1920s. Isauro Torres, also of the Radical Party, was deputy in 1926–41 and senator in 1941–65. Another Radical Party member, Carlos Melej, served as deputy from 1941 to 1953.

Unlike the great majority of Chilean labor unions, unions in the copper industry rapidly became stable, powerful institutions. To some extent, this was a result of copper's strategic economic and political importance for the nation and of the unique characteristics of the export sector. In the aftermath of the Great Depression, the copper industry replaced the nitrate industry as an important source of foreign income. By the late 1930s, the large-scale copper industry was producing an average of 400,000 tons of fine copper per year, reaching a record of 524,000 tons in 1944.[73] Adding to this was a growing industrial sector and an interventionist state, which grew increasingly dependent on the resources that issued from copper mining. Throughout the second half of the twentieth century, copper unions not only had more economic resources—because of higher wages and profit sharing—than other unions, but their position in a key economic sector gave them considerable political influence.

Unionism in the copper mines also gained strength and legitimacy through the intersections of the workplace and the community. In her study of Anaconda, Montana's Smelter City, historian Laurie Mercier described the existence of a strong bond between the community and the labor movement. She describes a "community unionism" that had developed in the city, whereby "the town's small size, cultural traditions, and relationship to

---

73. Reynolds, "Development Problems," 236–37.

its single industry demanded community cooperation and attention to local as well as workplace issues as strategy to ensure union survival."[74]

Although it was smaller than Anaconda, Potrerillos also evinced many features characteristic of this "community unionism." In Potrerillos, the small size of the camp and the company's control of urban space and the social infrastructure provided opportunities for local unions to play a role outside the workplace. Labor unions provided social and recreational spaces that were outside the direct control of the company and appropriated company resources to satisfy their members' leisure needs. Labor leaders used collective contracts and union resources to strengthen the local community and satisfy people's needs. In 1941, for example, the professional union helped to finance the summer camp for Potrerillos children in Chañaral.[75] By 1944, the Potrerillos plant union maintained a restaurant, a barber shop, a band, and a library.[76] Through parties, celebrations, and political meetings, the unions were present in the everyday life of the community. This involvement engendered a strong solidarity despite occupational divisions.

Conclusions

The construction of a company town and the industrial organization of production in Potrerillos had a tremendous impact on workers and their families. They created a dependent working community, in which Andes Copper played a major role as both employer and provider of social and urban services, and a workforce that was highly stratified along occupational lines. In a situation echoed in most company towns around the world, Andes Copper was everywhere, providing jobs, free housing, health care, transportation, and sports fields. Management presented these services as outstanding benefits, portraying Potrerillos as a model camp. The inherent contradictions of the model and the reality—the urban segregation of Chilean workers from foreign management, long lines at the company store, strict internal regulations, intrusive company inspectors, and isolation—made life a constant struggle, motivating workers to organize.

74. Laurie Mercier, *Anaconda: Labor, Community, and Culture in Montana's Smelter City* (Urbana: University of Illinois Press, 2001), 46.
75. *El Progreso* (Chañaral), December 27, 1941.
76. *La Usina* (Potrerillos), April 30, 1942.

By the late 1930s, lived experience in a company town, a clear understanding of the "other"—a foreign company and management that lived in a segregated neighborhood—and unsatisfactory working and economic conditions became the basis of a shared identity for Chilean copper workers and union members. To this was added the institutional impact of the Labor Code and the reformist, if not radical, political discourse of the Popular Front. On the eve of World War II, the copper workers' union movement transcended the immediate bread-and-butter struggle moving toward the reconfiguration of an influential social, labor, and political movement. This transition made copper workers critical actors in post–World War II Chile.

3 ★ Copper, Labor, and Political Repression, 1945–1952

Between 1945 and 1952, Chileans witnessed intense political debates, serious labor conflicts, and the consequences of shifts in world politics and the international economy. The deterioration of the terms of trade and the growing dependence on copper squeezed an economy struggling to industrialize. The postwar economic downturn and uncontrolled inflation had a dramatic impact on working people. In the period 1945–48, labor organizations and the Communist Party became increasingly dissatisfied with the pace of reforms, the orientation of the agenda of the Radical Party–led government, and broad political alliances more generally. Tensions within the government coalition, the labor movement, and the Left increased. The beginning of the Cold War ideological confrontation and, after 1946, pressures from the United States to outlaw Communist parties around Latin America aggravated the national political, labor, and social strife.[1]

In Potrerillos, the postwar instability of the international copper market and the depletion of the mine deteriorated living and working conditions, threatened job security, and sparked a wave of labor activism. The deterioration of the terms of trade for Chilean copper in the international market was accompanied by the depletion of the mine at Potrerillos. The crisis of Chilean copper and of the Potrerillos mine inspired a growing economic nationalism.[2] The outlawing of the Communist Party in 1948 and the authoritarianism of President Gabriel González Videla (1946–52) challenged local political alliances and labor strategies. Copper workers adjusted to the

---

1. For an overview of this period, see Paul W. Drake, "International Crises and Popular Movements in Latin America: Chile and Peru from the Great Depression to the Cold War," in *Latin America in the 1940s: War and Postwar Transitions*, edited by David Rock (Berkeley and Los Angeles: University of California Press, 1994).

2. For a discussion of this growing economic nationalism between 1945 and 1954, see Moran, *Multinational Corporations*, 57–88.

new political and economic climate, found refuge in trade unionism and industry-wide solidarity, and used the legal mechanisms of the Labor Code to defend their labor, social, and economic rights.

A Controversial Strike, 1945

On March 22, 1945, more than four thousand employees from Potrerillos went on strike.[3] They asked for a general wage increase, inclusion of sick days as days worked with respect to vacations, expansion of wage supplements such as a special two-peso bonus for workers who worked the night shift and a 10 percent bonus for those employees who completed twenty-four working days a month, a one-month service indemnity per year on dismissal, and job reclassifications. They also requested lower prices and better rations at the company store.[4] General manager Irl Greninger objected to the union demand for economic improvement, arguing that instability in the world market, low prices for copper, and the recent reduction of work at Potrerillos made acceding to worker's demands impossible. "The real cost of production," he claimed, "has been higher than the price of copper in the United States market, [and] the companies [Andes Copper Company and Potrerillos Railway Company] I represent are not in an economic situation to bear a new increase in the cost of production, whether it is because of higher salaries and wages or new benefits and exemptions on workers' behalf."[5] The government agreed with Greninger. Osvaldo Martínez, in a report on behalf of the Ministry of Labor, concluded that because of the international copper crisis, Andes Copper could not meet workers' economic demands.[6]

The strike received the strong support from the rank and file, the local community, national labor organizations, and the political Left. It was, as historian Daniel James explained for the case of Argentine workers in the 1950s, a collective experience reinforcing the unity and solidarity within the working community.[7] In Potrerillos, a strike committee was responsible

---

3. *El Progreso* (Chañaral), March 24, 1945.
4. *El Progreso* (Chañaral), January 4, 1945.
5. *El Progreso* (Chañaral), February 8, 1945.
6. *El Progreso* (Chañaral), April 5, 1945.
7. Daniel James, *Resistance and Integration: Peronism and the Argentine Working Class, 1946–1976* (New York: Cambridge University Press, 1993), 90–93.

for keeping the members actively involved in the conflict; finding solutions to daily problems; watching for any attempt at disorder, sabotage, or strike-breaking; and organizing general assemblies to inform the community. Independent shopkeepers reduced their prices and gave credit to the strikers' families, and local artists raised funds and sponsored special shows for the striking workers and their families. National labor organizations, labor unions around the country, and leftist political parties immediately supported the strike. Communist deputy and leader of the Industrial Mining Federation (Federación Industrial Minera, or FIM) José Díaz Iturrieta went to the mine to collaborate with the movement. Labor unions around the country raised funds for striking workers and their families.

Along with the men, women were also active in the strike. The local Committee of Women demanded that the government intervene and force Andes Copper to accept the workers' fair demands. "Our sons, the future men of our homeland," the committee declared, "deserve all kind of considerations from the government. Not to satisfy the fair *pliego de peticiones* [demands] means to accept the provocations of the company because the demands are completely necessary in order to live with a minimum of comfort."[8] The ways in which women became part of the strike is indicative of their place in the community. As Thomas Klubock and Janet Finn have clearly demonstrated in the cases of El Teniente and Chuquicamata, strikes were not only a male workers' responsibility but that of the entire community. As in El Teniente and Chuquicamata, women in Potrerillos made use of their traditional domestic roles of mothers, wives, and daughters to legitimate their demands and participation.[9]

After seventeen days on strike, workers accepted government arbitration and suspended their work stoppage. Poststrike negotiations dragged on for more than two months, and in June, a new union contract gave plant workers a fifteen-day service indemnity per year, improved rations in the company store, and a three- to four-peso general increase in daily wages.[10] The new contract resulted from the work of Moisés Poblete, the government-assigned mediator for the conflict. Poblete was the most prominent lawyer and expert in labor issues in Chile at the time. A prolific writer, he had also participated in the elaboration of the Labor Code; the

8. *El Siglo* (Santiago), March 28, 1945.
9. Finn, *Tracing the Veins*, 165–76;. Klubock, *Contested Communities*, 225–53.
10. *El Progreso* (Chañaral), June 14, 1945.

creation of the Labor Office; and multiple international conferences and organizations, including the International Labor Organization (ILO).

In October 1945, Anaconda started reducing production and also its labor force in the United States and at its Chilean subsidiaries. As World War II came to an end, Anaconda expected an imminent reduction in the international demand for copper. In Chile, Andes Copper and the Chile Exploration Company sued the unions for damages incurred during past strikes, overtly violating the last labor agreement and threatening the precarious understanding between management, labor, and the state.[11] Workers in Chuquicamata walked out on October 11, and in Potrerillos, a new strike started on October 20.

During this second strike, union leadership and sympathetic legislators emphasized workers' sacrifice during World War II to criticize Anaconda's position.[12] The war had reshaped local conditions in the copper mines. Copper workers had joined the enthusiastic foreign staff in the war effort, participated in public demonstrations against the Axis and joined the local office of the Unión para la Victoria.[13] Potrerillos and the port of Barquito were placed under military control to protect the production and shipment of copper, and the authorities introduced severe restrictions in the day-to-day life of the mining community.[14] The local community had objected to some of these restrictions because, as the local newspaper *La Usina* explained, they limited people's free mobility into and out of the camp.[15] The Chilean economy had also supported the war; the United States had considered copper a strategic war commodity, and copper companies in Chile sold their copper at a fixed price of 11.7 cents a pound to U.S. government agencies.

In October 1945, despite the unions' emphasis on Anaconda's unfair policies and on workers' contributions and sacrifices during World War II, the Chilean government showed little sympathy for a simultaneous strike in Potrerillos and Chuquicamata. During this nineteen-day stoppage, state authorities exerted enormous but unsuccessful pressure on workers to make them return to work.[16] In 1945, the government had several legal

---

11. Confederación de Trabajadores de Chile to Minister of Interior, October 5, 1945, ARNAD, Ministerio del Trabajo (hereafter MT), Providencias, 1945, vol. 2.
12. *El Siglo* (Santiago), November 4, 1945.
13. *El Progreso* (Chañaral), March 18, 1943.
14. *El Progreso* (Chañaral), February 9, 1943.
15. *La Usina* (Potrerillos), July 13, 1944.
16. *El Progreso* (Chañaral), November 3, 1945.

recourses to force workers to return to work. Article 547 of the 1931 Labor Code gave the government the right to decree a resumption of production (*reanudación de faenas*) when a strike threatened the "health or the socioeconomic life" of the population.[17] The "Internal Security" law of 1937 (Ley de Seguridad Interior del Estado, or law 6.026) severely punished illegal strikes by authorizing the detention, internal exile (*relegación*), and payment of fines for those who "promote, encourage, or maintain" illegal strikes.[18] Supplementing the internal security law adopted in 1937, law 7.200 (1942) authorized the president to declare a state of emergency—and eventually to send in military troops—in regions threatened by conflict, whether external or internal.[19]

Economic hardships created a very delicate situation in Potrerillos and Chuquicamata. In the first week of November 1945, the strike committee in Potrerillos announced its decision to evacuate children from the camps, since economic conditions had become critical. It is unclear whether children were finally evacuated, but the decision was used to show to the rest of the country the economic problems faced by striking workers. In response to workers' economic problems, national working-class organizations launched a campaign to raise funds in support of the strikers. This was the second long strike of the year, and workers were running out of financial resources. The Communist newspaper *El Siglo* noted in a dramatic article that "Potrerillos workers were cornered by hunger" and that "the company intends to defeat workers economically."[20] On November 7, the government decreed a resumption of production, and workers came back to work under the promise that Anaconda would comply with the contract.[21]

The strikes of March and October 1945 illustrate the local, national, and international difficulties faced by copper workers in Potrerillos after World War II. Management repeatedly used the existence of a system of social and economic benefits and the instability in the international market to delegitimate workers' demands. Workers, U.S. copper companies argued, were already entitled to a wide range of benefits (including housing and low prices at company stores), and their demands had no economic justification.

---

17. Poblete, *El derecho del trabajo*, 72.
18. Poblete, *El derecho del trabajo*, 73.
19. Brian Loveman and Elizabeth Lira, *Las ardientes cenizas del olvido: Vía chilena de reconciliación política, 1932–1994* (Santiago: LOM, 2000), 112–13.
20. *El Siglo* (Santiago), November 5, 1945.
21. *El Progreso* (Chañaral), November 3, 1945.

The growing state dependency on copper and its rising conservatism and antilabor ideology motivated a strong reaction against labor mobilizations. Internal security laws, and after 1948 the anti-Communist law, became favorite tools in the hands of public authorities eager to control strikes and demands from below and to depoliticize the labor movement.

Gabriel Gonzalez Videla and Anti-Communism

Elected in September 1946 with only 40.1 percent of the national vote and the support of the Communist Party, Gabriel González Videla represented the left wing of the Radical Party. He promised social reform and economic growth based on industrialization. He was a popular candidate in the copper camps, receiving 65.8 percent of the vote in Potrerillos.[22] In the copper mines his support derived from his nationalistic and pro-labor discourse and from the strong influence exerted on copper workers by the Popular Front since 1938. While the Popular Front as a political alliance between the Communist, Socialist, and Radical Parties formally ended in 1941, Communists supported the González Videla candidacy in 1946. In Potrerillos, workers believed that González Videla could restrict the power of foreign capital, defend workers' rights and demands, and break down the copper companies' hegemonic control of the camps and their inhabitants. In September 1946, mine workers celebrated what they perceived as the "beginning of a better Chile." A poem published in La Usina on the aftermath of the election illustrates workers' rising expectations following González Videla's victory:

> Farewell to the sorrows
> Now we sing victory
> Soon the speculators
> Will pass into sad history.
> Finally we will have potatoes
> Sugar, beans, and tea
> No more *mazamorra*
> Herb tea or coffee.
> They would have to spin very straight

22. Records of National Elections, 1946. Servicio Electoral, Centro de Documentación, Santiago.

> Our foreign friends
> And the ones who are now informants
> Would have to fly very fast.
> It will not be a Yankee State
> This beloved mine
> People will come without a pass
> Without saluting the general.[23]

Despite his initial popular support, President González Videla faced challenging labor and political conflicts. In 1947, there were 37 legal strikes involving 70 white-collar workers and 17,817 blue-collar workers and 127 illegal strikes with 483 white-collar and 51,169 blue-collar workers participating.[24] While most strikes stemmed from the government's inability to promptly meet workers' economic and social demands, lessen people's frustration, and assist in workers' efforts to improve material conditions at the local level, they were also a response to changes in the internal politics and strategies of the Communist Party.[25] Following its thirteenth national congress in December 1945, important groups within the party, led by Luis Reinoso, supported a shift in the party's orientation, from the broad political alliances that had inspired the Popular Front to "lucha de masas" (struggle of the masses). This tendency, known as Reinosismo (because of being proposed by Luis Reinoso), remained strong within the party until 1951.[26]

In the midst of a national political crisis and increasing international pressures, President González Videla became strongly anti-Communist. In April 1947, he expelled all Communist ministers from the government. On October 3, coal workers, a traditionally Communist enclave, went on strike, and three days later González Videla sent in troops to reestablish control in the area.[27] The government also censored the Communist newspaper *El Siglo*, ordered the arrest of the party's entire national and regional leadership—about one thousand people—and broke off diplomatic relations with the Soviet Union. In November 1947, workers engaged in an

---

23. *La Usina* (Potrerillos), November 2, 1946.
24. United States Department of Labor, Bureau of Labor Statistics, *Foreign Labor Information: Labor in Chile* (n.p.: U.S. Department of Labor, July 1956), 13.
25. Jorge Arrate and Eduardo Rojas, *Memoria de la Izquierda Chilena: Tomo I (1850–1970)* (Santiago: Javier Vergara Editor, 2003), 247.
26. Augusto Varas, ed., *El partido comunista en Chile* (Santiago: CESOC-FLACSO, 1988), 85–133.
27. On coal workers during this period, see Pavilack, "Black Gold in the Red Zone.

extremely difficult round of collective bargaining in Chuquicamata, in Sewell, and in the nitrate fields. González Videla blamed the Communist Party and Communist international forces for these strikes. In Potrerillos, labor negotiations were especially tense and long, lasting from October 2, 1947, to March 22, 1948.[28]

The government blamed the Communist Party for the social and labor unrest occurring in the nation, and in June 1948, the National Congress passed the Law for the Permanent Defense of Democracy to protect Chilean "democracy." Enacted in September 1948, law 8.987 outlawed the Communist Party, disenfranchised its members, and expelled them from the organized labor movement, the universities, and public office. *El Siglo* was banned from 1948 to 1952 and the Communist magazine *Principios* from 1947 to 1954. As labor lawyer Moisés Poblete explained in 1949, the aim of this law was to "construct a barrier against Communism, eliminating it as a political entity and trying to extirpate its influence on the labor movement and especially on the mining sectors."[29] It opened a decade of persecution, imprisonment, and underground politics in Chile. Internationally, the anti-Communist law was a response to the strong pressures of the United States and its Cold War policies in Chile and Latin America more generally.

The repressive anti-Communist legislation intensified tensions within the labor movement and the Socialist Party, dividing unions and political forces. Following the law's enactment, a sector of the Socialist Party, led by Bernardo Ibáñez and Juan Rossetti, left the party and created the Socialist Party of Chile (PSCh). The PSCh supported the law and the government of González Videla.[30] The remaining Socialist Party, under the name Popular Socialist Party (PSP) and led by Raúl Ampuero, criticized the government's decision, but without jeopardizing its own status, struggling, as Chilean socialist historian Julio César Jobet explained, to prevent the destruction of the party and save its members.[31] Most copper workers supported Ampuero and the PSP.

The anti-Communist legislation hit Potrerillos and other working communities hard. As union official Manuel Ovalle, himself a member of the

---

28. Dirección del Trabajo, Registro Conflictos Colectivos, 1947, ARNAD.
29. Poblete, *El derecho del trabajo*, 74.
30. Paul W. Drake, *Socialism and Populism in Chile, 1932–1952* (Urbana: University of Illinois Press, 1978), 292.
31. Julio César Jobet, *Historia del Partido Socialista de Chile*, 2d ed. (Santiago: Ediciones Documentas, 1987), 56–57, 199–203.

Socialist Party and not particularly close to Communist leaders, told Robert Alexander in an interview in August 1952: "The police came at one and two o'clock in the morning, knocked on the doors of all the communists, arrested the men, and wouldn't even let them set their personal affairs in order. As a result, whole families of these communist miners were left without any means of support. This had the result of course of arousing the spirit of solidarity of the miners, particularly in the face of these helpless women and children. It was *contrapoducente.*"[32] Local authorities put activists on trains and deported them to Pisagua, a town on the northern coast of Chile that became the most infamous destination for internal political exiles.[33] *La Usina,* though it claimed no political affiliation, was closed and its owner prosecuted.

Authorities not only persecuted, imprisoned, and sent to internal exile Communist leaders, but also, in tandem with management, used the anti-Communist law to repress most forms of political and labor activism.[34] The Law for the Permanent Defense of Democracy, explained Inter-American Labor Organization (Organización Interamericana del Trabajo, or ORIT) representative Luis López Aliaga in 1952, provided "powerful weapons to the big mining companies to keep the labor movement down by calling Communist-inspired every legitimate economic movement of their employees."[35] In Potrerillos, managers and public officers called workers who engaged in wildcat strikes "subversive elements." And under the law, those who called for or participated in illegal strikes were committing a crime against public order. Conscription of striking workers into military service, government decrees of "resumption of production," and close supervision of union elections became common strategies to control the labor movement.

The ways in which the government and management used the Law for the Permanent Defense of Democracy to repress labor activism was clear during the legal strike in Potrerillos of May 1949. Although the strike was legal, the government did not hesitate to decree a resumption of production and appointed Colonel Arturo Vergara to take charge of the mine.[36]

32. Robert Alexander, George Meany Memorial Archives (hereafter GMMA), International Affairs Department, Jay Lovestone Files 1939–74 (hereafter JLF), folder 2, box 10.
33. *El Progreso* (Chañaral), March 6, 1948.
34. Jorge Barría, *Historia de la CUT* (Santiago: Ediciones Pla, 1971), 28–29.
35. Luis López, "Brief History of the New Confederation of Copper Workers of Chile," *Labor News* 2, no. 1 (1952).
36. *El Progreso* (Chañaral), May 24, 1949 and May 26, 1949.

Vergara returned to Potrerillos in June 1951, to break an illegal general strike called by the recently organized Copper Workers Confederation (Confederación de Trabajadores del Cobre, or CTC). As it had in 1949, the government declared that if workers did not resume work, it would enforce the Law for the Permanent Defense of Democracy.[37] When in March 1951, twenty-seven workers from the Potrerillos electrical shop stopped working to demand better economic conditions, local political authorities responded promptly and imprisoned union director Félix González for breaking the Law for the Permanent Defense of Democracy.[38] As late as 1957, the Labor Office asked the *director general de investigaciones* to check into the political and electoral backgrounds of labor leaders elected to represent workers on the conciliation board.[39]

The Crisis of Chilean Copper

Between the end of World War II and the approval of the Nuevo Trato in 1954, conditions for Chilean copper deteriorated. In 1945, Anaconda expected a reduced international demand for copper and planned to reconvert the mining industry to adapt it to a peacetime economy.[40] Despite Anaconda's fear, the U.S. economy continued growing in the following decades. Indeed, it experienced a long economic boom (1945–73), fueled by postwar European reconstruction; the demands of the war industry, now oriented to fight the Cold War; and internal demographic increases. Yet the Chilean copper industry benefited little from this boom. The strategies of copper corporations, U.S. foreign and economic policies, and the characteristics of copper production prevented Chile from profiting from U.S. prosperity. The crisis, scholar Theodore Moran explained, affected the thinking of Chilean economists and policy makers. In the early 1950s, influential Chilean economists such as Aníbal Pinto criticized the role of copper in the national economy and argued that copper and foreign capital aggravated Chile's dependency on the export market.[41]

---

37. *El Progreso* (Chañaral), June 20, 1951.
38. *El Día* (Copiapó), March 7, 1951 and March 8, 1951.
39. Dirección General del Trabajo to Director General de Investigaciones, September 20, 1957, ADT.
40. Anaconda Copper Mining Company, *Annual Report* (1945).
41. Moran, *Multinational Corporations*, 62–63.

One of the big challenges to Chilean copper was the growth of the African copper industry. Demand from the war industry drove an expansion of copper mining in the African Copper Belt in the 1940s. Production continued to increase in the postwar period with the opening of new mines (Bancroft and Chibuluma) and the expansion of old ones. By the early 1950s, Northern and Southern Rhodesia (presently Zambia and Zimbabwe) and the Belgian Congo (now Democratic Republic of the Congo) were successfully competing against Chile. By 1954, Africa produced 16.16 percent of copper produced in the non-Communist world, and by 1960 Zambia was the leading producer of copper in the world.[42] The success of African copper lay not only in its high yield and quality, but also, and above all, in its low labor costs, including low wages and "sub-standard working conditions" as ORIT general secretary Luis Alberto Monge, explained in 1953. In Chile, wages and labor conditions were not outstanding but "much higher than those prevailing in Africa."[43]

Adding to changes in the international copper market, the Potrerillos mine started showing clear signs of depletion. In September 1945, Potrerillos produced less copper than during the war years and predicted a 40 percent reduction of its labor force. By July 1949, the mine had stopped producing oxide ore (about a third of the total production of Potrerillos), and Andes Copper had closed its leaching and electrolysis plants. From 1950 to 1955, the copper content of sulfide ore at Potrerillos dropped from 1 percent to 0.78 percent, compared with 1.49 percent in 1927. Production costs increased from 16.9 cents per pound of copper in 1950 to 23.4 cents per pound in 1954.[44]

The company's efforts to reduce production costs unleashed a wave of unemployment and economic insecurity; working and living conditions deteriorated at Potrerillos. The company reduced the blue-collar labor force from 4,517 in 1941 to 1,736 in 1950, and the white-collar force from 748 in 1941 to 426 in 1950 (see Table 5). Demographic changes in the camps also reflected the sharp decline in the labor force; the Potrerillos population dropped from 11,203 in 1940 to 4,587 in 1950.[45] Conditions remained stable

---

42. Jane L. Parpart, *Labor and Capital on the African Copperbelt* (Philadelphia: Temple University Press, 1983), 13–28.
43. "Monge Writes US State Department Concerning Surplus Chilean Copper," *Labor Bulletin* 9 (1953).
44. Bernardo Pizarro, "Monografía sobre el mineral de Potrerillos," *Minerales* 55 (1956).
45. Instituto Nacional de Estadísticas, *Población de los centro poblados de Chile, 1875–1992* (Santiago: Instituto Nacional de Estadística, n.d.), 36–37.

in the early 1950s, and the number of both blue- and white-collar workers increased again in 1956 with the construction of El Salvador.

The threat of unemployment mobilized local unions and concerned public authorities and legislators. The physical limitation of the mine, the crisis in Chilean copper, and the repressive national political climate shaped workers' responses. Labor unions sought guarantees that layoffs conformed to legal norms and that workers received economic benefits and compensation to which they were entitled. To do so, they used Article 91 of the Labor Code, which required employers to obtain public authorization when making substantial transformations in the workplace.[46] Labor unions in Potrerillos attempted to negotiate the number and names of workers to be fired, established the payment of service indemnities, and introduced the idea of reassigning workers. They found friendly allies among public officials and leftist legislators such as Baltazar Castro (Labor Party), Alejandro Chelén (Popular Socialist Party), and Manuel Magalhaes (Radical Party), who considered the companies' labor policies detrimental not only to workers but, since they represented an attempt to reduce production, also to the Chilean economy. Despite these efforts, their success was limited. In July 1949, the Ministry of Labor authorized Andes Copper to dismiss from the oxide plant 510 workers, who were to receive a fifteen-day service indemnity per year of service. The unions settled the names of some of the workers who were to be fired and replaced workers from the oxide plant with workers from the sulfur plant who voluntarily wanted to leave the company (they otherwise would not have had access to unemployment compensation). Through this mechanism, Andes Copper reassigned about sixty workers in 1949–50. Not only was the number low, but also many of these reassigned did not adjust to work in the sulfur plant and complained about the emissions, eventually leaving the company.[47]

The Copper Workers Confederation

In March 1951, recalled Luis Tapia, a former white-collar employee from Chuquicamata, "more than 150 union leaders of the copper industry, representing nearly twenty-five thousand workers in the North American

---

46. Gaete, *Código del Trabajo*, 71.
47. Mandiola to Inspección del Trabajo, May 11, 1950, ARNAD, DT, oficios, 1950, vol. 17.

companies, met in the city of Machalí. In an open challenge to President Gabriel González Videla and his Law for Permanent Defense of Democracy, referred to by the Left as the *ley maldita*, or accursed law, they traveled from Potrerillos and Chuquicamata to El Teniente. After tense hours of debate and looking to unify the actions of the mining labor movement, the Copper Workers Confederation was born."[48] Tapia remembered one of the most important institutional, political, and influential events in the history of the copper workers' labor movement: the organization of a confederation representing all blue- and white-collar workers in the large-scale and foreign-owned copper industry. For the following two decades, the Copper Workers Confederation (Confederación de Trabajadores del Cobre, or CTC), through solidarity and industry-wide strikes, political alliances, and meetings, struggled for the nationalization of copper and improved local living and working conditions. In the process, it emphasized the common experience of copper and export workers and built a distinctive collective identity based on solidarity, social justice, and economic nationalism.

Two men, Manuel Ovalle and Héctor Olivares, became emblematic of the politics and struggles of the CTC throughout the 1950s and 1960s. Both were members of the union board of directors for more than a decade, alternating between president and vice president. Militants of the Socialist Party, they successfully adapted to the political upheavals and challenges of their time, giving continuity to their movement.

Born in Potrerillos in 1920 into a blue-collar family, Manuel Ovalle attended a professional school for mining (Escuela de Minas) in Copiapó and started working as a white-collar employee in the Chemical Department of Andes Copper when he was eighteen years old. He joined the Socialist Party in 1938 and participated in the foundation of the professional union in Potrerillos.[49] Like many socialist union leaders, he supported Raúl Ampuero and the Popular Socialist Party when the party split from the Socialist Party in 1948. In 1951, in a evidence of the negotiations and tensions between labor and political parties, he quit the party, accusing the Socialists of trying to control the copper workers' labor movement, but he rejoined in the mid-1950s. Robert Alexander, who interviewed him in the 1950s, described him as someone who was "courted by all of the parties,

---

48. Luis Andrés Tapia, "Semblanzas de la Federación de Trabajadores del Cobre," *Cobre Chileno* 55 (April 2000), 28.
49. Alejandro Witker, ed., *Archivo Salvador Allende: Historia documental del PSCH, 1933–1993; Forjadores y signos de renovación* (Mexico City: IELCO, 1993), 56.

and dominated by none of them. He can keep the union free from subjection to any political party, and yet remain on more or less friendly terms with most of the parties."[50] In the 1960s, Ovalle became a strong supporter of the incorporation of copper workers into the Central Única de Trabajadores (CUT).

Héctor Olivares had a similar trajectory. Born in Rancagua in 1924, Olivares, like Ovalle, also attended the Escuela de Minas in Copiapó. He started working in the El Teniente mine in the late 1940s and became president of the miners' union in 1951. In contrast to Ovalle, Olivares was very involved in the Socialist Party and regional politics. After a successful career as a union leader, he ran for the National Congress for Rancagua in 1965 and won a house seat in 1965, 1969, and 1973.[51]

The CTC linked its demand for improved economic conditions at the local level with a demand for the nationalization of copper. In Machalí, union leaders drafted a proposal to the Senate, titled "Economic Discussions," in which they carefully exposed the companies' production costs and elaborated the economic needs of copper workers in Chuquicamata, Potrerillos, and El Teniente. The document began with an analysis of the overall costs of salaries and benefits and the claim that copper companies could afford a general increase in wages and salaries. The authors contested the traditional view that housing and social benefits were privileges for copper workers: "Regarding housing, electricity, and other benefits, it is necessary to point out that the nature of mining exploitation has incorporated these benefits into the workplace; even the modest industrialist in the small-scale mining provides these benefits to the mine worker."[52] The authors also discussed working and living conditions in the copper industry, pointing out that isolation of workers and their families, lack of educational opportunities, occupational diseases and accidents, and abuses by copper companies justified workers' aspiration for economic improvement. This concern for economic and local issues gave the CTC a strong presence in the mines and support from the rank and file.

In 1951, the CTC also emphasized the difficulties of enforcing national laws in foreign-owned camps. In the copper mines, the CTC explained, "there is a marked absence of constitutional rights and legal guarantees,

---

50. Robert Alexander, August 9, 1952, GMMA, JLF, box 2, folder 10.
51. De Ramón et al., *Biografías de chilenos*, vol. 3, 197.
52. Federación Nacional de Trabajadores del Cobre, "Discusiones económicas," Machalí, March 25, 1951, Fundación Justicia y Democracia, Archivo Radomiro Tomic, Santiago, Chile.

which makes work in the mining industry an unrewarding activity."[53] In Machalí, the leaders of the CTC agreed on the need to contest the repressive regulations imposed by copper companies in the camps and to press for the end of the company's subsidies to state employees and the contracting system.[54] In Chuquicamata, Potrerillos, and Sewell, copper companies regularly subsidized public schools and provided housing and other benefits for police officers and other public authorities living and working in the camps. According to labor leaders, this material contribution limited the neutrality of public officers. Copper leaders thus wanted the government and National Congress "to enforce constitutional guarantees in the territory under the jurisdiction of foreign companies, to enforce the legal dispositions in the copper milieu, and to revise the internal regulations of the companies in those aspects that these opposed the Constitution, the law, and social peace."[55]

As the document clearly suggested, economic improvement was a matter of social justice and the expansion of economic citizenship, a right that workers were entitled to through their hard work, productivity, and contributions to the national economy. Economic improvement also implied the expansion of social benefits such as family allowance, severance pay, and profit sharing.[56] In a context of national economic insecurity, the CTC endeavored to protect workers' economic gains at the national level. While they never achieved industry-wide bargaining, the strong solidarity among the unions and the schedule of labor negotiations homogenized union contracts in the three big copper mines.

The agenda of the CTC reveals a strong economic nationalism in the copper workers' labor movement. In 1951, the leaders of the CTC demanded that the government become directly involved in the copper industry and regulate the production and commercialization of copper. They also vowed

---

53. Federación Nacional de Trabajadores del Cobre, "Discusiones económicas."
54. López, "Brief History."
55. Federación Nacional de Trabajadores del Cobre, "Discusiones económicas."
56. While only white collar workers in the private sector were entitled to family allowance and service indemnity payments since 1942, some private companies had extended these benefits to their entire workforce. Family allowances were financed by contributions from workers and employers, and were paid monthly according to the number of family dependents. Employers made monthly contributions to their employees' service indemnity accounts, which could be cashed in case of involuntarily unemployment, retirement, or as a survivor's benefit. In 1953, a reform of the Labor Code extended family allowances and service indemnity programs to blue-collar workers. United States Department of Labor, Bureau of Labor Statistics, *Labor Law and Practice in Chile*, 62–64.

to struggle for the nationalization of copper.[57] They were not alone in this second endeavor. The deterioration of market conditions for the most important commodity Chile, in the middle of the import-substitution effort, had put copper policy at the center of the public agenda and political debates. In July 1951, Communist senators Salvador Ocampo and Elías Lafertte presented to the National Congress and the country the first project for the nationalization of copper.[58]

In 1951, the economic nationalism of the CTC challenged the efforts of the Chilean government to reach an agreement with U.S. copper companies. In 1950, tensions between foreign copper corporations and the Chilean state increased, following the U.S. government's decision to fix the price of Chilean copper at 24.5 cents after the outbreak of the Korean War in 1950. All sectors of Chilean society reacted against what was perceived as U.S. government abuse and demanded that President Gabriel González Videla protect Chilean economic interests.[59] In 1951, the Chilean government lobbied against the price ceiling established during the Korean War. The Treaty of Washington in May 1951 fixed the price for Chilean copper at 27.5 cents a pound—an increase of 3 cents from the 24.5 cents established after the outbreak of Korean War—and gave the Chilean state control over the commercialization of 20 percent of copper production.[60] U.S. companies agreed to increase production, and the Chilean government to modify taxation.[61]

The Treaty of Washington unleashed the first overt conflict between the state and the CTC. The conflict stemmed from workers' demand to have a voice in the negotiations between foreign capital and the state. They demanded that in the Treaty of Washington agreements there be incorporation of specific provisions to guarantee and increase workers' economic and social rights, rights that had been raised in discussions during the foundation of the CTC in March 1951. The Treaty of Washington therefore provided the CTC with an opportunity to discuss the confederation's agenda with both the government and management.

57. Tapia, "Semblanzas," 28–30.
58. Eduardo Novoa, *La batalla por el cobre: La nacionalización chilena del cobre; Comentarios y documentos* (Santiago: Quimantú, 1972), 14.
59. Joaquín Fermandois, "La larga marcha de la nacionalización: El cobre en Chile, 1945–1971," *Jahrbuch für Geschichte Lateinamerikas* 38 (2001): 287–312.
60. Mario Vera, *La política económica del cobre en Chile* (Santiago: Ediciones de la Universidad de Chile, 1961), 59–60.
61. United Nations, "Economic Survey of Latin America," years 1951–52 (combined volume), 200.

In mid-June 1951, the CTC called an industry-wide strike to increase pressure on the government and foreign management.[62] The confederation's extraordinary demands included a general increase in wages and salaries for blue- and white-collar workers throughout the copper industry, annual bonus (*gratificación*), family allowance, settlement payment of one month per year work for both blue- and white-collar workers, and strict respect for trade union immunity for union leaders (*fuero sindical*).[63] On June 18, 1951, the CTC elaborated the economic justifications for their demands, arguing that the Treaty of Washington gave enormous benefits to U.S. copper companies and that "it was fair to incorporate into the agreement benefits for the workers that produce those benefits." In addition, the confederation declared, not only could companies afford to do this, but the Chilean miner was underpaid.

> There is even more. This inferiority of the Chilean copper miner appears disconcerting in a comparison with the salaries that a similar worker makes in the mines of the United States; while the U.S. copper miner earns an average base salary of ten dollars per day, in our country the average salary is not even 50 percent of the North American salary, even including overtime, fringe benefits, and allotments. This is not all. Large companies, as in Potrerillos, for example, do not pay family allowances to their blue-collar workers. Thus, it is a matter of justice to defend the social peace with a decent and humane salary.[64]

A two-week strike reopened direct negotiations between the CTC and the government.[65] The negotiations between workers, the state, and foreign capital lasted almost four months. In September, a tripartite commission charged with finding a solution to the conflict agreed on a wage increase according to the price of copper and the payment of production bonuses.[66] Failure of copper companies to implement the new gains led to new waves of worker mobilization in the following months. In November, copper labor leaders met with President González Videla and demanded that he

62. López, "Brief History."
63. *Revista de los empleados de Chile* 5, no. 38 (1951).
64. *Revista de los empleados de Chile*.
65. López, "Brief History."
66. *El Progreso* (Chañaral), October 8, 1951.

intervene on behalf of workers.⁶⁷ González Videla called the general manager of Anaconda in New York directly and asked him to find a prompt solution to the impasse.⁶⁸ Although workers obtained a wage increase, the question of production bonuses remained unsettled, as copper companies continually played down their profits, which were the basis for calculating bonuses.

Events of the industry-wide strike of June 1951 clearly demonstrate how the CTC used workers' experiences in a foreign company to legitimate the confederation's demand for inclusion in the discussion of copper policy and the economic decisions of the industry. It also indicates how the state's constant efforts to deny workers a voice in negotiations between the state and copper companies turned the CTC toward industry-wide strikes and social mobilization throughout the 1950s and the 1960s.

International Solidarity

The Cold War created unique but controversial opportunities for international labor solidarity. During the early 1950s, the CTC leadership sought the strategic support of the U.S. labor movement, became an active member of the Inter-American Federation of Labor (ORIT), and established personal links with U.S. labor leaders such as Serafino Romualdi from the American Federation of Labor (AFL) and Paul Reed from the United Mine Workers (UMW). This alliance was representative of the CTC's efforts to obtain international support as well as a sign of its distance from the most radical sectors of the Chilean labor movement. Given the characteristics of the copper workers' labor movement, copper workers were attractive candidates for the agenda of U.S. labor in Latin America.

The ORIT, organized in 1949, was the result efforts by Romualdi and the AFL to create a regional non-Communist labor organization in Latin America within the U.S. ideological framework of the Cold War. Between July 1941 and September 1943, Romualdi traveled throughout South America and recommended that the AFL launch a campaign of "education and publicity" in the Americas.⁶⁹ During that period and continuing until 1944, Romualdi worked closely with the Labor Relations Division of the

---

67. *El Progreso* (Chañaral), November 16, 1951.
68. *El Progreso* (Chañaral), November 23, 1951.
69. "Suggestions for the Setting Up of a Latin American Desk at American Federation of Labor's National Headquarters," November 18, 1943, Kheel Center for Labor-Management

Coordinator of Inter-American Affairs (CIAA). Under the banner of Pan-Americanism, Nelson Rockefeller and the CIAA believed that "inter-American relations do constitute a major foundation of the lasting edifice of people's Pan-Americanism."[70] In 1948, the AFL sponsored the creation of the Inter-American Confederation of Workers (Confederación Interamericana del Trabajo, or CIT), and in 1951, the CIT merged into the ORIT. The ORIT was a member of the International Confederation of Free Trade Unions (ICFTU), an institution created in 1949 to recognize workers' contributions during World War II, defend workers' gains, and fight against Communism.[71]

Involvement of the AFL in Chilean labor politics dated from the mid-1940s.[72] Beginning in 1946, both the AFL and later the CIT helped, politically and economically, anti-Communist groups in Chile and supported Bernardo Ibáñez, leader of one of the fractions of the Chilean Workers Confederation (Confederación de Trabajadores de Chile, or CTCH).[73] During the critical years following the division of the CTCH (1946) and the enactment of the anti-Communist legislation (1948), the AFL maintained an intimate relationship with Ibáñez.[74] Contacts increased in the following years.

In 1952, the ORIT launched a campaign to "rescue" the Chilean labor movement from the influence of Communism and the populist threat represented by the presidential candidacy of General Carlos Ibáñez del Campo. The ORIT decided then to appoint international labor leaders to Chile, organize an educational campaign, and allocate extraordinary economic resources (the ORIT expected to raise not less than ten thousand dollars).[75] On the one hand, this campaign was a result of the ORIT's efforts, as Robert Alexander explained in 1952, to create "a non-political" and non-Communist trade union movement in Chile.[76] On the other hand, it also was a response to Bernardo Ibáñez's campaign to obtain international support for his own

---

Documentation and Archives (hereafter KC), Serafino Romualdi Collection (herafter SRC), box 9, folder 1.

70. Romualdi to Rockefeller, April 6, 1944, KC, SRC, box 9, folder 1.
71. Hobart Spalding, "US and Latin American Labor: The Dynamics of Imperialist Control," *Latin American Perspectives* 3, no. 1 (1976).
72. Drake, *Socialism and Populism*, 280.
73. Serafino Romualdi, *Presidents and Peons: Recollections of Labor Ambassador in Latin America* (New York: Frank and Wagnalis, 1967), 332.
74. Serafino Romualdi, memorandum, August 3, 1946; Romualdi to Free Trade Union Committee, May 6, 1946, both documents at KC, SRC, box 2, folder 11.
75. "Report of the Regional Secretary of the ORIT," December 17–18, 1951, KC, SRC, box 10, folder 1.
76. Alexander to Lovestone, August 10, 1952, GMMA, JLF, box 3, folder 1.

political agenda. During the meeting of the executive board of the ORIT in December 1951, Ibáñez was instrumental in bringing up the Chilean question and convincing the other board members that the so-called free trade union movement in Chile was in danger.

The formal contacts between the ORIT and copper workers started in November 1951, when Luis López Aliaga from the ORIT met with the leadership of the recently organized CTC "for the purpose of reaching an agreement on future trade union cooperation among the two groups."[77] In that meeting, the CTC leadership invited representatives of the U.S. labor movement and the ORIT to visit the country and the copper mines. The international union delegation arrived in Chile on July 20, 1952, integrated by Paul Reed (United Mine Workers), Serafino Romualdi (AFL), and Angelo Verdu (CIO, International Union of Mine, Mill and Smelter Workers).[78] At the airport, they were welcomed by Manuel Ovalle, the president of the CTC, and by representatives of the ORIT in Chile, the Chilean government, and the U.S. embassy.

They spent almost two weeks traveling around Chile and meeting with local labor leaders and workers. The visit became emblematic of the efforts of U.S. labor leaders to get in touch with local unions and the local reality, especially in the copper mines, and to share their own experience in organizing and bargaining in the United States. As noted in the report of the visit, "In all our interviews, conversations, meetings and addresses, we stressed that the purpose of our visit was mainly to strengthen the relationship between the workers of Chile and the labor movement of the United States. We explained the methods of collective bargaining prevailing in the United States; the gains achieved through the collective strength of trade unionism; the functioning of our Welfare and Retirement Funds; the provisions of the social security law, the wage and hour law, the National Labor Relations Board, and other aspects of the labor legislation in our country."[79]

The delegation spent almost a week in the south, where they visited the coalfields, the steel plant of Huachipato, several industries near Concepción,

77. Luis López Aliaga and Manuel Ovalle, "Agreement of Trade Union Cooperation Between the ORIT and the Confederation of Copper Workers of Chile," November 13, 1951, KC, SRC, box 2, folder 12.
78. Chile's Embassy in Washington to Minister of Foreign Relations, September 9, 1952. ARNAD, DT, Providencias, 1952, vol. 28.
79. "Report of the US Labor Delegation That Visited Chile and Peru," *Inter-American Labor Bulletin* 10 (1952).

and the copper mine at El Teniente. In Santiago, they met with President González Videla and the U.S. ambassador, Claude Bowers. From there, they traveled to Anaconda's properties in the north, Potrerillos and Chuquicamata, and the state-owned smelter plant at Paipote, Copiapó. ORIT members left Chile on August 5. Their trip enabled them

> to establish closer relationship with the labor movement in general, and in particularly with the Copper Mine Workers Confederation of Chile. With the leaders of that union we have planned future joint actions which will undoubtedly result in the strengthening of the union in its efforts to gain still better wages and working conditions. Our visit to Chile has contributed to eliminate [sic] to a certain extent misunderstandings and misconceptions about the international role of the U.S. labor movement. . . . We believe that the leadership of the Chilean labor movement, particularly of the Confederation of Copper Mine Workers, and a considerable section of the rank and file have now a better understanding of the basic philosophy of the American labor movement, of its effectiveness and of its constructive role in promoting not only the welfare of the working people, but the prosperity of industry and the interest of the nation as well.[80]

The ORIT viewed the union leadership of the CTC as "pro-Democratic, definitely anti-communist and openly in favor of international democratic trade union cooperation."[81] The anti-Communism of the CTC, however, was more instrumental than real and was representative of the complexity of Chilean politics in the 1950s. The Communist legislation of 1948 had purged the labor movement of Communist leaders, and still in 1951–53 Communists could not legally be union leaders. Many former Communists, however, participated in the unions as independents or under different labels.

In the following years, the CTC developed an instrumental relationship with the ORIT. Politically and economically, the ORIT supported copper workers' trade union militancy and strikes. It denounced the attitude of U.S. copper companies in Chile. The antilabor attitude of copper management was palpable in the ways in which foreign companies, and especially

---

80. "Report of the US Labor Delegation."
81. "Report of the US Labor Delegation."

Anaconda, approached collective bargaining in the early 1950s. The U.S. labor leaders visiting Chile in 1952 were stunned by Anaconda's labor relations policy and how company management acted toward labor leaders. They overtly denounced Anaconda, explaining that in Chile the company had not met basic labor standards and had "not yet accepted the union as a necessary and constructive factor for the welfare of the industry itself beyond what the law of the land prescribes."[82] Similarly, that same year the *United Mine Workers Journal* published an extensive article on conditions in Chilean mines, accusing Anaconda of "ruthless anti-labor policies" that were sabotaging the "U.S. 'Good Neighbor' role" in South America.[83]

The success of the ORIT in Chile was partial, and the organization was unable to shape the decisions and actions of the labor movement, especially the CTC, showing the limits of U.S. labor's efforts to control Chilean labor organizations. In 1954, Romualdi was again concerned that despite all the efforts and resources, the Communists remained strong in the Chilean labor movement, even in those labor unions affiliated with the ORIT.[84] The only Chilean unions still affiliated to the ORIT were the CTC, the National Federation of Bakers, and the National Federation of Chemical and Pharmaceutical Workers. The ORIT maintained some contact with the Federation of Petroleum Workers and the Maritime Confederation of Workers (COMACH); the latter would become one of ORIT's most important members throughout the 1960s and early 1970s.[85] In 1955, the CTC withdrew from the ORIT, arguing that too little support was received from this international organization in the past strikes.[86]

The decline in ORIT's influence on Chilean unions was a result of new political alliances and changes in the national political climate and in national labor politics. In 1952, the Communist Party supported the first presidential candidacy of Salvador Allende and joined the Socialists in a new political alliance, the Frente del Nacional Pueblo (People's National Front). In February 1953, the founding of the Central Única de Trabajadores (CUT) under the charismatic leadership of Clotario Blest, a white-collar-union

---

82. "Report of the US Labor Delegation."
83. *United Mine Workers Journal*, September 15, 1952.
84. Romualdi to Ibáñez, September 15, 1954, KC, SRC, box 10, folder 9.
85. Luis Alberto Monge, General Secretary ORIT, "Plan for Organization Activity in Chile," c. 1955, KC, SRC, box 2, folder 12.
86. Hugo Salazar, "Informe sobre la situación de la Confederación de Trabajadores del Cobre," 1955, GMMA, International Affairs Department, Serafino Romualdi's Files, 1945–61 (herafter SRF), box 1.

leader, provided new opportunities and voices for Chilean labor unions. While the Law for the Permanent Defense of Democracy was only abolished in 1958, after 1952 Communist leaders found alternatives that allowed them participate in local elections and in union activities and overcame the political isolation of the last six years.

Rising Economic Demands

In October 1953, copper workers in Potrerillos and Chuquicamata struck again. They demanded a 75 percent wage increase, a production bonus, and an increase in service indemnity payments and school and family allowances.[87] The strike lasted fifty-three days and involved about seventy-five hundred blue- and white-collar workers in the two Anaconda mines. The strike unleashed a passionate debate in the country as workers, politicians, state authorities, and management debated and disagreed on the conditions that existed in the copper camps and on the right of copper workers to demand a wage increase. The most contentious issue was the extent to which a national increase in the costs of living affected workers in the isolated copper mines because of their company store privileges: essential products were sold at the fixed prices of 1932. As confrontations increased, the strike raised critical questions about the investment conditions enjoyed by foreign companies.

In 1953, copper workers emphasized their rights to have higher salaries and benefits. They contested Anaconda's arguments about favorable economic conditions existing in the copper camps and their inability to absorb production costs. For example, in the case of the company store, workers denounced the poor supply and bad quality of products, which forced them to buy products on the open market. In the midst of the strike, a delegation from Chuquicamata explained to *El Siglo*: "The companies . . . make a show of their claims that we enjoy a privileged economic situation because we have benefit from frozen prices at the company stores. But in reality we find out that the quality of the products sold there is so bad that most of what we need we need to buy in the free market, where there is an unrestrained speculation that escapes any control. With the daily salaries of 130 pesos that we earn we cannot finance our family budget."[88]

---

87. *El Siglo* (Santiago), August 8, 1953.
88. *El Siglo* (Santiago), October 14, 1953.

Representatives of the Socialist and Radical Parties agreed with workers' economic demands, which they saw as fair and felt were essential to maintaining decent working and living conditions in the mines. Ideas of economic nationalism, state intervention, and the country's right to own its natural resources also shaped the legislators' support for copper workers' demands. Deputies Baltazar Castro (Labor Party) and Ramón Silva (Popular Socialist Party) emphasized the foreign ownership of the copper industry and the imperialistic attitude of the companies. Castro explained that U.S. copper companies monopolized the international market and were indifferent to the fate of the local labor force. He urged the government to protect and enforce workers' rights in the mines; he noted that copper workers suffered not only from international-market fluctuations and abusive labor practices, but also from harsh living and environmental conditions. Castro's intervention in the congressional debate clearly shows the ways in which nationalism was used to legitimate copper workers' demands. The state, argued Castro, should "make the companies obey their commitments" and "give this country the respect that it deserves for its past contributions to the cause of world democracies."[89]

Some politicians perceived copper workers' economic demands as a threat to the industry and eventually to the national economy. Juan Eduardo Puentes (Liberal Party) tried to delegitimate workers' demands, arguing that national inflation and the rise in the cost of living did not affect workers in the copper mining camps, as they did other Chilean workers, because the former profited from frozen prices in the company stores. Manuel Bart (Agrarian Labor Party), a legislator representing the south, called copper workers "proletarian princes," because they ignored that "in the south, their fellows wander around the countryside and the cities without work and anything to eat. And here we see the selfishness of the people of the north who want to live at the expense of others' poverty." Bart was especially concerned with the development of copper industries in Africa and the ability of Chilean copper to compete against cheap producers. He asked copper workers, as many would do in the following years, to give up their economic demands on behalf of the nation: "We cannot discuss the problem of copper from a sentimental point of view," Bart argued, because "our economy is in a critical time, and, therefore, we must make sacrifices and leave aside selfish attitudes to face reality."[90]

---

89. Baltazar Castro, Cámara de Diputados, *Diario de Sesiones*, October 28, 1953, 372, 374.
90. Manuel Bart, Cámara de Diputados, *Diario de Sesiones*, October 28, 1953, 370, 369.

The government, through its new minister of labor Oscar Herrera, struggled to find a solution to the strike. This conciliatory position was an indication of the political changes in the country at the time. Elected in September 1952 with nearly 46 percent of the national vote, President Carlos Ibáñez offered Chileans the image of a strong leader who could solve the nation's political, social, and economic crisis. In 1952–53, he incorporated the Popular Socialist Party into the government and implemented a pro-labor agenda. In 1953, the government approved the family allowance law for blue-collar workers (Decreto con Fuerza de Ley [Decree Having Force of Law, or DFL] 245) and established a minimum salary for agricultural workers. In this context, the national labor movement was able to reorganize, leading to the foundation of the CUT in February 1953. The government also presented a nationalistic agenda; the most popular graffiti of the campaign read, "Copper for Chile: Ibáñez."[91]

The 1953 strike was aggravated by Anaconda's efforts to make the resolution of it contingent on changes in taxation. Anaconda, explained union leader Manuel Ovalle, argued that the company was suffering from high production costs, high investment, an expensive taxation system, and a low exchange rate. In addition, they "said they do not have cash, because they have not been able to sell the stockpiles."[92] After long negotiations, management and workers agreed on the solution proposed by Minister Herrera. The settlement guaranteed a wage increase of 32–48 percent; a 50 percent increase in family allowances; 30 days' service indemnity; and gains in vacation, education, holiday, and night shift bonuses.[93] Because of high inflation rates (see Table 7), these increases did not mean an increase in real income.

The strike of 1953 illustrates the changes experienced by copper workers in 1945–53. As the political debate suggests, the workers' economic demands became more controversial and the gap between conditions in the copper industry and in other Chilean industries was used to criticize the legitimacy of their demands. The strike also shows the growing power of the CTC and points to increasing trade solidarity. During the entire conflict, CTC president Manuel Ovalle negotiated with public authorities and met with President Carlos Ibáñez to find a solution to the strike. Finally, the strike clearly indicates the ways in which local conflicts intertwined

91. *El Siglo* (Santiago), November 3, 1953.
92. *La Nación* (Santiago), November 21, 1953.
93. *El Siglo* (Santiago), December 1, 1953.

Table 7 Consumer price index, 1950–1963

Year	Index (1950=100)	Percent Change (Year to Year)
1950	100	
1951	122.3	22.3
1952	148.7	21.6
1953	187.6	26.2
1954	293.1	56.2
1955	516.7	76.3
1956	856.9	65.8
1957	1,102.9	28.7
1958	1,388.9	25.9
1959	1,944.9	38.6
1960	2,148.6	11.6

SOURCE: Peter Gregory, *Industrial Wages in Chile* (Ithaca: Cornell University, 1967), 2.

with national copper policies and the role of the copper industry in the national economy.

Conclusions

The political and economic tensions of the post–World War II period destroyed the precarious political consensus that had inspired the Popular Front in 1936–41. Tensions and confrontations between political parties and within the Left and the labor movement increased. In March 1946, the national labor confederation CTCH split into two political factions: a Communist wing led by Bernardo Araya and a small socialist faction under Bernardo Ibáñez. In 1948, the anti-Communist law of 1948 outlawed the Communist Party, persecuted its militants, and repressed the labor movement.

The growing importance of copper for the national economy put copper and copper workers at the center of the national political and economic debate. The crisis of Chilean copper raised critical questions about the role of the industry in the national economy, Chile's dependency on the export market, and the need for a serious copper policy.

In Potrerillos, as in the rest of the country, workers experienced intense labor conflicts, economic hardship, and political and labor repression. Yet in their struggle against the deterioration of working, living, and employment conditions, union power and trade solidarity grew and copper workers built a unique labor tradition. In 1951, they built the foundations of the CTC, and in 1952, they joined the ORIT. By 1955, the CTC had a membership of almost eighteen thousand workers and began to provide the resources, solidarity, and power that copper unions needed to protect their members, enforce union contracts, and improve economic and working conditions.

4. Making a New Deal: Copper Laws, Modernization, and Workers' Rights, 1955–1958

In February 1956, Roy Glover, vice president of the Anaconda Copper Company, traveled to Chile to meet with national authorities and visit the company's properties. Glover was a well-known figure in Chile and had visited the country several times. In 1955, he received the Order of Merit from President Carlos Ibáñez for his contributions to the national economy and to the progress of the copper industry.[1] He also played a critical role in most negotiations between the Chilean government and Anaconda and, according to Anaconda historian Isaac Marcosson, had "developed a friendship" with President Ibáñez.[2] In 1956, Glover announced an investment of $52,950,000 in the mining deposit of Indio Muerto, an action taken as part of the El Salvador project, whereby the El Salvador mine was intended to replace Potrerillos and keep Anaconda's subsidiary Andes Copper, viable for at least the following decade.

Glover's announcement symbolized the beginning of years of optimism in the Chilean copper industry. From the perspective of the national state, the El Salvador project represented the success of the Nuevo Trato, or New Deal (1955), an agreement signed between the Chilean state and U.S. capital to increase investment and reduce taxation in the copper industry. To Anaconda, El Salvador was emblematic of the modernization of the copper industry and indicated a strategy, both economic and political, aimed at protecting its stake in Chilean mining. Workers, by contrast, faced the new order with ambivalence. The construction of the new mine opened clear and immediate opportunities to increase pay and improve working conditions, and labor unions successfully used the Nuevo Trato to expand their

---

1. *The Montana Standard* (Butte), April 8, 1955.
2. Marcosson, *Anaconda*, 319.

rights and benefits. Yet efforts to implement stabilization programs and build good relationships with U.S. capital led President Ibáñez to repress workers' increasing local and industry-wide activism. By 1958, copper workers were reconciling their struggle for economic benefits with larger national aspirations and a demand for inclusion in the political debate.

The Nuevo Trato

The Nuevo Trato was law 11.828, which defined the relationship between foreign copper companies and the Chilean state between 1955 and 1964. The new law imposed a tax on large-scale copper companies. The tax was composed of 50 percent based on profit and 25 percent adjustable according to investment and production. To calculate the adjustable tax, the agreement established a production base equivalent to 95 percent of the average company production between 1949 and 1953. The production base for Chuquicamata was 339,654,498 pounds a year; for Potrerillos, 93,577,734 pounds a year; and for Kennecott's property, El Teniente, 301,685,204 pounds a year.[3] An increase above the production base would receive a tax reduction.

The Nuevo Trato eliminated exchange rate regulations and government control over pricing and marketing. It also created the Department of Copper, which under the control of the new Ministry of Mining (created in March 1953) was in charge of studying copper policies and the international copper market and finding mechanisms to encourage foreign companies to obtain their supplies, especially domestic industrial goods, locally. The Department of Copper trained a generation of experts in copper policies and marketing; as Theodore Moran explains, these individuals would play key roles in the Chileanization (1964–70) and nationalization (1971) of copper.[4]

The administration of Carlos Ibáñez and the Chilean business class conceived the Nuevo Trato as a response to the failure of previous copper agreements, Chile's increasing dependency on copper, and U.S. pressure to redefine the terms of investment. Beginning in the 1940s, Chile perceived that the differences between the price of copper in the United States and that in the rest of the Western world (traded at the London Metal Exchange) as well as Cold War market restrictions that mandated selling copper to

---

3. On the Nuevo Trato, see Vera, *La política económica*, 72–86; Moran, *Multinational Corporations*, 89–118.
4. Moran, *Multinational Corporations*, 125–26.

only non-Communist countries were damaging Chilean interests. In 1952, the Chilean government did not renew the Treaty of Washington and instead the Chilean Central Bank took control of all copper sales. In 1953–55, copper policies became especially erratic, and copper companies used labor conflicts to put pressure on the government. To make things worse, Chileans were witnessing a decline in copper production and investment. While the copper industry still accounted for 66 percent of the value of Chile's exports in 1955, production had fallen about 0.9 percent a year since the end of World War II.[5] In addition, during the entire period, U.S. copper companies compelled the Chilean government to create a more favorable investment environment and eliminate state control of price and commercialization, threatening to withdraw from the country.

The Nuevo Trato was also an attempt to solve the limitations of import-substitution and industrialization efforts by increasing state revenues and private investment. Since the Popular Front (1938–41) and particularly under the presidency of Gabriel González Videla (1946–52), Chilean governments influenced by ideas of state capitalism promoted and financed industrialization programs.[6] In 1950–51, President González Videla inaugurated the three jewels of the state industrialization effort: the steel mill of Huachipato in Concepción; an oil refinery in Con-Con; and a copper smelter in Paipote, Copiapó. In addition to state enterprises, the state supported private investors and, through the Development Corporation (Corporación de Fomento Fabril, or CORFO), lent money to important private industries such as the Manufactura de Metales (Metal Manufacturers, or MADEMSA) and the Manufactura de Cobre (Copper Manufacturers, or MADECO).[7] However, like other nations in most industrialization efforts in Latin America, the country remained strongly dependent on foreign loans and the traditional export sector, the copper industry.

In the mid-1950s, the process of import substitution was reaching its limit, and Chile, like many Latin American countries, faced the challenge of making a leap from the "easy" phase of import substitution toward the production of durable consumer and capital goods.[8] Chilean industry had a

---

5. *Economic Survey of Latin America* (United Nations), 1956.
6. On the history of Chilean industrialization and its contradictions, see Oscar Muñoz, *Chile y su industrialización: Pasado, crisis y opciones* (Santiago: CIEPLAN, 1986).
7. Simon Collier and William Sater, *A History of Chile, 1808–1994* (Cambridge: Cambridge University Press, 1996), 269–74.
8. Victor Bulmer-Thomas, *The Economic History of Latin America Since Independence* (New York: Cambridge University Press, 1994), 278–88.

series of bottlenecks that were causing serious difficulties, including its inability to offer enough employment opportunities and lack of sufficient capital to expand.[9] Inflation increased from 12 percent in 1952 to more than 84 percent in 1955, reinforcing a sense of economic failure and the need for drastic measures. While Chilean businesses blamed excessive state intervention in the economy and the country's generous wage policies, the political Left highlighted the structural contradictions of the national economy: a strong dependency on the export market and lack of modernization in the countryside, including an unequal distribution of land.

Confronting a challenging economic crossroads, Chilean policy makers argued that the Nuevo Trato would encourage copper companies to invest in Chile and increase production, supporting the industrialization of copper within the country and creating markets for industrial goods produced there. An increase in state revenues, by contrast, would allow Chile to support other industrialization projects and pay its increasing foreign debt. With these arguments, they reasserted the importance of foreign investors and—temporarily—moved away from the economic nationalism that had inspired the Treaty of Washington and control over sales, seen in the early 1950s.

After the uncertainties of the early 1950s, copper companies welcomed the Nuevo Trato, because it abolished the unpopular discriminatory exchange rate, gave companies absolute control over production and commercialization, and eventually reduced taxation. In its annual report of 1955, Anaconda explained to its shareholders the benefits of the new legislation: "In previous reports we have referred to legislation which it was hoped would give relief from the unfortunate tax, exchange and marketing situation which was applicable to the large copper producers in Chile, including the subsidiaries of your Company. This legislation, which was sponsored by the Administration . . . should be of great importance to the Republic of Chile in the re-establishment of a favorable climate for investment, as well as to its mining industry."[10] In 1960, reflecting on the company's decisions during the past five years, Anaconda recognized that this copper policy had been instrumental in creating "an investment climate conductive to make large risk investments possible."[11]

---

9. Ricardo Ffrench-Davis, *Políticas económicas en Chile, 1952–1970* (Santiago: Ediciones Nueva Universidad, 1973), 23.
10. Anaconda Copper Mining Company, *Annual Report* (1955), 17.
11. Clyde E. Weed, "El Salvador," *Engineering and Mining Journal* 340 (April 1960).

The agreement became an opportunity for Anaconda to reframe its public image. In an effort to improve its presence in Chile and respond to the attacks of nationalistic groups and labor organizations, Anaconda used the Nuevo Trato to demonstrate its contributions to the Chilean economy and the country. In the company newspapers *Andino* (Potrerillos) and *Oasis* (Chuquicamata) and in regional papers such as *El Día*, Anaconda advertised its commitment to the copper agreements, portraying foreign investors as the engine of Chile's economic growth and industrialization. It attempted to reach a local audience by insisting on the positive, modernizing, and necessary roles played by foreign investment in the country.[12]

Two graphics that Andes Copper published in *Andino*, picturing the Nuevo Trato as a favorable alliance between Chile and foreign capital, clearly reveal the new company discourse. The first depicts a man, who clearly resembles a friendly Uncle Sam, saying: "A machine produces when its three wheels are coordinated and synchronized"; and the three wheels were "white- and blue-collar workers," "stockholders," and "consumers" (Fig. 1).[13] In the second image, Andes Copper graphically explains the mechanisms of the Nuevo Trato: "With a base production of copper, each dollar of profit is divided into 75 cents for the government and 25 cents for the company" (Fig. 2).[14] This graphic, however, clearly disregards the fact that most companies, because of production and investment, were paying less than 75 percent in taxes.

Important sectors of Chilean society criticized the government's copper policy because it represented a turn to the right and moved away from previous efforts to exert control over the sale of copper. Believing in the importance of state intervention and control, which had inspired the industrialization effort of the Popular Front, the Left and workers' organizations argued that the solution to Chile's economic problems was the complete nationalization of the export sector and the implementation of structural social and economic reforms. By compromising with foreign capital, Chile was delaying its economic independence. From the Senate,

---

12. Historian Julio Moreno described a similar situation in the case of U.S. business companies investing in Mexico in the 1940s. Julio Moreno, *Yankee Don't Go Home! Mexican Nationalism, American Business Culture, and the Shaping of Modern Mexico, 1920–1950* (Chapel Hill: University of North Carolina Press, 2003).
13. *Andino* (Potrerillos), December 15, 1956.
14. *Andino* (Potrerillos), March 20, 1957.

Figure 1.

Salvador Allende argued that the project protected the interests of foreign companies and did not defend the nation's interest.[15]

Throughout the 1960s, criticism against the Nuevo Trato increased, and as Moran argued, the treaty "came to be considered a 'failure' by almost

15. Fermandois, "La larga marcha."

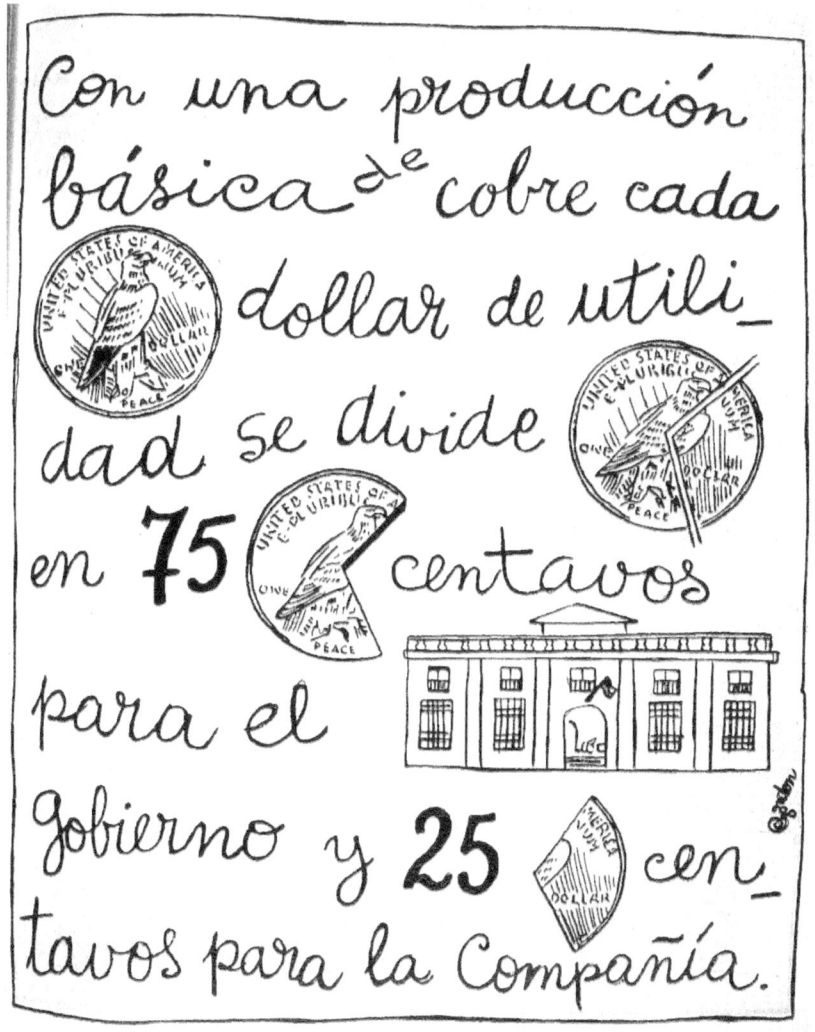

Figure 2.

all segments of Chilean society."[16] In 1961, Chilean socialist economist Mario Vera heavily criticized the Nuevo Trato for its failure to convince foreign copper companies to invest their profits in the country and for not establishing a bridge between the national economy and so-called foreign enclaves.[17] A critical point was the refining of copper, which did not increase but, rather, declined from 87 percent of the total production in 1950 to 55

16. Moran, *Multinational Corporations*, 98.
17. Vera, *La política económica*, 181–88.

percent in 1954 to 47 percent in 1963.[18] One clearly evident flaw of the Nuevo Trato was that the base production had been determined during a time of crisis, making it easier for foreign companies to receive tax breaks. El Salvador was a major investment, but it only restored Andes Copper's investment and production to levels preceding the depletion of Potrerillos. Anaconda, however, received generous tax breaks. The failure of the Nuevo Trato was apparent, and Chile began to look for new, more radical solutions to the already old copper question.[19] In 1961, Socialists senators Salvador Allende, Raúl Ampuero, Salomón Corbalán, Aniceto Rodríguez, Luis Alberto Quinteros, Alejandro Chelén, and Galvarino Palacios presented a new project of nationalization.[20]

A Labor Deal: Workers and the State

On the eve of the Nuevo Trato negotiations, copper workers constituted a powerful and militant labor movement and played a central role in national politics. They demanded their right to maintain and protect their standard of living, the recognition of the unique characteristics of the large-scale copper industry, and a share of benefits from the new copper prosperity. Their rising economic demands limited the enforcement of anti-inflationary and stabilization policies, and long bargaining processes and increasing strike activity threatened production and state revenues. Their strong nationalism contrasted with the government's efforts to compromise with foreign capital. The activism of the new Copper Workers Confederation (Confederación de Trabajadores del Cobre, or CTC), organized in 1951, and the state's de facto recognition of its role as representative of all copper workers challenged the boundaries of the national labor legislation.

The economic and labor rights of copper workers and their unions became especially controversial during the discussion of the Nuevo Trato. As the country prepared to reexamine copper policies, workers asked to be included in the negotiations and demanded the recognition and guarantee of their historical gains. Article 22 of the Nuevo Trato authorized President Ibáñez to organize a commission to discuss special legislation for copper workers. Similar to what had happened during the debate that preceded the Treaty

18. Moran, *Multinational Corporations*, 102.
19. Moran, *Multinational Corporations*, 18
20. Novoa, *La batalla por el cobre*, 115.

of Washington in 1951, a tripartite commission was appointed. Representatives of executive power, copper companies, and the CTC met ten times between August and December 1955 to discuss the future of copper workers.[21]

The political shift of the government and enforcement of new anti-inflation economic policies complicated negotiations between workers, the government, and foreign capital. In 1952–53, President Ibáñez had implemented a popular style of government, enforced relatively friendly labor policies, and introduced important labor and social reforms; in 1954, however, the government was becoming increasingly conservative. High inflation accompanied by growing strike activity was creating a serious political crisis. As the cost of living rose drastically that year (see Table 7), Ibáñez began loosing the popular support that had brought him to power in 1952. In September 1954, for instance, strikes involved workers in the copper mines of El Teniente and Potrerillos, public school teachers, bank clerks, and graphic art workers. On September 3, President Ibáñez warned labor organizations that he would not accept any illegal or solidarity strike, and six days later, he declared a state of emergency in the provinces of O'Higgins, Concepción, Antofagasta, Santiago, and Valparaíso and attempted, unsuccessfully, to obtain from the National Congress extraordinary powers. Tensions continued to escalate during the first half of 1955, as manifested in a twenty-four-hour national strike called by the Central Única de Trabajadores (CUT) on July 6. In the process, Ibáñez became more authoritarian, deliberating whether to maintain his alliance with the labor movement and the Left or turn—as he finally did—to the business sector and the Right.[22]

The reactionary, antilabor orientation of the second half of the Ibáñez administration paralleled the debate about the need to enforce unpopular strict economic stabilization policies. In July 1955, the government hired the private U.S. firm Klein-Sacks to conduct a supposedly "neutral" and "nonpolitical" study of the Chilean economy and, specifically, of inflation. The Klein-Sacks mission had been in Peru in the late 1940s, where it came to be known for its strong, orthodox laissez-faire, as described by Chilean economist Aníbal Pinto in his denunciation.[23] The mission obtained the

---

21. *El Siglo* (Santiago), December 14, 1955.
22. Sofía Correa et al., *Historia del siglo XX chileno: Balance paradojal* (Santiago: Editorial Sudamericana, 2001), 199–202.
23. Alberto Hirschman, "Inflation in Chile," in *Money Doctors, Foreign Debts, and Economic Reforms in Latin America: From the 1890s to the Present,* edited by Paul W. Drake (Wilmington: SR Books. 1994), 133–48.

warm support of the Chilean political Right, who felt it would eliminate the chaos and disorganization of the national economy. Foreign economists and members of the Chilean conservative party shared a distrust for what they saw as "excessive" state intervention in the economy, a politically driven public investment in social infrastructure, and a populist wage policy.

The economic mission worked in Chile from September 1955 to mid-1958. It recommended reduction in public expenditure; implementation of liberal economic policies; and elimination of automatic wage increases—which had been popular since the late 1940s—state subsidies, and price controls. In the pages of the Communist *El Siglo*, the mission was called the "Klein-Sakeo" (a play on words meaning Klein-Looting). In 1956, the National Congress, following the recommendations of the Klein-Sacks mission, approved a law to regulate prices, wages, and pensions (Ley de Estabilización de Precios, Remuneraciones y Pensiones). The law eliminated automatic wage increases for public, white-collar, and agricultural workers and limited wage and pension increases for blue-collar workers to half the hikes in the cost of living between December 1954 and January 1956. To ameliorate the impact of the stabilization programs, it established a minimum wage for blue-collar workers equivalent to 45 percent of the minimum wage for white-collar workers.[24] The enforcement of the stabilization program led to increasing popular unrest, and the government unleashed a new wave of repression, revitalizing Gabriel González Videla's Law for the Permanent Defense of Democracy.[25]

Under the critical political and economic conditions of 1955, the economic and legal demands of copper workers met strong resistance, and labor representatives witnessed how, as observer Robert Alexander noted, "government representatives combined against the workers."[26] Anaconda and Kennecott strongly opposed any change in the labor legislation and questioned the intentions of the government to reform the Labor Code and give special rights to copper workers. In October 1955, confronting the failure of the Tripartite Committee to reach a consensus, an authoritarian Ibáñez attempted to break the impasse by dictating special legislation, a statute, for copper workers. The new statute included all the recommendations set forth by copper companies, but it ignored workers' demands. Among the most serious

---

24. Ffrench-Davis, *Políticas económicas en Chile*, 200.
25. Correa et al., *Historia del siglo XX*, 203–4.
26. Robert J. Alexander, "The Copper Workers Strike in Chile," *Inter-American Labor Bulletin* 2 (1956).

and threatening aspects of the government-proposed statute were the legal dissolution of all copper labor unions and their reorganization under new regulations, which prohibited reelection of union officers, thus representing a serious threat to experienced and politically connected leadership. Despite the fact that in November the Contraloría General de la República (Office of the Attorney General) determined that the new statute was illegal, the government made no effort to change it.[27]

On December 14, 1955, responding to the unilateral decision of the government and voicing concern about how the statute would undermine workers' historical rights, gains, and benefits, copper workers called a general and industry-wide strike. Specifically, the CTC demanded revision of the copper legislation and agreements, a profit-sharing arrangement equivalent to six minimum salaries for both blue- and white-collar workers, and new legislation regulating the copper industry.

While the strike had an important economic motivation, it also directly questioned the recent agreements between foreign companies and the state. It also demonstrated the articulation of a powerful nationalistic discourse within the copper labor movement. On the eve of the strike, the CTC declared:

> Law 11.828 [Nuevo Trato] has reduced taxes, and it has given them [copper companies] unusual conditions to increase their profits and investments. We are not against foreign investment for its own sake. We believe that, in any civilized country, the laws or the agreements subscribed between a government and a foreign company should not only provide better conditions for capital but also protect the rights of workers. We combat the idea that there is a monopoly on patriotism; some people invoke patriotism though they do not truly feel it. Chile not only gives [to foreign capital] its most valuable natural resource, copper, but also the cooperation of its best human resource, the miner.[28]

As the CTC declared in *El Siglo*, copper workers were defending not only their own interests but those of the "entire country."[29] During the strike, labor organizations opposed the Nuevo Trato, considering it a law "enacted

27. *El Siglo* (Santiago), December 14, 1955.
28. *El Popular* (Antofagasta), December 14, 1955.
29. *El Siglo* (Santiago), December 11, 1955.

and intended to benefit the Companies and accelerate the exploitation of Chilean copper."[30] While U.S. copper companies had received enormous privileges under the Nuevo Trato, the CTC leadership argued, the government had not advanced workers' rights. Similarly, the CTC restated the valuable contribution of copper workers to the industry and the national economy. These workers' contributions, therefore, justified their demands for economic improvement.

The strike lasted about three weeks, from December 14 to January 5–6, and involved at its height about sixteen thousand white- and blue-collar copper workers from the three big mines. Despite the risks of joining an illegal strike, the rank and file maintained a strong unity during the conflict.[31] In the mining camps, workers and community organizations guaranteed the success of the movement. In Chuquicamata, a Women's Committee was organized to prevent the entrance of strikebreakers.[32] National labor organizations such as the Industrial Mining Federation (Federación Industrial Minera, or FIM) and the CUT strongly supported the copper workers' movement. In a declaration issued on December 15, the leaders of the FIM referred to the copper strike as a "patriotic" movement in defense of labor rights and "national sovereignty."[33]

Adding to the strong militancy and solidarity at the local level, copper workers received the warm support of legislators representing copper districts such as the socialists Ramón Silva and Roberto Flores; Juan de Dios Carmona from the Falange Nacional; and Manuel Magalhaes, the Radical Party's representative from Chañaral. Legislators accused the government of delaying a solution to the conflict, ignoring workers' legal rights, and enforcing unnecessary repressive measures.[34] In the process, politicians challenged a presidential style that had become increasingly authoritarian. On December 23, legislators representing mining districts stated: "We believe that threatening [workers] with arbitrary and illegal measures such the military draft, which in times of peace is only authorized for aims of military training, does not protect the principle of authority."[35]

30. *El Popular* (Antofagasta), December 14, 1955.
31. *El Popular* (Antofagasta), December 16, 1955.
32. *El Siglo* (Santiago), December 29, 1955.
33. *El Siglo* (Santiago), December 16, 1955.
34. *El Siglo* (Santiago), December 24, 1955.
35. The statement was also signed by Raúl Hernán Brücher (Radical Party), José Cueto, Víctor Galleguillos (Communist Party), Pedro Cisternas (Popular Socialist Party), Baltazar

The strikers also received the assistance of international labor organizations. On December 19, Eduardo Delfín, president of the CTC, asked the Inter-American Regional Organization (ORIT) for political and economic aid. In the subsequent days, the ORIT authorized a contribution of a thousand dollars to the Chilean copper unions. In addition, Paul Reed, leader of the United Mine Workers (UMW), agreed to contact both the president of Anaconda and the U.S. Department of State to inform "them of the mounting concern on the part of organized labor in the U.S. for the continuance of the copper strike in Chile and urging steps to bring about an early satisfactory solution."[36]

The government reacted energetically against an illegal movement that challenged its authority, threatened the recent agreement with copper companies, and harmed public finances. President Ibáñez was "furious," as William Thayer, then a CTC lawyer and later a minister of labor under the presidency of Eduardo Frei, recalled, and the president used legal recourse, authoritarian mechanisms, and the progovernment media to undermine the movement.[37] On December 15, Ibáñez decreed a resumption of production, threatened to enforce military conscription against strikers, placed mining districts under martial law, and appointed military interventors in the three mines.[38]

At the local level, management threatened workers, as Robert Alexander noted, "with permanent dismissal from their jobs" and "menaced [them] with being thrown out of their houses."[39] In the days that followed, using the Law for the Defense of Democracy, the government ordered the arrest of the main leaders of the CTC and local unions, including thirty union leaders from Potrerillos, among them the ex-president of the CTC and white-collar leader Manuel Ovalle.[40] When the local police took the imprisoned leaders to the railway station in Potrerillos, men and women sang the national anthem in protest against the repressive measures.[41] The repression had little success. In Chuquicamata, after thirteen days of strike, only twenty-seven workers had

---

Castro (Labor Party), René Jerez (Socialist Party), Sebastián Santandreau (Radical Party), and Armando Jaramillo (Liberal Party). *El Siglo* (Santiago), December 24, 1955.
  36. Romualdi to Brown, December 29, 1955, GMMA, SRF, box 1, folder 15.
  37. William Thayer, *Segunda Fila* (Santiago: Editorial Jurídica, n.d.), 33.
  38. *El Siglo* (Santiago), December 16, 1955.
  39. Alexander, "Copper Workers Strike."
  40. Potrerillos Labor Unions to Benjamín Videla, Santiago, May 22, 1956, ARNAD, DT, Providencias, vol. 18, 1956.
  41. *El Siglo* (Santiago), December 28, 1955.

returned to work.[42] In Potrerillos, the unions reported only one strikebreaker during the entire conflict.[43]

Ibáñez used the pages of the government-sponsored newspaper *La Nación* to argue the inconsistencies in the workers' petitions and to show the political content of their demands. During the strike, *La Nación* published critical editorials against copper workers. Highlighting the economic costs of the strike, journalists called it a selfish action that harmed the national interest. The paper's editor pointed out: "If the strikers obtained higher salaries, we would have less money to import the oil that moves the machines of the industry and less dollars to buy the products that Chile does not produce. Each day of this unjust strike costs 200 million pesos. Each household in the country is paying 150 pesos every day."[44] In other words, *La Nación* portrayed copper workers as striking against Chile and its working class and threatening the nation's prosperity and industrialization. Similarly, the right-wing *El Diario Ilustrado* blamed the strike on political activists and called copper workers "Soviet servants" and the strike a Communist maneuver. By exacerbating economic difficulties and impoverishing the country, the newspaper declared, the Communist Party hoped "to take advantage of people's miseries to obtain their unspoken goals."[45] The strike, however, was successful: copper companies agreed to increase profit sharing, President Ibáñez accepted reopening discussions on the copper stature, and labor leaders in prisons were set free.[46]

Enacted in April 1956, the new Statute of Copper Workers recognized copper workers as a distinctive and influential labor group and reframed labor relations in the copper industry. It shortened the bargaining period, strengthened local unions' power by guaranteeing cooperation between plant and professional unions (both unions could present a common list of demands), and reinforced the presence of the state as an actor in mediating labor relations in the copper industry. A special arbitration board (Junta de Conciliación para la Gran Minería del Cobre) guaranteed the participation of the state by incorporating two ministers (Labor and Mining) and one important public authority in every labor negotiation. The statute legalized the CTC, an institution that became a bridge between the local unions and

---

42. *El Siglo* (Santiago), December 26, 1955.
43. *El Siglo* (Santiago), January 4, 1956.
44. *La Nación* (Santiago), December 23, 1955.
45. *El Diario Ilustrado* (Santiago), December 16, 1955.
46. Alexander, "Copper Workers Strike."

national authorities and the three large mines (Chuquicamata, El Teniente, and Potrerillos). It also recognized the workers' right to receive an annual profit-sharing payment from the companies that could not exceed 20 percent of their wage per day worked.[47]

The Chilean state viewed the statute as a means of decreasing conflict in the rich copper mines and incorporating the organized working class into a controlled system of labor relations. By forcing plant and professional unions to present a common list of demands and establishing fifteen-month union contracts, the state aimed to diminish the frequency of labor disputes and strikes and to control wage increases.

From the workers' perspective, the statute had some limitations. First, it forbade unions from bringing to the bargaining table subjects not included in their previous contracts. In other words, they could improve conditions but not create new rights. Long contracts forced labor leaders to negotiate wage salaries through speculating on the increase in costs of living for the following fifteen months. Before 1966, labor leaders did not have access to the companies' accounting information, limiting their ability to bargain. Finally, by prohibiting industry-wide contracts, the statute made the first collective bargaining of the year especially important, since it would set standards for the following two mines.

The statute per se did not improve economic conditions for copper workers and thus did not contradict the government's stabilization policies. But the empowerment and growing solidarity among copper workers and the development of a copper workers' trade identity made the statute a useful tool for improving economic conditions. In sum, the statute neither decreased levels of conflict nor prevented the construction of a radical labor discourse, but it reinforced the power and autonomy of the copper workers' labor movement. In the following years, labor conflicts continued to be intense and frequent in the copper industry (see Chapter 5).

The El Salvador Project, 1956–1959

Following the visit of Roy Glover and the negotiations of the Copper Workers' Statute, Anaconda embarked on its largest and most ambitious project in Chile since the 1920s. Inaugurated in 1959, El Salvador, announced

---

47. "Estatuto de los trabajadores del cobre," Santiago, April 30, 1956.

Anaconda, marked the "advent of the largest new copper-producing mine and plant anywhere in the world since 1943."[48] The El Salvador project included the construction of an underground mine, additional railway lines, primary and secondary crushing plants, a concentrator, a molybdenum plant, and a model town. Ultimately, the project made possible a new company discourse about labor and the country.

The future looked auspicious. According to announcements made in November 1956, the mine had a reserve of 200 million tons of ore containing about 1.6 percent copper. In November, the company had increased its initial budget, planning at this point to invest more than 80 million dollars in bringing El Salvador into production, of which more than one-third would be spent in Chile, and less than two-thirds in importing machinery and supplies.[49] According to the Nuevo Trato, the Department of Copper worked closely with Andes Copper to facilitate the purchase of Chilean materials and manufactured products such as cement, steel, wires, and lumber.[50] Only when Chilean products were not available did the Department of Copper authorize the company to import.

International and local forces led Anaconda to launch a new investment program in Chile. From a global perspective, Anaconda used "modernization" to overcome two serious threats of the Cold War period. First, the development of aluminum and plastic as cheaper substitutes for copper in the electrical and pipe industries was threatening the copper market. Second, the growth of mines outside the control of big corporations was challenging the latter's power over prices and copper ore stocks. In this context, the construction of El Salvador was part of Anaconda's international effort of modernization, diversification, and expansion. By reducing production costs, Anaconda would be able to compete against plastic and aluminum.

The most important of Anaconda's projects included the Greater Butte Project in Montana, which modernized Butte's mines; the construction of a new production plant in Cananea, Mexico; the opening of the Yerington mine in Nevada, its first venture into the aluminum industry; and an extensive program of geological exploration throughout the United States, Canada, and Latin America. These projects incorporated ideas of scientific

---

48. Anaconda Copper Mining Company, *Annual Report* (1959), 6.

49. Anaconda Company, "News from Anaconda," November 5, 1956, AHC, AGDC, box 85709.

50. Stewart Carpenter, "Plant Construction and Procurement of Supplies," *Engineering and Mining Journal*, April 1960.

management, introduced new technology and equipment, and improved transportation.[51] The threat of Chilean nationalism and pressure from the U.S. government to guarantee supply of this strategic metal had initially motivated Anaconda to develop and expand copper deposits in the United States, as in the case with the Greater Butte Project and the Yerington mine.[52] Despite the expansion of investment within the United States, Chile continued to be the most important source of unrefined copper for Anaconda.

From a national perspective, the quest for modernization became urgent as the Chilean state increased its pressures on foreign capital to increase investment and industrialization. The El Salvador project was part of the company's efforts to satisfy the demands of the Chilean state, show its commitment to the Nuevo Trato legislation, and benefit from the tax breaks offered in the new copper policies.

The basis of Anaconda's program of expansion and modernization was geological exploration. Anaconda mines had a geological unit that not only provided the logistics for mine exploitation but also carried on its own exploration projects in the surrounding areas. In the post–World War II period, Anaconda was looking for any mine from which it could "make money" and organized several prospecting projects both in the United States and in Latin America. The main interest of the company was copper because, as chief geologist Vincent Perry noted, "an adequate supply of cheap copper is essential to the company's prosperity."[53] The company also considered other nonferrous metals such as gold, lead, zinc, and manganese; and in the following two decades, oil and uranium.

Between 1946 and 1949, Anaconda had unsuccessfully explored the Gurupi mine in Maranhao, Brazil, and the Eagle Mountain and Omai areas in British Guiana.[54] In the north of Chile, the company considered La Disputada and Río Blanco, and in Peru, it explored the Cerro Verde property.[55] The failure of exploration in other Latin American countries reinforced the importance of Chilean ore reserves, creating a future dangerous dependency on Chilean copper. Fear of competition also motivated Anaconda's exploration in Chile. In 1952, the rumor that a U.S. copper company had asked the Areo

---

51. "How Modernization Benefits the Mine and the Man," *Engineering and Mining Journal* 159 (1958).
52. Finn, *Tracing the Veins*, 49.
53. Perry to Mulchay, January 12, 1949, AHC, AGDC, box 81403.
54. Perry to Hurst, February 2, 1948, AHC, AGDC, box 93503, folder 1.
55. Perry to Weed, May 16, 1952, AHC, AGDC, box 85709; March to Perry, October 15, 1946, AHC, AGDC, box 85709.

Survey Company "to do an extensive job of aerial photography and aerial reconnaissance mapping of Chile" made William Swayne, from the Compañía Sudamericana de Minas and close collaborator of Anaconda, wonder whether "this [could] mean some real competition, possibly Kennecott?"[56]

The exploration and development of El Salvador was part of this international effort. Anaconda's geologists had explored and acknowledged the existence of copper mineralization in the Indio Muerto peak as early as the 1920s. Indio Muerto, renamed El Salvador in the 1950s, was located about twenty-eight miles northwest of Potrerillos, at 7,825 feet above sea level; before the construction of roads in 1956, it was completely isolated. The distance between Indio Muerto and Potrerillos and the exploitation of Potrerillos had discouraged further exploration until the 1940s. In 1942, a team of geologists led by Walter March reexplored the area, and in 1944, Andes Copper bought seven mining claims. Unsure about the magnitude of the deposit, the company continued exploring and evaluating other properties in the area, including two mines near Chañaral owned by French capital.[57] In 1954, a team of geologists finally discovered the ore body in Indio Muerto, and by mid-1955, Andes Copper had acquired options to all mining claims in the area and started drilling.[58]

Between 1956 and 1959, the company built a mine, two crushing plants, a concentrator, a molybdenum plant, and several shops and auxiliary services. As in the case of the Yerington mine, El Salvador was started from scratch and planned as a whole. Works expanded rapidly. By March 1956, there were 730 men working on preliminary road construction and drill station preparation,[59] and in July, Charles Brinckerhoff reported, "more than 1,300 men scattered out over the various phases of the project" and equipment arrived in "greater quantities."[60] As it had during the construction of Potrerillos in the 1920s, the company hired many foreign technicians, engineers, and skilled workers. Nine foreign supervisors, 15 Chilean crew supervisors, and an estimated 234 crew workers, for instance, carried on the construction of the mine tunnel in 1956.[61] Chilean private contractors,

56. Swayne to Perry, November 12, 1951, AHC, AGDC, box 69903, folder 1.
57. Weed to Sales, June 23, 1944, AHC, AGDC, box 85709.
58. Perry to Weed, January 29, 1957, AHC, AGDC, box 69810, folder 22.
59. Brinckerhoff to Perry, March 5, 1956, AHC, AGDC, box 70102, folder 2.
60. Brinckerhoff to Campbell, July 23, 1956, AHC, AGDC, box 70102, folder 2.
61. Robbins and Staff, "Tunneling at El Salvador, in Andes Copper Mining Company," in Andes Copper Mining Company, *Articles on Mining Operations* (1957), Museo El Salvador, Salvador, Chile.

by contrast, were in charge of plant, road, and housing construction. At the peak of activity, 1957–58, there were twenty independent contractors employing about 4,150 workers.[62]

There is little information about construction workers during these years. The company relied on private contractors, whom they paid a unit price for specific work and who subcontracted their own labor force, hiring them also on a unit-price basis.[63] Workers lived in temporary facilities housing 100–120 single men and located next to the construction site. There was no room for family members in the construction camp. Workers hung out in the cantinas or mess halls for food and went to Pueblo Hundido for entertainment. Working and living conditions were precarious, hard, unpleasant, and dangerous. On the roads, truck accidents were frequent.[64] There is little evidence of major labor problems with the construction crew, and according to project manager Stewart Carpenter, "the entire job was accomplished without work stoppage."[65] It should be noted, though, that strikes involving company workers in Potrerillos had only an indirect impact on construction when shutting down offices and shops.[66]

Some of the most successful and experienced mining experts from Anaconda managed the construction project. Charles M. Brinckerhoff, the project's director, had a degree in metallurgy from Columbia University and more than twenty years of mining experience in the United States, Mexico, and Chile. He had spent eleven years in Potrerillos, serving as assistant mine superintendent, mine superintendent, and general manager (1945–48). He became general manager of Chile Exploration in 1948, executive vice president of Chile Exploration Company and Andes Copper Mining Company in 1955, and president and director of Anaconda and president of the two Chilean subsidiaries in 1958.[67] In charge of the supervision of the project were Norbert Francis Koepel, Andes Copper general manager, and H. E. Robbins, general superintendent. Koepel was also an Anaconda old-timer. A mining engineer from the University of Michigan, prior to moving to Potrerillos in 1919, he had worked for Anaconda in Montana. After thirty

62. Carpenter, "Plant Construction."
63. Carpenter, "Plant Construction."
64. See, for instance, *El Día* (Copiapó), December 11, 1957 and August 13, 1958.
65. Carpenter, "Plant Construction."
66. Swayne to Perry, September 14, 1954, AHC, AGDC, box 69903, folder 1; Brinckerhoff to Perry, December 27,1955, AHC, AGDC box 70102, folder 2.
67. *Diccionario biográfico*, 9th ed. (Santiago: Empresa Periodística, 1953–55), s.v. "Charles M. Brinckerhoff."

years in Potrerillos, he became general manager.⁶⁸ Two geologists directed and supervised work: William Swayne and Frank Trask.⁶⁹

The characteristics of the ore body made the design and construction of the mine a challenging task. Although the ore body was of "extraordinary lateral extent and unusual thickness," it was "also characterized by local irregularities" and by abrupt variations in the elevation.⁷⁰ The solution to these problems was a system of block caving, in which the ore was dropped "from upper gathering levels through ore passes." The mine operated simultaneously on two levels, 2,600 and 2,660 meters, and one adit, located at a level 2,400 meters above sea level. From the adit, the electric railway transported the ore to the primary crushing plant, and the belt conveyors to the secondary crushing plant and finally to the concentration plant or flotation section. The copper concentrate was pumped through a 13.75-mile gravity pipeline to Llanta and transported by railway to the smelter in Potrerillos.⁷¹

More than the size of the investment, what distinguished El Salvador as a modern experiment was the introduction of the latest trends in industrial and mining design. Wilbur Jurden of Anaconda-Jurden Associates, "Anaconda's master builder," designed the plants. Anaconda-Jurden was a subsidiary of Anaconda that performed designing, engineering, and construction. Jurden had designed all Anaconda's major projects, including the new sulphide plant at Chuquicamata in 1952 and the Yerington mine at Nevada in 1953. Designed as a model modern industrial site, Jurden explained that El Salvador's several units were arranged "into a compact layout which will perform efficiently, be economical to build, and allow for possible expansion."⁷² The compact layout had multiple advantages; its simplicity guaranteed low maintenance costs, "ease of operation, and higher tonnage per man-day, all adding up to a lower per ton treatment cost."⁷³

Jurden represented a new tendency in industrial design, and El Salvador was emblematic of changes in the world copper industry, resembling other

68. *El Día* (Copiapó), June 29, 1955.
69. Perry to Weed, January 29, 1957, AHC, AGDC, box 69810, folder 22.
70. Robbins, Dunstan, and Dudley, "Development of El Salvador Mine," January 12, 1960, AHC, AGDC, box 69810, folder 15.
71. Julian L. Hayes, "Brief Description of El Salvador Mine Project of Andes Copper Mining Company," November 6, 1956, AHC, AGDC, box 85709; Robbins, Dunstan, and Dudley, "Development of El Salvador Mine."
72. "How Anaconda-Jurden Associates Achieve Modern Industrial Planning," *Engineering and Mining Journal* 159, no. 11 (1958).
73. "How Anaconda-Jurden Associates Achieve Planning."

modern mines built at the time, among them San Manuel, Arizona, and Yerington, Nevada.[74] In November 1958, the *Engineering and Mining Journal* explained, the world copper industry was experiencing a wave of modernization to "increase productivity, cut costs and maintain a good profit margin." Modernization would make "mines and mineral processing plants better, safer, cleaner, more comfortable, less arduous for the man."[75] New technology and equipment, mechanization, and better transportation would reduce high labor costs. Especially important was to save costs of transportation and fuel, which required a careful design of the plants and their location. For example, in the case of El Salvador, company engineers had initially planned to transport the ore from the new mine to the concentrator in Potrerillos, 12.5 miles away. However, high transportation costs led the company to build a new concentrator in Potrerillos and transport the copper concentrate through a pipeline.

In Chile, the modernization of the plants required a new effort by the company to break down employee work habits. In the mid-1950s, copper companies such as Andes Copper faced high rates of labor turnover, absenteeism, and wildcat strikes. Historians of the nineteenth century have viewed these behaviors as patterns of resistance to industrial discipline and a result of continuous migration from traditional rural areas to urban and mining regions.[76] However, by the 1950s copper workers numbered among the most proletarian sectors of the Chilean labor force and these behaviors, as historian Juan Luis Sariego suggests for the case of Mexican miners in Real del Monte and Pachuca, were more a response to working conditions, labor abuses, work risks, and economic insecurity than an expression of preindustrial cultural values.[77]

Motivated by the ideal of modernization, Andes Copper attempted once again to reshape the labor force and increase labor discipline, efficiency, and workers' commitment to production. While the goals were not new and had

---

74. The San Manuel mine in Arizona, owned by Magna Copper Corporation and inaugurated in 1956, also had a so-called modern design and an efficient layout that guaranteed a rapid and clean flow. "San Manuel . . . America's Newest Large Copper Producer," *Engineering and Mining Journal* 159, no. 4 (1958).

75. "How Modernization Benefits."

76. Herbert G. Gutman, *Work, Culture, and Society in Industrializing America: Essays in American Working-Class and Social History* (New York: Knopf, 1976); Pinto, *Trabajos y rebeldías*; French, *A Peaceful and Working People*.

77. Juan Luis Sariego, "Los mineros de la Real del Monte: Un proletariado en formación y transición," *Revista Mexicana de Sociología* 4 (1980).

inspired managerial policies since the beginning of the twentieth century, the 1950s brought new ideas. In the 1920s, the company had organized a Welfare Department and a security system to create a proletarian and efficient labor force. By encouraging families and repressing alcoholism, gambling, and promiscuity, it had tried to decrease absenteeism, labor turnover, violence, and accidents. In the 1950s, while the moral tone did not completely disappear, the company used a scientific approach to labor relations and sought instead to incorporate workers more thoroughly into the company's plans. Similarly, it put a new emphasis on the layout of the workplace and on the relationship between space, work, and managerial control. This new labor discourse paralleled the company's efforts to improve its national image described above.

Between 1955 and 1958, Andes Copper published a series of images that demonstrated its new labor discourse, portraying the importance of the production bonus and the relationship between workers' commitment to production and workers' salaries. Since production was the result of a team effort, Andes Copper asked workers to fight against those workers who did not produce. In January 1957, a graphic published in *Andino* claims: "The absentee harms his co-worker."[78] The poster pictured the absentee as a lazy, well-fed man, called a "fallero," whose attitude affected the "good," "responsible" hardworking man (Fig. 3). A second image shows the consequences of male workers' lethargy not only for their families but for the entire nation. "This man supports his family, and his inactivity affects his family. This man provides for a group of families, and his inactivity undermines a region. This man contributes resources to the nation, and his inactivity affects his family, weakens a region, and damages Chile" (Fig. 4).[79] Similarly, a third image illustrates the problem of breaking machines and the value of work efficiency. "Breaking a machine is a waste of time, and time is gold."[80] The image conveys three ideas: disruption of production caused by breaking a machine, workers' responsibility in maintaining machines, and the impact of a decline in production on workers' income (Fig. 5). This new discourse, however, had serious limitations. As the company's management did not make efforts to improve relationships with labor unions or change its attitude toward collective bargaining, labor conflicts mounted throughout the following decades.

78. *Andino* (Potrerillos), January 12, 1957.
79. *Andino* (Potrerillos), February 23, 1957.
80. *Andino* (Potrerillos), January 26, 1957.

Figure 3.

In El Salvador, the construction of the change house, where miners could wash up after work, represented the reorganization of the working space. Located on the surface next to the mine entrance, the change house provided workers a clean place to shower and change clothes. Workers received two open-metal baskets, one each for their work and street clothes. While the change house per se was nothing more than a useful facility, the ways in which the company described it suggests its new corporate discourse. Andes Copper viewed it as a means for improving workers' hygiene and

Figure 4

sense of order, believing that these were "important elements in the good functioning of a company." Management saw it as a big improvement in working conditions that would allow workers "to return home perfectly clean and in order."[81]

81. *Andino* (Potrerillos), April 2, 1960.

Figure 5.

In May 1959, El Salvador sent its first copper concentrate to the smelter. Six months later, on November 12, Anaconda officially inaugurated El Salvador "with considerable fanfare," as the U.S. embassy described it.[82] President Jorge Alessandri cancelled his visit at the last minute, but in the crowd were prominent national and international figures. The ceremony included speeches from Clyde Weed (president of Anaconda's board of directors), Charles Brinckerhoff (president of Anaconda), Roberto Vergara

82. U.S. Embassy, November 13, 1959, NARA, GR, Chile 1955–59, box 3027.

(minister of finance), and Manuel Magalhaes (deputy of the Radical Party from Chañaral). Following the speeches, the guests visited the new facilities and attended a cocktail party and a lunch at the company store.

The inauguration ceremony clearly shows the ways in which Anaconda used El Salvador to demonstrate its commitment to Chile's economic development. In his speech, Weed described El Salvador as a turning point in the history of Chilean mining; he also celebrated the Nuevo Trato as an agreement that had made possible the growth of the copper industry and the state's revenues. Believing that Anaconda would be in Chile for at least another fifty years, Weed referred to Anaconda's "intimate and cordial association with the [Chilean] state," expressing his "pride that our industry constitutes one of the essential basis of the development and progress of the national economy."[83] Charles Brinckerhoff also emphasized the contributions of Anaconda to the national economy. Contesting the argument that Anaconda only left "holes" in Chile, Brinckerhoff explained that his company had invested about 460 million dollars in its Chilean subsidiaries. Like Weed, Brinckerhoff emphasized Anaconda's relationship with the Chilean state and the existence of a "single mutual and inseparable interest between the state and the producer, in which the state receives the greater proportion of the benefits."[84]

However, the ceremony also highlighted the Chilean state's efforts to attract foreign capital and increase copper production. El Salvador, according to Minister Roberto Vergara, would increase Chilean exports, contributing to the general economic goals of the government. A strong supporter of foreign investment, he believed that investments such as those in El Salvador would help Chile to achieve economic development and prosperity. He also made a special reference to workers, claiming that "workers' prosperity and the improvement of workers' living and working conditions depend, fundamentally, on increased production."[85]

Although the impact of El Salvador on the national economy was limited, the construction of the new mine had immediate benefits for the department of Chañaral; the transportation of goods and people and the general business activity around the construction created job and business opportunities in an economically depressed region. As noted by William Swayne when construction began, the company hired local truckers for the "transportation of

83. *La Nación* (Santiago), November 13, 1959.
84. *El Mercurio* (Santiago), November 13, 1959.
85. *La Nación* (Santiago), November 13, 1959.

equipment, water, and supplies."[86] Consequently, as reported by the Ministry of Housing, employment in business and transportation in the department of Chañaral increased about 65 percent in 1952–60.[87] Similarly, on the eve of the inauguration ceremony, *El Mercurio* explained that Andes Copper had spent about 27 million pesos during the construction of El Salvador. Local expenses included salaries and supplies.[88]

In Pueblo Hundido, the impact of the construction activity was evident. Workers and contractors crowded the once-abandoned streets of the town in search of goods and entertainment. Members of a young, male labor force eased their long hours of loneliness by visiting the traditional bars and brothels. Businesses opened in Pueblo Hundido to satisfy the newcomers' needs, and many locals became prosperous entrepreneurs, among them Alamiro Castillo Cerda. Castillo invested 5 million pesos to open the first gas station in town.[89] The population of Pueblo Hundido increased from 906 inhabitants in 1952 to 2,123 in 1960 and 6,187 in 1972. With a housing shortage in the camps, many company workers decided to live in Pueblo Hundido as well. This new prosperity, however, was problematic. Since the only important investments were drugstores, hotels, restaurants, storage spaces, and transportation, employment remained precarious and unstable, offering few possibilities for expansion.

El Salvador: A Modern Mining Camp

In the 1950s, the modernizing ideas that inspired exploration, construction, and the reorganization of the labor force in the mining industry influenced the construction of mining camps. Mining companies started replacing traditional mining camps with "modern town sites," "to attract high quality staffs and workers, and to cut down on high turn-over costs."[90] They adopted some principles of modernism, a tendency that was changing the ways in which architects and urban planners talked about and designed cities and housing. Modernism advocated efficiency, functionality, and standardization in housing and urban spaces. Using pure concepts and geometrical designs, modernists

86. Swayne, AHC, AGDC, box 69810, folder 10.
87. Ministerio de Vivienda y Urbanismo, *Chañaral*.
88. *El Mercurio* (Santiago), November 11, 1959.
89. *El Día* (Copiapó), July 19, 1957.
90. "How Modernization Benefits."

believed in the possibility of using planning to solve social problems and achieve progress.[91] In this context, new industrial towns were precious opportunities to plan from scratch and became symbols of the new architectural and urban tendencies.[92] However, as with many modernist experiments, El Salvador failed to remold its inhabitants.

El Salvador embodied the spirit of the new era. It was "a modern village."[93] Its good urban infrastructure, decent housing, and innovative layout satisfied, at least temporarily, residents' demands and visitors' expectations. Inspired by the agenda of architects and urban planners, Anaconda built a modernist camp to change the labor force and overcome the social and political tensions that had affected experiences in previous camps. In doing so, the company was ultimately looking to increase production and efficiency.

Modernism in El Salvador was present in the camp's layout, architecture, zoning, materials, quality and availability of services, and housing distribution and—above all—in the company's urban discourse. El Salvador was shaped in a curve, similar to that of an amphitheater; the goal, said its architect, Raymond Olson, was "to avoid the monotony displayed in many strictly gridiron pattern town-sites" (Fig. 6).[94] Nevertheless, with the most prominent streets converging in the central plaza, the location of office headquarters, the layout reinforced the symbolic dimension of company power.[95]

In yet another attempt to avoid monotony, the concrete houses of the camp were painted in "ten different compatible pastel colors," from turquoise blue to light yellow. Overall, Olson claimed, the "pastel-colored exteriors with gleaming white-chip marble roof tops (to reflect the heat)" would give "El Salvador eye-appeal akin to that exhibited by Bermuda's white-roofed, pink and white cottages."[96] Under the environmental conditions of the camp, however, the pastel exteriors were rapidly covered with dust. Houses

---

91. On planning and modernism, see James Holston, *The Modernist City: An Anthropological Critique of Brasilia* (Chicago: University of Chicago Press, 1990); James C. Scott, *Seeing Like a State: How Certain Schemes to Improve the Human Conditions Have Failed* (New Haven: Yale University Press, 1999).
92. Miles Glendenning, "The New Town 'Tradition': Past, Present—and Future?" in *Back from the Utopia: The Challenge of the Modern Movement*, ed. Hubert-Jan Henket and Hilde Henyen (Rotterdam: 010 Publishers, 2002), 206–15.
93. Julian L. Hayes, "Brief Description of El Salvador Mine Project of Andes Copper Mining Company," November 6, 1956, AHC, AGDC, box 69810, folder 15.
94. "How Anaconda-Jurden Associates Achieve Planning."
95. "El Salvador, ciudad minera proyectada como tal," *AURA* 5 (1996).
96. "How Anaconda-Jurden Associates Achieve Planning."

Figure 6.

included all the modern comforts: gas, electricity, and private bathrooms. They were a big improvement from what was available in previous camps.

In the El Salvador camp a clear physical separation was established between industrial and living areas.[97] The town site was located about six and a half miles from the mine, and employees commuted in company buses.[98] Services were also separated from the residential area. The company store, the church, the theater, small retail shops, and public offices were located near the central plaza, "within easy walking distance of all homes."[99] Recreational areas and facilities were important components of the town-site plan and located within the residential area. The school was located on the periphery of the town, in a safe, traffic-free area. With this, Anaconda emphasized the residential character of the camp.

The company used a wide range of urban symbolic elements to reinforce its image. The town planners carefully named streets after Chilean

97. Douglas Porteous, "Social Class in Atacama Company-Towns," *Annals of the Association of American Geographers* 3 (1974).
98. Robbins, Dunstan, and Dudley, "Development of El Salvador Mine," January 12, 1960, AHC, AGDC, box 69810, folder 15.
99. "How Anaconda-Jurden Associates Achieve Planning."

and U.S. heroes to overcome the traditional distance between the company and the native labor force.[100] Street names emphasized the mining character of the camp, the role of U.S. mining companies in the development of copper mining in Chile, and the universal character of U.S. democracy. The two main parallel and only straight streets celebrated the independence days of both countries in their names, 18 de Septiembre for Chile and 4 de Julio for the United States. The two streets crossed the town and ended in Bernardo O'Higgins Street, named in honor of the most popular leader of the Chilean independence movement. The names of other prominent Chilean national heroes, such as Carrera, Bulnes, Baquedano, and Prat, were used for short streets that crossed 18 de Septiembre Street and 4 de Julio Street. The five largest circular streets were called Andes, Cornelius Kelly (after an important figure in the early history of Anaconda), Anaconda, Chuquicamata (after the other Anaconda property in Chile), and Potrerillos. The other streets had names that recalled the most famous mines in Chilean history (Tamaya, Caracoles, El Teniente), important figures of Chilean political history (Portales, Balmaceda), Chilean intellectuals (Abate Molina, Benjamín Vicuña Mackenna), old mining crafts (El Cateador, or mining prospector), and people who had played an important role in the development of mining in Chile (William Braden). Finally, there was a group of streets named after the "creators of the concept of democracy" (George Washington, Thomas Jefferson, Abraham Lincoln, and Franklin D. Roosevelt).[101] The strong ideological content of the names, however, made them vulnerable to ownership and political changes. After copper nationalization in 1971, Anaconda Avenue was renamed 11 de Julio Avenue. In 1973, after the coup, the new military authorities renamed the street Diego Portales, the military's favorite civilian and authoritarian figure.

The layout of El Salvador was an attempt to diminish the strong segregation that characterized other company towns. "Chastened by the anticompany feelings of copper workers and Chileans at large," wrote geographer J. Douglas Porteous, management improved housing integration.[102] In El Salvador, unlike in previous camps, houses for blue- and white-collar workers and public employees were intermixed and located within the curved part of the city. This section had duplex houses for married workers, buildings

---

100. *Andino* (Potrerillos), November 12, 1959.
101. *Andino* (Potrerillos), November 12, 1959.
102. Porteous, "Social Class."

for single male and female employees, separate dining halls for white- and blue-collar workers, union halls, social clubs, and a playground area.

The company did not abandon its desire to shape the community. Moving away from traditional repressive and paternalist methods, it opened new services. In 1956, for example, Andes Copper started publishing its first company newspaper, *Andino*, to reinforce its corporate and modernist image. *Andino* attempted to reach the community by reporting social events, festivities, sport games, and school events. It informed its readers about the company's achievements and new constructions, providing a clean image of the community. Although labor conflicts and strikes were absent from the pages of *Andino*, it reported the social role of labor unions, such as their participation in cultural and social events.

Women remained an important component of the corporate ideology. In the 1950s, Andes Copper not only encouraged workers to live within traditional family structures, but also attempted to reach and incorporate women in modern activities. The company organized new vocational schools that reinforced traditional middle-class women's roles and images. In 1956, the courses included domestic economy, child care, fashion, and handcrafts.[103] Young women were encouraged to play sports and study. Many young women were employed as secretaries and clerks, revealing the feminization of office work in an otherwise dominant male world. *Andino* played an important role in advertising the traditional middle-class values of domesticity and the company's programs. Representative of this new company discourse was a section of *Andino* titled *An Old Lady Who Knows: Aunt Paulina* (*Una viejita que sabe: La Tía Paulina*). This was a woman's section intending to give advice on personal fashion, housekeeping, and cooking. Nevertheless, the gap between the foreign company's image of the "ideal woman" and the reality of mining camps was enormous, limiting the impact of the company's discourse.[104]

Despite its improvements, El Salvador had many urban and social contradictions. It maintained strict segregation between the Chilean and American camps. Foreign employees lived in an area located on the west side of the city. This section included forty houses for married employees, a manager's house, a director's house, a guest house, six double-occupancy

103. *Andino* (Potrerillos), August 25, 1956.
104. Finn, *Tracing the Veins*; Klubock, *Contested Communities*.

single employees' houses, a school, a dining hall, a social club, a golf course, and tennis courts. Like traditional company towns, El Salvador enforced a clear division between the inside and the outside. Police officers maintained strict control over vehicles entering the town; at checkpoints, the license plate, cargo, passengers, and origin of every vehicle were recorded.[105] Unlike those who built new company towns in the United States, Andes Copper did not encourage home ownership and its camps remained the company's private property. In many ways, frequently the new industrial towns "were still closely bound with the older traditions of town planning."[106] In El Salvador, this older tradition meant segregation, exclusion, and control.

Despite the contradictions, visitors admired the new town, its modernist design, and the quality of living conditions. Socialist senator Alejandro Chelén, who persistently denounced Andes Copper's abusive labor attitudes, recognized that El Salvador had "all the necessary comforts for its blue- and white-collar workers." About this he was extremely enthusiastic, believing that in this ideal environment a worker could "dedicate himself, with more enthusiasm, to activities proper to the spirit."[107] For many of the new residents, however, the modernist layout of El Salvador was too far from their previous urban experiences. People complained about the impersonal structure of the town, the lack of public spaces, and the uniformity of constructions. At the beginning, local historian Héctor Maldonado recalled, all the houses looked the same and people had a hard time finding their residence.[108]

As the years passed, El Salvador expanded. In 1963, Andes Copper announced the construction of twenty-five buildings, or fifty household units. By December 1966, the population had almost doubled and Andes Copper began planning the construction of high-density buildings that had little resemblance with what was present in the master plan.[109] In 1967, it approved the construction of two hundred family houses. Despite all the changes, in the 1990s, architects still considered the camp a "valuable contribution to solving the problem of mining-industrial cities."[110]

---

105. *Andino* (Potrerillos), March 15, 1958.
106. Glendenning, "New Town 'Tradition.'"
107. Alejandro Chelén, Cámara de Senadores, *Diario de Sesiones*, June 9, 1959.
108. Héctor Maldonado, *Albores de el mineral El Salvador* (Potrerillos, Chile: Imprenta Cobresal, 1989), 115.
109. Fiorenza Sartori and Eugenio Garcés, "Evolución histórica del asentamiento minero de El Salvador (1956–1994)" (paper presented at the conference "Asentamientos mineros del cobre en Chile: Realides y proyecciones," Universidad Católica de Chile, September 2000).
110. "El Salvador, ciudad minera proyectada como tal."

Conclusions

The mid-1950s was a unique time in the Chilean copper industry. In 1955, the Chilean government redefined copper policies, offering foreign companies a new deal: a reduction of taxation in exchange for an increase in investment and production. The Nuevo Trato was a unique solution to the specific dilemmas of the Chilean economy: strong dependency on copper exports and a need to overcome the bottlenecks caused by import-substitution efforts. The new arrangements, however, required the cooperation of labor. Facing serious labor tensions in the copper mines, including a nineteen-day industry-wide strike in 1955, the government offered a new pact to copper workers, the Statute for Copper Workers.

At the local level, the construction of El Salvador represented Anaconda's efforts of to respond to increasing national pressures and its dependency on Chilean copper. The company used and advertised its new investment and the good quality of the urban infrastructure and housing at El Salvador to show workers, and the country more generally, its commitment to Chile's economic growth and workers' welfare. Anaconda's strategy fell short. Although El Salvador opened new employment and business opportunities and improved living conditions, the camp suffered from internal contradictions, such as segregation of Chilean workers and foreign management.

In the long run, the prosperity was fragile. The Nuevo Trato did not solve the economic troubles of Chile, inspiring radical solutions to Chile's dependency on copper. Similarly, the Statute of Copper Workers did not solve labor tensions and instead helped to consolidate the power of the CTC, the alliance between blue- and white-collar copper workers, and a labor discourse that included both the demands for better economic conditions and for the nationalization of copper. At the local level, labor relations did not improve and strike activity remained high. By 1958, the political victory of the Right (in the election of Jorge Alessandri), the reunification of the political Left under the leadership of Salvador Allende, the structural limitations of the Chilean economy, and the consequences for labor of modernization shaped the demands and political alliances of copper workers, leading them toward more radical positions.

5 Nationalism and Radicalization, 1958–1970

In April 1962, the leaders of the Copper Workers Confederation (CTC) held an extraordinary meeting in Santiago to discuss the "exceptionally difficult conditions" encountered by their members since their last meeting in May 1961. The Braden and Anaconda companies were denounced by the CTC leadership for carrying out a "policy of arrogance, abuses, and conflict against union leaders," which made "impossible a friendly and loyal understanding to approach, with calm and sense of justice, the diverse problems that unions face every day." Copper companies, the meeting's report stated, disregarded national copper policies, laid off workers, ignored union agreements, and made efforts to reduce production costs. In addition, they launched a media campaign to delegitimate the labor movement, arguing that union demands were politically motivated and would only increase production costs and undermine Chilean copper's position in the international market. The CTC condemned the lack of commitment from public authorities, who had neither shown "enough energy nor acted with a strong hand to prevent companies from disregarding the law or simply eluding the agreements that we have signed with them." In the midst of these adverse conditions, CTC directors highlighted the existence of a "clear, defined, and active" union agenda; "the support and the affection" demonstrated by the rank and file; and the strong solidarity expressed by national labor organizations. During the three-day meeting, labor leaders participated in several working groups addressing a wide range of issues, from housing needs to national copper policy.[1]

---

1. Confederación de Trabajadores del Cobre, "Primer Congreso Nacional Extraordinario" (1962), Biblioteca de la Federación de Trabajadores del Cobre, Santiago, Chile.

The CTC's 1962 report reveals the difficulties and challenges experienced by workers in the large-scale copper industry during the 1960s. Yet it also suggests the strength and legitimacy of the labor movement in the copper camps and its efforts to combine bread-and-butter demands with larger political claims. Throughout the 1960s, labor tensions continued to mount in the copper mines, and labor unions maintained a permanent activism to defend workers' historical victories, protect their jobs, and expand their economic rights. In Chuquicamata, El Teniente, Potrerillos, and El Salvador, copper companies improved productivity by introducing new technology and rationalizing the company's administration, but workers became the first victims of these management schemes as jobs became less secure and working and employment conditions deteriorated. The hostility of employers, the ambivalence of the state toward protecting workers' rights, and economic insecurity convinced many leaders and union members of the need to introduce radical reforms.

Copper workers' lives, struggles, and politics continued to be shaped by the foreign ownership of the copper industry, the debate over the nationalization of this key sector of the economy, and the singular importance of copper exports for the country. From the late 1950s until the complete takeover of the mines by the Chilean state in 1970, the question of copper nationalization reached its highest point. Workers became a central part of this debate. As the country failed to draft and enforce an effective copper policy, copper workers became more dissatisfied with official policies and articulated an alternative discourse of economic nationalism and development, demanding the complete nationalization of the mines and workers' incorporation into the new public enterprises.

To understand the complex interaction of local, national, and transnational forces in Potrerillos and El Salvador, one needs to examine the difficulties faced by copper workers, their demands, and the controversies around them. Local demands such as housing, work safety, and job security were entangled with larger issues regarding the foreign ownership of the copper industry, debates on the best production modalities, and increasing national political and economic tensions. In this chapter I describe the radicalization, polarization, and rising economic nationalism (anti-imperialist discourse) in the copper mines. I argue that these transformations and demands were collective responses to the contradictions of the local copper industry and the international copper market, the crisis of the national economy, shortcomings in copper policies, and the lack of state commitment to protect workers' rights.

A Controversial Collective Bargaining Agenda

In May 1961, workers at Potrerillos, El Salvador, and Barquito demanded a 40 percent increase in basic wages and salaries and expansion of bonuses and fringe benefits.[2] General manager William Bennett rejected workers' petitions, claiming, "[These] demands tend to increase workers' salaries and living conditions beyond any limit and above the present ones that are, as we have said, among the best in the world."[3] On August 11, more than three thousand Andes Copper employees went on strike. The CTC then called a sympathy strike in the rest of the copper industry and, as the U.S. embassy reported, "the Andes problem assumed great national importance."[4] After intense government lobbying, the strike ended, on September 10. Negotiations lasted two more months, and on November 16, a new collective contract secured a 15 percent increase in wages and salaries and improvement of benefits and bonuses and gave each worker a onetime payment of 50–120 escudos.[5]

The strike of 1961 was emblematic of the rising labor tensions and confrontations in the copper industry. Every fifteen months, local unions renegotiated salaries, benefits, and living conditions. Through collective bargaining and strikes, copper workers sought to achieve and consolidate substantial economic benefits in a time of increasing inflationary pressures and job insecurity (see Table 8). Given management's opposition to increasing wages and improving conditions in the mines, labor negotiations were long and complicated, and legal and illegal strikes occurred frequently. Despite government opposition, growing solidarity among labor unions throughout the large-scale copper industry and the effective work of the CTC transformed local strikes into industry-wide conflicts and into de facto industry-wide negotiations. The impact of strikes on the national economy and state revenues eroded the always precarious understanding

---

2. "Pliego de peticiones trabajadores Andes," May 2, 1961, ADT.
3. Bennett to the Unions, May 9, 1961, ADT.
4. U.S. Embassy, October 20, 1961, NARA, GR, Chile 1960–63, box 2394.
5. U.S. Embassy, November 17, 1961, NARA, GR, Chile 1960–63, box 2394.

Table 8 Andes Copper wage increases, 1959–1970

Contract (15-Month)	Workers' Demands (Percentage)	Wage Increase Obtained (Percentage)	Year	Official Wage Increase, Private Sector (Percentage)	Increase in Inflation (Percentage)
1959–60		100	1959	28	38.6
1960–61	60	21	1960	15	11.6
1961–62	40	15.1	1961	16.6	7.7
1962–64	25–30	21.1	1962	15	13.9
			1963	15	44.3
1964–65	100	Scale	1964		46.0
1965–66	85	Scale	1965	38.4	28.8
1966–67	Scale	Scale	1966	25.9	22.9
1967–69	60	30	1967		18.1
			1968	21.9	26.6
1969–70		38	1969		30.7

SOURCES: Data for workers' demands from Pliego de Peticiones, Archivo de la Dirección del Trabajo; data for wage increase obtained and for official wage increase, private sector, from Jorge Barría, *Los sindicatos de la Gran Minería del Cobre* (Santiago: INSORA, 1970), 123; data for increase in inflation from Barbara Stallings, *Class Conflict and Economic Development in Chile, 1958–1973* (Stanford: Stanford University Press, 1978), 247.

between labor and the state and politicized local conditions. Labor conflicts in the copper industry were aggravated by the efforts of the government, management, and the conservative media to use the economic gap between copper workers and the rest of the Chilean working class to question the legitimacy of copper workers' demands. Ultimately, the conflict between capital, labor, and the state evidenced major tensions in Chilean society: the crisis of a model of economic development that could not reconcile economic growth and social justice.

The strike activity in the copper industry and the language used by the different actors involved illustrate the intensity of labor conflicts in the mines. Between 1955 and 1964, 124 strikes took place in the Chilean large-scale copper industry.[6] In Andes Copper, between 1960 and 1969, five out of the eight contract negotiations involved a strike, and strikes usually lasted more than a month. Workers in Potrerillos also joined one industry-wide strike, one solidarity strike, and one national strike (see Table 9). There were also numerous wildcat strikes motivated by disagreements on

---

6. "Chilean Copper Miners Approve 60% Pay Rise," *New York Times*, September 25, 1964.

Table 9 Strikes at Andes Copper Company, 1960–1969

Year	Days of Strike	Motive	Character
1960	26	Collective Bargaining	Legal
1961	31	Collective Bargaining	Legal
1962	37	Collective Bargaining	Legal
1964	48	Collective Bargaining	Legal
1965	37	Against Chileanization laws	Illegal Industry-Wide Strike
1966	12	Solidarity with El Teniente's workers	Illegal Solidarity Strike
1967	34	Collective Bargaining	Legal
1969	1	In protest against the attempted military coup "tacnazo"	Illegal National Strike called by the CUT

SOURCE: Jorge Barría, *Los sindicatos de la Gran Minería del Cobre* (Santiago: INSORA, 1970), 136–38.

the shop floor about such issues as levels of dust inside the mine, foremen's attitudes, and general working conditions and also over bonus payments. Unfortunately, the information regarding these illegal and local strikes is scattered. According to a study by Rodrigo González and Alonso Daire, wildcat strikes affecting the entire large-scale copper industry increased consistently throughout the 1960s: from 16 in 1963, to 32 in 1964, to 194 in 1966–67.[7] Chilean historian Jorge Barría, by contrast, registered 11 serious wildcat strikes in Andes Copper between 1966 and 1970, but he provided no information for the previous years.[8]

As in the rest of the country, the main issue behind legal strikes continued to be wage negotiations. Because of high rates of inflation and the length of union contracts (fifteen months), wage demands in the copper industry were traditionally high (see Table 9). High economic demands were ways to accommodate to the characteristics of the copper industry and life in mining camps. Living in a company town; working under unsatisfactory health conditions; and having little access to the state's services, social plans, or alternative sources of income, unions looked at bread-and-butter demands as fair compensation for workers' sacrifices. Copper workers also argued that they deserved the best wages and working conditions because

---

7. Rodrigo González and Alonso Daire, *Los paros nacionales en Chile (1919–1973)* (Santiago: Centro de Estudios Democráticos de América Latina [CEDAL], 1984), 138.
8. Barría, "Organización y políticas laborales," 208.

of their high levels of productivity and contributions to the national economy. As employees of a foreign company, they compared their productivity and salaries with those earned by similar miners in developed countries and argued that Chilean miners were underpaid. In 1965, the front page of the CTC newspaper *Cobre* published a comparison of Chilean and U.S. copper workers by salary and productivity. The image depicted two characters. On the left, a copper worker representing the United States says, "A North American worker earns eight times more and produces less"; on the right a Chilean miner announces, "A Chilean worker earns eight times less and works more."[9]

Facing soaring workers' demands and labor pressures, management insisted that copper workers were the best-paid workers in the country and received outstanding benefits. "Our workers" stated Andes in its response to the 1962 *pliego de peticiones* (opening proposal in contract bargaining), "enjoyed an exceptionally high system of wages, higher than the wages earned by other workers in the country and comparable only to workers' wages in countries that have achieved a higher level of economic development than Chile."[10] This discourse is representative of the company's strategies, whereby it sought to question the reasons behind workers' economic demands. In the same way, the U.S. embassy explained strikes in the copper industry as driven by political and electoral interests. During the 1960 strike in Potrerillos and El Salvador, Norman Pearson, the U.S. labor attaché in Chile, concluded: "In view of the extent of the offer rejected by the unions at a time when the wage line was being restricted throughout all of Chilean industry, and in view of the apparent lack of interest by the unions in settling through making virtually ridiculous proposals, one must look to other factors for the principal cause of the strike at the Andes Mining Company. It is believed that this cause lies in the political field."[11]

To what extent were copper workers successful? In the 1960s, local unions achieved substantial benefits and improved living and working conditions for their members. A comparison of inflation levels, wage increases in the copper industry, and official wage increases in the private sector suggests that local unions were able to protect their members from economic instability. Similarly, as a former union leader from the port of Barquito put it, "Around

9. *Cobre* (Santiago) 3, no. 28 (1965).
10. Andes Copper, "Oferta de Andes Copper Mining Company a sus empleados y obreros," October 19, 1962, ADT.
11. Pearson, May 20, 1960, NARA, GR, Chile 1960–63, box 2397.

1962 the labor movement became more stable, we got the benefits, we got what we wanted."[12] This economic security, however, was threatened by job instability, production restructuring, and the company's efforts to reduce the costs of production.

Defending Jobs and Working Conditions, 1960–1964

In January 1961, general manager William Bennett warned public authorities about a crisis in the international copper market. Bennett declared that falling international prices, increase in copper world production, and extensive use of copper substitutes might force the company to reduce production in Potrerillos and El Salvador. Responding to Anaconda's orders, Bennett suspended work on Sundays and holidays and eliminated overtime.[13] In April, Edmundo Espinoza and Luis Toro, inspectors at the Department of Labor (Oficina del Trabajo), informed the minister of labor of a policy entailing "reduction of the costs of production" in the Anaconda mines El Salvador and Chuquicamata. Espinoza and Toro reported that Anaconda's subsidiaries were laying off, reassigning, and retiring workers. Although the labor inspectors were not critical of the companies' policies, they noticed increasing unrest among workers and union leaders.[14] In November, Andes Copper announced the elimination of about eight hundred job positions. Again, the increase in the costs of production, management argued, made it impossible to "maintain job positions that are not strictly necessary."[15]

In December 1961, the union leaders of Potrerillos, El Salvador, and Barquito addressed the minister of labor in a detailed report on the current layoffs (Table 10); denounced the illegality of the company's measures; and asked the government to force Andes Copper to "present all the economic, technical, and social antecedents" that justified its current policy.[16] Their demand was based on the legal obligation of the company, according to the Labor Code, to ask for authorization when firing more than ten employees.

12. Guido Soriano, conversation with the author, 26 July 2000.
13. Bennett, January 26, 1961, ARNAD, MT, Providencias, 1961, vol. 6.
14. Espinoza and Toro to Minister of Labor, April 28, 1961, ARNAD, MT, Providencias, 1961, vol. 6.
15. *La Nación* (Santiago), November 23, 1961.
16. Labor Unions to Gálvez, Minister of Labor, December 14, 1961, ARNAD, MM, Providencias, 1962, vol. 1-300.

Table 10 Proposed layoffs in Potrerillos, El Salvador, and Barquito, December 1961

Department	Total Workforce	Jobs to Be Eliminated
Mechanical	489	104
Electrical	216	57
Plant	154	38
Engineering	135	49
Warehouse	81	42
Welfare	172	69
Company Store	55	10
Construction	48	36
General Offices	78	21
Mine	124	8
Arsenal	37	23
Other	113	13
Total	1702	470

SOURCE: Labor Unions to Hugo Gálvez, Minister of Labor, Santiago, 14 December 1961, Records of the Ministerio de Minería, Providencias, 1962, vol. 1-300.

Among the people fired and reassigned during 1961 was Luis López, a blue-collar worker in Potrerillos, who was let go because the department where he worked had "an excess of employees." Eight days later, the company offered him a job in the El Salvador mine.[17] Similarly that year, Benigno Brilladeros, a white-collar employee in the Electric Department earning 155 escudos a month, was reassigned by Andes Copper as a blue-collar worker in the mine (underground), and his monthly salary was cut to 107 escudos. Manuel Rodríguez, a blue-collar worker with five years of service, was also transferred from the Electric Department to the mine, and his daily wage reduced from 3.28 to 3.21 escudos.[18] In addition to the loss of good jobs and reassignment of workers, labor unions complained, the reorganization of the workplace was leading in many sections to dramatic work intensification. In the company port Barquito, where the pace of work varied in relation to the arrival and departure of boats, overwork became an acute problem. Since Andes Copper had reduced the workforce employed

17. Letter from the Andes Copper Mining Company, quoted by Manuel Magalhaes. Manuel Magalhaes, Cámara de Diputados, *Diario de Sesiones*, December 6, 1961, 1790.
18. Espinoza and Toro to Minister of Labor, April 28,1961, ARNAD, MT, Providencias, 1961, vol. 6.

in the port, most employees were working overtime and could not take their legal vacations.[19]

The stories of Luis López, Benigno Brilladeros, Manuel Rodríguez, and the workers at Barquito evidenced the impact of the world economy on people's lives. They confirmed workers' sense of their historical vulnerability and powerlessness not only in confronting the "international market," but also in the face of management's arbitrary decisions. Job instability had created a permanent migration of people and a strong sense of insecurity among workers, especially unskilled blue-collar workers. Unlike what had been achieved in the United States, in Chile workers had failed to introduce seniority as a formal right to protect older workers from layoffs.[20] In 1957, two social workers who had conducted research in Chuquicamata concluded, "Most workers feel insecure in their job and fear being fired at any moment. Faced with any fluctuation in the price of copper in the world market, they fear a reduction of personnel, and neither their efficiency nor their seniority is a guarantee."[21] In 1961, Espinoza and Toro noted in Potrerillos a strong feeling of "insecurity and fear" among workers.[22] Similarly, in 1962, labor unions described a "psycho-neurosis" among their members.[23]

The layoffs provoked a militant response from the union leadership, who organized a local and national campaign to defend the right to work and to job security. Labor unions contested the reasons for reductions in the labor force and for the restructuring of labor conditions, revealing the contradictions of U.S. investment in Chile and reinforcing workers' demands for the nationalization of the industry. In doing so, they criticized a model of modernization that sacrificed workers' welfare on behalf of profit and productivity. This struggle was emblematic of the power of labor in the 1960s and the legal and political limits to the imposition of what, ten years later, would be the neoliberal agenda of the Chilean military and the country's economic elite.

19. Labor Unions to Gálvez, Minister of Labor, December 14, 1961, ARNAD, MM, Providencias, 1962, vol. 1-300.
20. For a discussion of seniority in the United States, see Ronald W. Schatz, *The Electrical Workers: A History of Labor at General Electric and Westinghouse, 1923–60* (Urbana: University of Illinois, 1983).
21. Eliana Galaz and María Angélica Alvear, "Factores de trabajo en Chuquicamata" (Memoria, Universidad Católica de Chile, 1957), 86.
22. Espinoza and Toro to Minister of Labor, April 28, 1961, ARNAD, MT, Providencias, 1961, vol. 6.
23. *El Día* (Copiapó), March 3, 1962.

The experience of layoffs and arbitrary company policies convinced union leaders of the need to exert direct influence on the administration of the company and to be part of the decision-making process. Manuel Ovalle, Potrerillos union official and CTC director, for one, contested the attitude of management and their power to make unilateral decisions about the administration of the company, the unions, he believed, had to be consulted "on the reassignment of workers and the efficiency studies themselves." As he put it to U.S. diplomats in 1961, one of the major issues in the past layoffs was "the manner of doing it."[24] The quest for workers participation raised the issue of the freedom enjoyed by employers in administering their business; in this, as general manager William Bennett remarked in 1964, unions went beyond the issues covered by collective bargaining and sanctioned by the Labor Code.[25] By asking management to take into consideration not only market conditions but also workers' lives, future, and contributions, unions took labor-management relations to a new level. In doing so, they were not questioning modernization per se, but offering an alternative view of economic growth.[26] This demand, albeit not yet fully articulated, for worker participation was revolutionary and became an integral part of the program of *participación popular*, worker representation on boards of directors, and the nationalization of the copper industry during the three years of the Popular Unity (1970–73) (see Chapter 6).

Aware of the need to have a national response and state intervention, union leaders took the drama of employment insecurity from the isolated mines to the capital city, forcing legislators and government officials to find answers. The CTC launched a public campaign to denounce the massive firing in El Teniente, Potrerillos, and El Salvador.[27] Through political lobbying, use of the media, and formal protests, the confederation drew national attention. Working-class and leftist newspapers, such as *El Siglo, Cobre*, and *Punto Final*, published several articles, provoking national awareness of the plight of copper workers. In December, local leaders from Potrerillos and El Salvador addressed a formal complaint to the minister of labor.

In an indication of the importance of the industry and the power of its labor movement for Chile, national political authorities quickly responded to the crisis in the copper industry. On December 6, 1961, deputies questioned

---

24. Memorandum, May 26, 1961, NARA, GR, Chile 1960–63, box 2397.
25. Bennett to Union Officers, February 8, 1964, DT.
26. For a comparison, see Schatz, *Electrical Workers*, 111
27. *Cobre* (Santiago), October 1964.

the reasons behind the mass firings and the companies' economic rationale, and they unanimously approved petitions directed at the Ministries of Mining and Labor to stop the layoffs, to the Copper Commission to inspect the mines, and to the National Health Service to carry out extensive medical inspections of the labor force.[28] Representative of the state's concern were the declarations of the minister of labor, Hugo Gálvez. Although Gálvez did not overtly question the reasons behind the layoffs, he believed that Andes Copper should reduce the labor force in a less rapid and conflictive way and develop mechanisms such as gradual layoffs, hiring freezes, and the pensioning off of older workers. Similarly, Gálvez accused Andes Copper of undermining social peace in Chile and U.S. policy toward Latin America. While the U.S. government, in the context of the Alliance for Progress, encouraged substantial socioeconomic reforms, Gálvez explained, "the companies appear to be resisting the taxes imposed by the public authorities and to be creating a climate of social unrest that could be serious."[29]

The employment policies of copper companies and the unions' successful labor campaign degraded the companies' position in Chile in the midst of nationalistic pressures. It did not help that the massive layoffs coincided with the approval of new taxation. Between 1960 and 1961, the National Congress had approved new income taxes on copper companies (laws 14.603 and 14.688). In copper companies' attitudes toward their workers, many Chileans perceived a sign of the failure of foreign capital to contribute to Chile's development. As Norman Pearson, counselor for political affairs at the U.S. embassy, recognized in late 1961, conditions for U.S. copper companies were clearly deteriorating; the majority of Chileans believed that copper companies should increase investments, production, and copper manufacturing. There was also, Pearson noted, "a general feeling that the large companies are acting so as to derogate the sovereignty of Chile."[30]

Production and Company Restructuring

The 1961–62 layoffs were part of a general production restructuring of the copper industry. Throughout the 1960s, Anaconda introduced technological

---

28. Cámara de Diputados, *Diario de Sesiones*, December 6, 1961, 1785–1828.
29. U.S. Embassy, December 28, 1961, NARA, GR, Chile 1960–63, box 2397.
30. U.S. Embassy, July 5, 1961, NARA, GR, Chile 1960–63, box 2397.

innovations in an attempt both to satisfy the national demand for investment and industrialization and to decrease production costs. The quest for modernization became urgent as nationalism and labor tensions mounted and the international market became more competitive. The restructuring of copper mines had an important impact on productivity: between 1956 and 1966, productivity in the large-scale copper mines increased 15.6 percent.[31] With the quality of the ore remaining stable, efficiency and productivity increased mainly because of changes in the organization of production and introduction of new technology. But, as in many other economic sectors, in the copper industry, the attempt to increase productivity had a negative impact on employment and threatened job security and economic benefits.[32]

The first component of this reorganization focused on production. The changes did not imply an increase in production capacity but instead an improvement in the production processes, whereby traditional levels of output were maintained at a lower cost. To do this, Anaconda built new facilities and introduced technology that reduced labor costs. In 1960, Andes Copper opened a molybdenum recovery plant—molybdenum was found together with sulfide copper ore and was a valuable metal used in the steel industry—and a hydroelectric plant that produced about seventeen hundred kilowatts.[33] Important advances in the mine included the introduction of ammonium nitrate (explosive), changes in the layout of ore blocks, and a new underground ore-handling system. The smelter incorporated automatic features for material handling.[34] Similar changes were introduced in Chuquicamata, where Chile Exploration implemented an automatic system of control and operation and electronic instruments to record production in the sulfur plant and updated trucks, drills, and mechanical shelves.[35] Along with modernizing the production processes, Andes Copper launched a project of rationalization of the administration of the camps, clerical work, and shops. Unlike efforts of production flexibilization in the 1990s, the changes introduced in the 1960s did not entail a complete restructuring of the workplace or a change in traditional job hierarchies.

---

31. Barrera, *El conflicto obrero*, 20.
32. Francisco Zapata, ed., *¿Flexibles y productivos? Estudios sobre flexibilidad laboral en México* (Mexico City: El Colegio de México, 1998), 21–22.
33. Anaconda Copper Mining Company, *Annual Report* (1961).
34. Anaconda Copper Mining Company, *Annual Report* (1961, 1963).
35. Chile Exploration Company, *Chuquicamata: El esfuerzo industrial de Chile* (Chuquicamata, Chile: Chilex, n.d.), 9–16.

In some sections, the introduction of new machines led to the elimination of jobs. In Potrerillos and El Salvador, the company store brought in machines to label products and automatic scales that made work faster.³⁶ The acquisition of bread machines in El Salvador's company bakery made traditional bakers' skills unnecessary.³⁷ In other departments, the introduction of private contracting reduced employment opportunities for company workers and their families. In the Welfare Department of Potrerillos, for instance, Andes Copper began using the services of Carlos Sánchez, a private contractor, for all the maintenance work in the Chilean and the American camps, reducing the Welfare Department's workforce by 40 percent in 1961.³⁸ Private contracting also affected informal employment opportunities. In 1967, two restaurants run by private concessionaries prepared meals for blue- and white-collar workers, replacing local women (most of them wives of company workers) who, as a way to supplement their family income, previously had cooked lunch for single workers.³⁹

In other sections, the replacement of machinery created tensions when workers viewed the transition as an increase in their responsibilities. In 1956, when the IBM Accounting Machines Department introduced new machines, its thirteen white-collar employees walked off the job. They asked for a wage increase, a workweek of five and a half days (*sábado inglés*), and holidays. These demands were a response to the effects of the recent reorganization of work. The changes required the IBM employees, they said, "to work excessive shifts above the limits set by the legislation, absorbing our rest hours and having a heavy impact on our health, as well as the fact that the new machines have too many defects that are not the responsibility of the operator and that demand more work."⁴⁰

The most controversial work transformation was the increase in subcontracting, defined as a capital scheme to achieve production flexibility so as to adapt to unstable market conditions. The introduction of contract workers was consistent with changes in the labor structure of the world economy. Historically, the characteristics of industrial mining and its

---

36. *Andino* (Potrerillos), January 2, 1960.
37. *Andino* (Potrerillos), January 2, 1960.
38. Labor Unions to Gálvez, December 14, 1961, ARNAD, MM, Providencias, 1962, vol. 1-300.
39. *Andino* (Potrerillos), January 28, 1967.
40. IBM Employees to Campbell, April 27, 1956; Bennett to Cárdenas, May 4, 1956; Bennett to Cárdenas, 9 May 1956; Bertoglia, June 19, 1956. All the documents in ARNAD, DT, Providencias, 1956, vol. 15.

requirement for large capital investment limited subcontracting to construction work, but overtime it expanded to maintenance and some administrative functions. Beginning in the mid-1950s, copper companies began using contractors more extensively. Contract workers were a cheap, vulnerable, poorly organized, unskilled, disposable labor force. Many contractor companies were in a precarious economic position, owed money to Andes Copper, and held workers' salaries for unusually long periods, and few paid social benefits.[41]

In El Salvador, as Socialist senator Alejandro Chelén remarked, contract workers lived in provisional, "unhealthy, and unhygienic" bunkhouses at the outskirts of the camp, this complex of dwellings surrounded by "a wire fence like [a] concentration [camp]."[42] These workers did not have access to the company's social services and urban infrastructure, and the long distances between the camps and major cities made most public services inaccessible. Many of them moved with their families, creating acute social problems for which the company assumed no responsibility. Following a visit to El Salvador and Potrerillos, a journalist from *El Cobre* summarized the contract system: "This system is lucrative to contractors because of the brutal and unlimited exploitation of the workers employed in these works. They [the workers] are not organized in labor unions and do not have any kind of power. As in the nitrate fields at the beginning of the century, they are hired with miserable salaries, without benefits, living conditions are indecent, pile up like animals."[43]

While consistent information is lacking on the exact number of contractors in the large-scale copper industry, the growing concern of local unions and the CTC suggests its impact on the employment structure. In 1961, in the midst of the national debate about layoffs, *El Día* denounced Anaconda for its plan to allow the participation of private contractors in the mine. *El Día* reported that this strategy benefited only foreign companies, since salaries would decline and the cost of living would increase.[44] In 1963, the CTC denounced contractors as "modern vultures of the desert" and part of a cheap strategy to "reduce the costs of production."[45] In 1967, the

---

41. Bertoglia to Director General del Trabajo, February 13, 1958, ARNAD, DT, Providencias, 1958, vol. 8.
42. Alejandro Chelén, Cámara de Senadores, *Diario de Sesiones*, January 17, 1962, 2566–67.
43. *Cobre* (Santiago), October 1963.
44. *El Día* (Copiapó), May 2, 1961.
45. *Cobre* (Santiago), October 1963.

CTC again called attention to the problem of private contracting and temporary workers, demanding that contract workers earn the same salary and have the same employment conditions as company workers.[46] In the years that followed, unions asked management to permanently abolish outsourcing and to rehire contract workers as company employees. For copper workers, the massive use of contracting in construction and maintenance—two areas that, copper workers argued, were part of the production process—was a clear sign of the contradictions inherent in the rationalization of administration and production, demonstrating the inconsistency of the layoffs.

In an effort to reduce costs, copper companies began to withdraw from the administration of the camps, turning over to the government many social and urban-based responsibilities.[47] This withdrawal was representative of changes in managers' attitudes and their doubts that rigid company towns were an effective instrument of labor and social control. In the 1960s, high maintenance costs and increasing pressures from the national state and the labor community made rigid company towns unpopular; for example, late in the decade, administering the camps represented about 14 percent of labor costs and created enormous conflicts between management and the working community.[48] Foreign capital was thus convinced of the benefits of a switch from company to public services. This transition, however, was also a result of legal reforms. After 1956, mining camps were not considered "private properties" but subject to the jurisdiction of the municipal government.[49]

In El Salvador and Potrerillos, Andes Copper began passing responsibilities on to the state. These changes reduced employment opportunities for company workers. In one example, where previously at the crushing plant at Potrerillos three private guards had been employed, by 1961 Andes Copper had shifted the responsibility for security onto the local police.[50] The geographical characteristics and isolation of El Salvador and Potrerillos limited the urban and social choices of Andes Copper. In contrast, both El Teniente and Chuquicamata started to resettle workers in urban centers,

---

46. *Cobre* (Santiago), May 1967.
47. Robert J. Alexander, "Changes in Chuquicamata," GMMA, International Affairs Department, Country Files 1945–71 (hereafter CF), box 18, folder 11.
48. Aurelio Butelmann, "Productivity and Wage Determination: A Microeconomic Model for the Gran Minería of Copper in Chile" (master's thesis, Cornell University, 1969).
49. Barrera, *El conflicto obrero*, 49.
50. Labor Unions to Gálvez, December 14, 1961, MM, Providencias, 1962, vol. 1-300.

diminishing the importance of company towns.[51] In 1966–67, El Teniente started "Operación Valle" (Plan 280), a scheme to move the population from Sewell to Rancagua, where workers could buy a house and live in a "normal" urban environment.[52] Similarly, Chuquicamata launched a project to move part of the working population to Calama, where it financed the development of Villa Ayquina. By 1970, 14.91 percent of the labor force lived in Villa Ayquina and another 31.76 percent in Calama.[53]

Not all reforms implemented by companies had a negative impact. The main advance in copper production accomplished by Andes Copper in the 1960s was the construction of a copper refining facility in Potrerillos. The refinery represented a victory for the Chilean state and its effort to increase the industrialization of copper in the country. Copper refining was traditionally a controversial issue in the large-scale copper industry and a source of major conflicts between copper companies and the Chilean state. Like Andes Copper, most foreign companies investing in developing countries did not build refineries, but preferred to refine blister copper in industrialized countries. Because the costs of transportation of unrefined and refined copper were similar, copper companies around the world had few reasons to build refineries next to ore-production sites, preferring to build them closer to consumer centers.

In contrast, the refining of copper was a critical issue for the Chilean state. Not only were refineries viewed as an essential component of industrialization, but also the price of refined copper was higher than that of unrefined, affecting state revenues and the balance of payments.[54] Similarly, as Jaime Claro from the Department of Copper argued in 1962, "by refining Chilean copper in the United States and then sending it to Europe, we are paying transportation costs twice, which increases the costs of refining from about 0.9 to 1.0 cents per pound." Prior to 1964, Andes Copper had refined its copper in an Anaconda plant in Perth Amboy, New Jersey. The Perth Amboy refinery was highly dependent on Chilean copper, to the extent that, noted Claro, it would have to reduce its capacity if Andes Copper started

---

51. Porteous, "Social Class."

52. Eugenio Garcés, "Las ciudades del cobre: Del campamento de montaña al hotel minero como variaciones de la company town," *Revista de Estudios Urbanos Regionales (EURE)* 88 (2003).

53. Clorinda Marín and Sonia Trivick, "Servicio social en la Gran Minería del Cobre: Chuquicamata" (Memoria, Universidad de Chile de Antofagasta, 1970), 65–66.

54. Vera, *La política económica*, 110–12.

refining its own copper.⁵⁵ In the 1950s, the Nuevo Trato and the construction of El Salvador led Andes Copper to consider the possibility of building a refinery in the port of Chañaral. The local community strongly supported the project, seeing it as the basis for the economic development of the region. The company postponed the project until May 1962, when it announced the investment of 25 million dollars in the construction of the expected electrolytic refinery. The new refinery, however, would be located in Potrerillos, dashing the expectations of the local community of Chañaral.⁵⁶ Inaugurated in 1964, the Potrerillos refinery, with a productive capacity of about thirty-six thousand tons of copper annually, produced wire bars and cathodes and shipped them from Barquito to different markets around the world. By 1967, Potrerillos refined 80 percent of its copper production. In 1968, motivated by the 1966 copper laws, Chuquicamata inaugurated a new electrolytic refinery, which, claimed the Sociedad Nacional de Minería (National Mining Society, or SONAMI), was a step forward in the modernization of the large-scale copper industry.⁵⁷

In addition, there were positive effects for the country, as seen in increased hiring of Chilean professionals to replace foreign staff.⁵⁸ The reasons for replacing foreign staff were both economical and political. Hiring foreign professionals in the copper industry was expensive, involving traveling costs, housing, wages paid in dollars, and outstanding benefits.⁵⁹ Similarly, Chile pressured foreign companies to hire local professionals. In Potrerillos, the number of foreign staff declined from sixty-six in May 1960 to forty-five in July 1962.⁶⁰ Adam Dutton, superintendent of smelting in Potrerillos, remembered that "over the years Chileans gradually replaced foreign positions except for key positions in management. . . . During the decade

55. Jaime Claro, Department of Copper, June 12, 1962, ARNAD, MM, Providencias, 1964, vol. 780-849.
56. U.S. Embassy, May 8, 1962, NARA, GR, Chile 1960–63, box 2396.
57. *Boletín Minero*, October–December 1968.
58. This has been a common strategy among foreign companies facing national pressures and high labor costs. In the case of U.S.-owned maquiladoras in the U.S.-Mexican border, as sociologist Leslie Salzinger explains, the decision of foreign employers to build a local "managerial workforce" has been a response to pressures from the national state and local elites and efforts to "lower labor costs, increase local expertise, and placate indigenous power-holders. Leslie Salzinger, *Genders in Production: Making Workers in Mexico's Global Factories* (Berkeley and Los Angeles: University of California Press, 2003), 77.
59. Reynolds, "Development Problems," 268.
60. "Estadística Minera y Metalúrgica: Resumen de Personal," May 1960, ARNAD, MM, Providencia, 1960; "Estadística Minera y Metalúrgica: Resumen de Personal," July 1962, ARNAD, MM, Providencia, 1962, vol. 845-1272.

1960–70, foreign staff at Potrerillos never exceeded 18–20 and towards the end this number was further reduced to about 10."[61] The situation in the other two large-scale mines was similar. Chuquicamata reduced foreign employees from eighty-nine in May 1960 to fifty-eight in July 1962. In El Teniente, foreign personnel remained a small minority, varying between eleven and twenty in number throughout the 1960s.[62]

The incorporation of Chilean professionals did not completely challenge the "national" division of labor. Foreigners remained in the top management positions, and Chilean professionals remained in an ambiguous social and work position. Chilean professionals became part of the American camp and English-language social and cultural life. When Chilean professional Carlos Munchemeyer accepted a job offer in the Geological Department of El Salvador in 1967, Anaconda offered him not only the "opportunity to learn a lot of geology," but also a chance to "improve his English."[63] Further, Chilean professionals were paid in dollars, a privilege that created enormous tensions during the nationalization of the copper industry in 1971. The growing number of Chileans in managerial and technical positions helped to increase what Theodore Moran called the "Chilean confidence in the domestic ability to run the copper industry at the production stage and (evidently) to set copper policy on the international level as well."[64] Although many supervisors disagreed with the nationalization and opposed the government of Salvador Allende, others stayed and made possible the transition from a foreign to a national administration.

Politicization, Radicalization, and Nationalism Under Eduardo Frei, 1964–1970

The presidential election of 1964 was a turning point in Chile's history, opening a decade of social reform and popular mobilization. That year, the majority of Chilean citizens supported the reformist agenda of Christian Democrat Eduardo Frei Montalva and voted him into office. Frei's victory

---

61. Adam Dutton, e-mail message to the author, 18 November 2003.
62. "Estadística Minera y Metalúrgica: Resumen de Personal," May 1960, ARNAD, MM, Providencia, 1960; "Estadística Minera y Metalúrgica: Resumen de Personal," July 1962, ARNAD, MM, Providencia, 1962, vol. 845-1272.
63. Gustafson to Munchmeyer, August 23, 1967, AHC, AGDC, box 70002, folder 3.
64. Moran, *Multinational Corporations*, 121.

pointed to new, emergent electoral forces, among them women, poor urban dwellers, peasants, and youth. Elected with 56 percent of the national vote and with strong support from the United States, Frei offered Chile a "Revolution in Liberty," promising to improve living standards; achieve economic growth; support industrialization; and respect the rights and freedoms of all Chileans, especially property rights. Frei attempted to help the poor by expanding social programs and assistance, improving public services, and creating employment opportunities. Through a program of agrarian reform, Frei expected to modernize the countryside, augment rural production, and increase the size of the internal market by giving economic resources to thousands of poor peasants. Frei's promises created great expectations, thus mobilizing vast sectors of society. By 1967, however, shortcomings in his government's reformist agenda and the reappearance of inflation politicized and radicalized Chilean society.[65]

Eduardo Frei received strong electoral support in mining camps, especially among women, through the appeal of his program pressing for social, economic, and labor reform (Table 11). Yet unlike previous presidential elections, that of 1964 saw growing political polarization in the copper mines. Whereas in the past, presidential candidates such as Pedro Aguirre Cerda, Gabriel González Videla, and Carlos Ibáñez had won strong, uncontested majorities in mining cities, the election of 1964 confirmed the polarization of Chilean politics and the emergence of two strong, popular, competing alternatives: Eduardo Frei and Salvador Allende. Tension was evident in the political differences between blue- and white-collar unions and, eventually, between men and women.

The initial electoral support for Eduardo Frei did not guarantee an alliance between copper workers and the recently elected government, and the influence of Christian Democrats on the copper workers' labor unions and labor leaders remained largely limited to white-collar labor unions. Indeed, Frei faced some of the most serious labor crises in the copper mines. The conflict between the government and the copper movement was emblematic of an old tension between Christian Democracy and the traditional labor movement and of the internal divisions within the government party.[66] Lacking a

---

65. Michael Fleet, *The Rise and Fall of Chilean Christian Democracy* (Princeton: Princeton University Press, 1985). Also on this period, see Tinsman, *Partners in Conflict*, 83–208.

66. For a discussion of the relationship between the labor movement and Eduardo Frei, see Patrick V. Peppe, *The Frei Government and the Chilean Labor Movement* (New York: New York University, Ibero-American Language and Area Center, 1974).

Table 11 Presidential election, 1964, Potrerillos and El Salvador

District	Salvador Allende	Julio Durán	Eduardo Frei	TOTAL
Potrerillos				
Men	662	150	687	1,499
Women	319	79	594	992
Total	981	229	1,281	2,491
El Salvador				
Men	862	144	630	1,636
Women	257	105	432	794
Total	1,119	249	1,062	2,430
Total	2,100	478	2,343	4,921

SOURCE: Records of National Elections, 1964, Servicio Electoral, Centro de Documentación, Santiago.

tradition within the union movement, Frei had sought the support of non- or less-organized sectors of society, such as poor urban dwellers, women, and peasants. In 1965, the government launched its program Promoción Popular, encouraging the political and social organization of the urban poor.[67] In contrast, Frei's relationship with the traditional labor movement remained tense during his administration a situation aggravated in the last three years by Frei's wage and stabilization programs and *mano dura* (hard hand) policy against the labor and the popular movements. Rejecting any sort of agreement with leftist union leaders, the government, especially its minister of labor, William Thayer, maintained a contentious relationship with the Central Única de Trabajadores (CUT) and attempted, unsuccessfully, to develop parallel union structures.

In the copper mines, the government resented the intensity and length of labor conflicts, and especially actions—for instance, solidarity and industry-wide strikes—that ignored legal frameworks. The potency of labor conflict in the copper mines challenged Frei's economic and copper policies. Attempting to control the rising demands from below, Frei repressed conflicts and demands on the part of workers that did not follow strict legal regulations. The confrontation between copper workers and the government reached its height in March 1966, and relations only deteriorated in the following years.

67. Fleet, *Rise and Fall*, 87.

On January 1, 1966, workers from El Teniente started a legal strike after three months of unsuccessful bargaining with Braden Copper. The conflict in El Teniente was the first collective bargaining of the year and would set the standards for upcoming negotiations in El Salvador (May) and Chuquicamata (October).[68] By late February, the CTC called a solidarity strike to force the government to find a solution to the conflict in El Teniente. Solidarity strikes were illegal and had major political and economic implications. On March 1, the great majority of workers in Potrerillos and El Salvador walked out in solidarity with El Teniente, while workers in Chuquicamata remained deeply divided on this issue.

Because of the strike's illegality, President Eduardo Frei did not hesitate to decree a resumption in production and a state of emergency. On March 3, the police detained six union directors from Potrerillos and El Salvador, sending them to La Serena, where they remained incommunicado. In the face of a refusal to return to work, Andes Copper fired eighty workers and threatened to do the same with the rest of the strikers.[69] On March 11, military troops occupied the union's local office in El Salvador. Their subsequent violent operation left eight dead (six men and two women) and thirty-five wounded. In the days that followed, Andes Copper fired about 120 workers. Fifteen labor activists from El Salvador and Potrerillos were fired and faced legal charges, including CTC leaders Manuel Ovalle and Pedro Samuel Gutiérrez.[70] The government blamed the Left for politicizing the conflict, and in a speech that marked the beginning of the *mano dura* policy, President Frei warned, "The government's hand will not tremble in its efforts to maintain its authority and protect citizens' rights." Meanwhile, leftist legislators flew to the camps in support of the victims.[71]

Labor organizations responded to the repression in El Salvador with new waves of activism. On March 14, copper workers started a forty-eight-hour-strike and were joined the following day by about twenty labor organizations affiliated with the CUT. The authorities' aggressive actions in El Salvador, like those in Puerto Montt three years later, antagonized many labor groups. "The massacre of the workers of El Salvador is an insult that

---

68. *El Siglo* (Santiago), March 6, 1966.
69. *El Siglo* (Santiago), March 9, 1966.
70. Among the union leaders fired were Juan Arancibia (independent) from Potrerillos and Carlos Gómez (Socialist Party), Jaime Sotelo (Socialist Party), and Guillermo Henríquez (Communist Party) from the plant union of El Salvador. "A defender la organización sindical," Potrerillos, April 1966, Biblioteca Nacional.
71. Loveman and Lira, *Las ardientes cenizas del olvido*, 266.

will not be erased in the history of the Christian Democratic government," declared copper labor leader Jorge Castillo. "The blood of the working class spilled only sixteen months after Mister Frei was elected announced very bad times for the freedom of the country."[72] Locally, the repression undermined the influence of Christian Democracy, and the party lost its only two seats in the 1966 union election in El Salvador.[73] Nationally, events in El Salvador not only created a strong reaction against the government but also aggravated internal divisions within the Christian Democratic Party.

The discussion of copper policies intensified conflict between labor unions and the government of Eduardo Frei and made clear the existence of different economic nationalisms. In 1964, the Christian Democratic Party proposed a gradual increase in state participation in the copper industry, rejecting the idea of complete nationalization.[74] Christian Democrats felt that because the copper industry required the cooperation of foreign technicians, spare parts for foreign machines, and knowledge of the international copper market, a confrontation with U.S. capital could be detrimental to the interests of Chile. As an alternative, they proposed creating joint ventures between foreign capital and the state, a halfway nationalization. This scheme would increase the state's direct participation in the administration of the large-scale copper companies without jeopardizing foreign investments and cooperation. Although the "Chileanization" project assumed the collaboration and goodwill of foreign corporations, it could not guarantee foreign investors that future changes in domestic politics would not threaten the agreements.

Conversations with foreign companies started in 1965. In January 25, 1966, law 16.425 approved the Chileanization of copper, promising copper companies that copper policies would remain stable for the following twenty years. The Kennecott Corporation agreed to sell 51 percent of El Teniente to the Chilean government and to launch a program of expansion. In exchange, Kennecott received additional tax breaks and exploitation rights and remained in charge of the administration of El Teniente.[75] The Chileanization agreement also included the Cerro de Pasco Corporation. Cerro had been investing in Chile since 1955, when it acquired some shares

---

72. *El Siglo* (Santiago), March 12, 1966.
73. Peppe, *Frei Government*, 6.
74. The ideas of Chileanization had already been articulated in the early 1950s; see, for instance, "El cobre: La Falange da a Chile una política del cobre," Falange Nacional, Santiago, Chile, 1953.
75. Moran, *Multinational Corporations*, 132–36.

of the Rio Blanco property, a mine near Santiago. Between 1955 and 1964, Cerro explored the mine and did some drilling, waiting for a favorable agreement with the Chilean government.[76] In 1966, Cerro agreed to sell 25 percent to the Chilean state and organized the joint venture Compañía Minera Andina (Andina Mining Company).

Negotiations with Anaconda were more difficult than with the other companies. Strongly dependent on Chilean copper, Anaconda rejected the alternative of selling some of the company stocks to the Chilean government. It agreed, however, to double its production and electrolytic copper refining capacity in Chuquicamata and El Salvador.[77] In addition, it sold to the Chilean government 25 percent of La Exótica mine, a new mining venture located next to Chuquicamata. This was a small mine, by 1971 producing an average of twenty-six thousand tons a day and with a total labor force of 388 employees: 258 white-collar workers, 110 blue-collar workers, and 20 supervisors.[78] As part of the 1964 agreements, Anaconda agreed to create the Compañía Exploradora Cordillera to conduct exploration in Chile. In return, Anaconda received a substantial reduction in taxation.

The government copper project met strong resistance from the Left and labor organizations, increasing the politicization of the copper question. In an official document, the Socialist Party accused the Frei administration of offering the country "nothing new" in terms of copper policy and criticized the government's concessions and tax breaks. What Frei "called Chileanization," the party declared, was "the Americanization of the Chilean State" and "shameful concessions to imperialism."[79] In the process, the Socialist Party presented complete nationalization as the only solution to the copper problem.[80] In August 1961, Socialist senator Salvador Allende addressed the National Congress and submitted a new nationalization project.[81]

From the perspective of labor, the new project, like the 1951 Treaty of Washington and the 1955 Nuevo Trato, ignored worker rights. In December 1964, Frei addressed the nation and introduced his new policy on Chilean

---

76. Cerro de Pasco Corporation, *Annual Report* (1960, 1964).
77. Girvan, *Copper in Chile*, 40.
78. Liliana Muñoz, *Estudio ocupacional de la minería del cobre* (Santiago: Servicio Nacional del Empleo, 1971), 155–56.
79. *Arauco* (Santiago), September 1965.
80. *Arauco* (Santiago), August 1965.
81. The project was presented by a group of socialist senators, including Salvador Allende, Raúl Ampuero, Aniceto Rodríguez, Luis Alberto Quinteros, Alejandro Chelén, and Galvarino Palacios on August 8, 1961. Novoa, *La batalla por el cobre*, 115.

copper, making vague references to the status of copper workers. Frei promised to guarantee living conditions in the mining camps, but in terms of labor rights and economic conditions, his position was ambiguous. The CTC, Frei explained, "in whose organization and patriotic spirit I feel confident, will have an extraordinary responsibility in the conduction of the social policy to be developed in the large copper exploitation."[82] The meanings of these responsibilities remained unclear in Frei's speech.

The lack of clear benefits for workers in the Chileanization project increased tensions in the copper towns. In March 1965, representatives of the U.S. embassy traveled to the north of Chile and met with labor leaders from Chuquicamata. Walter Alfaro, president of the professional union in Chuquicamata and a militant in the Socialist Party, explained to the U.S. visitors that copper workers opposed the Chileanization project because it did "not take into account the needs of workers." Alfaro also questioned the patriotism of the government, since only the foreign companies would benefit from the agreements.[83] For less militant workers, the transition to a state-owned company also raised questions about the economic consequences of joining the ranks of public employees.[84]

Tensions escalated in the months that followed. In October, the CTC called its third general strike to protest the Chileanization laws. The strike, starting on October 25 in Chuquicamata and El Teniente and on October 27 in El Salvador and Potrerillos, lasted thirty-seven days. It had a strong impact on production; between October 26 and December 2, 1965, 19,430,000 pounds of production was lost in El Salvador, 80 million pounds in Chuquicamata, and 37 million pounds in El Teniente.[85] Successful labor mobilization in the mines entailed critical political costs for the government. As the U.S. embassy reported, because of the "ineptitude of the government," the leadership of the CTC "is coming out of the strike reinforced and what little chance the Christian Democrats had, in the past, to increase their influence among copper workers, is now reduced to almost zero."[86]

The CTC protested the government's position vis-à-vis foreign copper companies and demanded an improvement in workers' legal and economic

---

82. Eduardo Frei, "New Policy for Chilean Copper," December 21, 1964, Chilean Subject Collection, 1933–97, Hoover Institutional Archives, Stanford, Calif.
83. U.S. Embassy, April 9, 1965, NARA, GR, Chile 1964–66, box 1288.
84. *El Sol de México* (Mexico City), June 28, 1969.
85. Brinckerhoff to Romualdi, April 26, 1966, KC, SRP, box 2, folder 11.
86. Memorandum, November 9, 1965, NARA, GR, Chile 1964–66, box 2026, folder 12.

status. As reported by a U.S. embassy secretary, the CTC indicated that it was particularly concerned with three issues. First, it criticized the reduction of tax levels included in the program of Chileanization. Second, it demanded not an increase in refining, as the government proposed, but that companies did "all refining" in Chile. Finally, it asked for a reform of the Statute of Copper Workers (1956) as a way to solve socioeconomic problems faced by labor.[87] From a broader perspective, the leaders of the CTC declared in November, the strikers demanded respect for the country's national sovereignty, dignity, and justice.[88] The strike thus had both a political and an economic dimension and demonstrated how entangled these two elements were by the mid-1960s.

As had happened in 1951 and 1955, the CTC questioned the national commitment of the Chilean government and demanded that changes in copper policies benefit not only capital but also Chile and its workers. In this way, copper workers offered an alternative view of nationalism. The government reacted by defending its own patriotism while, like the press, questioning that of copper workers. During the general strike, minister of labor William Thayer asserted that the government was not undermining the "sovereignty of the country" but was fulfilling its "social and revolutionary project"; similarly at the end of the strike *La Nación* editorialized that the workers' action had been antipatriotic, since it caused economic consequences for the country.[89]

Echoing President Carlos Ibáñez in 1955, President Eduardo Frei heavily criticized and repressed the strike, blaming the left-wing coalition Frente de Acción Popular (FRAP) and calling attention to its economic costs. Accusing copper workers of demanding wage increases beyond the capabilities of the country and the industry, Frei pronounced his belief that the strike had a "clear political meaning" and was "detrimental to the national interest." The government portrayed the strike as a movement to achieve "economic privileges": describing copper workers as the best-paid workers in the country, it accused the CTC of demanding "extraordinary" economic benefits. The Left and the Central Única de Trabajadores (CUT) strongly supported the demands of copper workers and opposed the copper agreements. In January 1965, consistent with the resolutions of its 1962 third

---

87. Prochnick, Second Secretary, June 23, 1965, NARA, GR, Chile 1964–66, box 1288.
88. *Cobre* (Santiago), November 1965.
89. *La Nación* (Santiago), October 27, 1965; October 30, 1965.

national congress, the CUT reiterated its commitment to fight for the complete nationalization of the copper industry.[90] During the conflict, a group of senators representing copper districts signed a declaration in which they insisted that the government find a rapid solution to the conflict. Legitimating workers' demands, they noted that while the government gave enormous benefits to foreign copper companies, it "rejected the fair demands of those workers who produced that richness [copper]."[91]

The government's resistance to engaging in dialogue with the copper workers aggravated the conflict. Accused of breaking the internal security law, labor leaders were harassed and imprisoned. Manuel Ovalle was in prison for nineteen days, during five of which he remained incommunicado. Despite the government's acts of repression, the strike continued to enjoy massive support from the union rank and file; ultimately, the industry-wide stoppage forced the government to introduce some labor reforms. In 1966, it revised the Statute of Copper Workers (Decreto con Fuerza de Ley [Decree Having Force of Law, or DFL] 426, 1966). Among the most important reforms was giving unions freedom in collective bargaining to address social, labor, and economic issues. The Copper Corporation was renamed the Department of Copper, incorporating two representatives of copper workers (a blue-collar and a white-collar worker). The Special Arbitration Board was restructured, and the minister of mining and the vice president of the new Copper Corporation were added.[92] The reforms, however, did not alter the basics of labor relations in the copper industry and prohibited industry-wide contracts.

The unsolved question of copper nationalization continued to mobilize copper workers and polarize Chileans in the following years. In 1969, Héctor Olivares, writing in *Punto Final*, emphatically restated the commitment of the CTC "to struggle for copper NATIONALIZATION as the only mechanism of economic liberation and dignified sovereignty in decisions about the production, pricing, and fabrication of our basic resource."[93] In that same year, the government reopened negotiations with Anaconda,

---

90. *La Nación* (Santiago), October 26, 1965; October 27, 1965; October 26, 1965; *Chiflón* (Santiago), January 1965.

91. The declaration was signed by Jonás Gómez (Radical Party), Julieta Campusano (Communist Party), Tomás Chadwick (Socialist Party), Hermes Ahumada (Radical Party), Raúl Ampuero (Socialist Party), Salomón Corbalán (Socialist Party), Armando Jaramillo (Liberal Party), and Víctor Contreras (Communist Party). *Cobre*, November 1965.

92. Barría, "Organización y políticas laborales," 197.

93. Héctor Olivares, "La Confederación de Trabajadores del Cobre en todos los frentes," *Punto Final*, July 1969.

demanding that the company sell 51 per cent of its shares. Anaconda had few options: its strong dependency on Chilean copper and the large amount of capital invested in 1964–69 forced it to agree to nationalization, with compensation.[94]

Chileanization had two phases. In 1970, Anaconda would sell 51 percent of its two companies in Chile: Chile Exploration and Andes Copper. "The final stage of the sale," Anaconda explained to its shareholders, would take place between 1972 and 1981.[95] The nationalization by agreement guaranteed Anaconda full compensation and time to find new copper supplies, and it offered the government a nonconfrontational solution to the copper problem.

In the U.S. media, the arrangement was seen as a "preferable" alternative to complete expropriation. Its opinion shaped by recent events in Peru, where a military regime led by Juan Velasco Alvarado had nationalized the properties of the International Petroleum Company in 1968, the *New York Times* described "Chileanization" as "the only alternative on a continent of burgeoning nationalism."[96] The U.S. embassy and U.S. capital, however, were skeptical about the consequences of the agreements. For the U.S. embassy, "favorable acceptance of the Anaconda accords by groups which have traditionally opposed 'statism' and favored close political and economic ties with the United States provides another indication of the rapid and pervasive growth of nationalism in this country." The reaction was nervousness. Edwin Trench, a longtime Anaconda employee at the port of Barguito, remembered that in Potrerillos, following approval of the nationalization project, "the Americans got scared and wanted to leave." As fear increased, Trench recalled, a company staff member named Robinson "went into a panic over international Marxism."[97]

In Chile, the nationalization-by-agreement measure was controversial. For Christian Democrats, it was Chile's "second independence." Minister of mining Alejandro Hales defended the project as a peaceful transition from complete foreign to mixed ownership, stressing that "the nationalization by agreement allows the State to reach, peacefully, the same objectives and advantages of an expropriation law, and avoids all the direct and indirect upheavals and damage of a nationalization imposed by the law."

94. Moran, *Multinational Corporations*, 146–47.
95. Anaconda Copper Mining Company, *Annual Report* (1970).
96. Editorial, *New York Times*, May 29, 1969.
97. U.S. Embassy, October 8, 1969, NARA, GR, Chile 1967–69, box 1981; Edwin Trench, conversation with the author, 26 July 2000.

In contrast, the Left (including the Socialist, Communist, and Radical Parties and the Movimiento de Acción Popular Unitaria [Unitary People's Action Movement, or MAPU]) called the agreement with Anaconda a "fraud" and not a coherent copper policy, since it did not affect all the large-scale copper mines but only the mines of Chuquicamata and El Salvador, creating a legal gap between El Teniente and Anaconda's properties. In addition, it gave the state limited power over the decision-making process and omitted "the participation of the workers in the management of the new companies."[98]

Conclusions

The period 1958–70 was a time of change and conflict in the copper industry. The limitations of the national economy, the shortcomings of copper policies, and the attitude of copper companies prevented the possibility of building a stable system for labor relations in the copper mines. Anaconda accommodated these forces of changes by restructuring production, reorganizing labor, and introducing new technology. These measures, however, had a strong impact on working and employment conditions. The limitations on achieving complete flexibility illustrate the existence of legal, labor, and political structures that prevented the complete erosion of workers' rights in predictatorship Chile.[99]

A rapid decline in occupational citizenship mobilized workers and reinforced their traditional alliance with the Left, paving the way for their support for Allende and the Chilean road to socialism in 1970. In the following years, the failure of the "Revolution in Liberty" to overcome the traditional constraints of the Chilean economy alienated the organized labor movement. Despite efforts to stimulate private and foreign investments, the Chilean economy did not grow as expected; rather, by 1967, it showed clear signs of stagnation. High rates of inflation reappeared in the last two years of Eduardo Frei's administration, unleashing a vast wave of popular discontent. On the eve of the 1970 presidential election, many Chilean workers, disenchanted with Frei, demanded a radical transformation of society.

98. "La controversia de la nacionalización pactada," *Panorama Económico*, July 1969.
99. Graciela Bensuán, "Los determinantes institucionales de la flexibilidad laboral en México," in Zapata, *¿Flexibles y productivos?* 39–67.

6. Experiencing Nationalization and Socialism, 1970-1973

The electoral victory of Salvador Allende, the first democratically elected Socialist president, in September 1970 introduced substantial changes in copper workers' daily lives. In the following three years, the nationalization of the copper industry, the incorporation of workers into the administration of the company, the Battle for Production, and the democratization of social and urban services transformed labor and social relations in the copper camps. Despite the popularity of these measures, their implementation was far from easy. Indeed, the recently elected socialist and revolutionary government faced serious social and labor conflicts in the copper mines, including supervisors' strikes, frequent wildcat strikes in Chuquicamata, and a watershed strike in El Teniente in April–June 1973. In addition, the deterioration of the national economy threatened copper production and food supply in the camps, unleashing protests from local communities.

Despite these problems, many copper workers, especially in Potrerillos and El Salvador, welcomed Chilean administrators, were ready to work overtime to increase production, and supported the popular government and the process of nationalization. In this chapter I examine the changes brought by nationalization and socialism in the copper mines. I look at implementation of the Program of Popular Participation (Participación Popular), changes in living conditions, and the problem of labor relations in the period between the election of Allende in September 1970 and the military coup of September 1973.

Salvador Allende and the Nationalization of the Copper Industry

Elected with 36.4 percent of the popular vote, Salvador Allende and his government coalition, the Popular Unity (Unidad Popular, or UP), supported a radical but peaceful and legal transformation of Chilean society and a political transition to socialism.[1] The revolutionary agenda of the UP proposed to benefit the poorest of Chilean people through income redistribution, reallocation of public investment, and reorganization of the national economy. According to the government program, the national economy would be reorganized in three sectors: the social sector (*área de propiedad social*), the mixed sector (*área de propiedad mixta*), and the private sector (*área de propiedad privada*). The construction of a social sector of the economy, one of the most controversial elements of the new government's economic program, included about 250 industries that were foreign owned, part of large monopolies, or strategically important. Nationalization of natural resources, massive agrarian reform, and state intervention in key sectors of the economy formed the bases of a long-term industrialization process. Allende and the UP were also planning the construction of a socialist country, symbolized in the phrases "new society" (*nueva sociedad*) and "new human being" (*hombre nuevo*).

Salvador Allende was a well-known figure to workers in El Salvador and Potrerillos. He had run for the presidency four times since 1952 and had been a member of the Senate since 1945. As a presidential candidate and a senator, he had visited the camps on numerous occasions and showed sympathy for copper workers' struggles. Consistent with the anti-imperialist discourse of the Socialist Party, Allende had argued for nationalization of the mines and denounced, in the National Congress, the imperialism and abuses of North American corporations.

Given the long local history of electoral commitment to leftist candidates, the successful campaign of the UP, and the deteriorating image of Christian Democracy at the end of Frei's administration, Allende received massive electoral support in the copper mining camps in September 1970 (Table 12).

The program put forth by the UP had great appeal for copper workers, and their electoral support for Salvador Allende was emblematic of the radicalization occurring in the copper workers' labor movement. The UP's victory symbolized the promise of complete nationalization, the recognition of miners' long labor struggles, the legitimacy of labor demands, and political inclusion. It meant the end of repression by the state, a state that

---

1. The political parties that were initially part of the Popular Unity were Socialist Party, Communist Party, Radical Party, Movement for United Popular Action (MAPU), Independent Popular Action (API), and Social Democratic Party (PSD). In 1972, the Christian Left Party (IC) joined the coalition.

Table 12 Electoral results for Salvador Allende in mining electoral districts, 1952–1970

District	1952	1958	1964	1970
Potrerillos	37	650	981	1,100
Men		568	662	770
Women		82	319	330
Total votes	1,503	1,620	2,491	2,344
El Salvador			1,119	1,480
Men		862	1,083	
Women		257	397	
Total votes		2,430	2,563	

SOURCE: Records of National Elections, Servicio Electoral, Centro de Documentación, Santiago.

had traditionally suppressed strikes, imprisoned and exiled labor leaders, and favored foreign companies. The triumph of the UP, which included political parties that had usually stood in defense of workers' rights in the National Congress as well as on picket lines, created enormous expectations. From a broader perspective, the UP symbolized the empowerment of working people, the participation of workers in the administration of companies, and the commitment to full employment. Above all, copper workers were voting for a better Chile, better salaries and working conditions, access to housing and social benefits, and more opportunities for themselves and their families. Their bread-and-butter demands were intertwined with calls for social justice.

The nationalization of the copper industry was the most durable reform introduced by the UP. On July 11, 1971, the National Congress unanimously approved a constitutional reform that authorized the government to nationalize the large-scale copper mines.[2] In September 1971, the government ruled that U.S. copper companies were not entitled to compensation, because of their "excess profits."[3] Nationalization was no surprise, but, rather, the result of a long history of negotiation between the Chilean government and U.S. corporations, during which the Chilean state had

---

2. On the nationalization of copper, see Norman Gall, "Chile: The Struggle in the Copper Mines," *Dissent* (Winter 1973); Al Gedicks, "The Nationalization of Copper in Chile: Antecedents and Consequences," *Review of Radical Political Economics* 5 (1973); Girvan, *Copper in Chile*; Novoa, *La batalla por el cobre*.

3. Novoa, *La batalla por el cobre*, 208–22.

consistently increased taxation and regulations.⁴ A fifty-year history of increasing state dependence on the mining industry and incomplete attempts to reduce, or at least control, the power of foreign capital had created a foundation for a national political consensus.

Nationalization without compensation, however, was a break with the traditional policy of negotiation that had characterized the previous decades, overturned agreements made during the Frei administration, and provoked a long international legal conflict with Anaconda and Kennecott. In 1972, Kennecott launched a legal campaign that seriously damaged Chile's opportunities to sell copper abroad.

The nationalization of natural resources was a crucial point in the UP's program and in the construction of a "new economy." Included among the UP's "Forty Immediate Measures," it constituted both a battle against U.S. imperialism and the basis for projected income redistribution and other social and economic transformations.⁵ Through nationalization, Salvador Allende explained in December 1970, Chile would affirm its "sovereignty" and show that its "dignity and independence are beyond price, beyond pressure, and beyond threat."⁶ The government attempted to increase copper production as a way to sustain public programs and encourage industrialization, copper being, in the words of the slogan promoting nationalization, "the wage of Chile" (*el sueldo de Chile*). Nationalization, Allende explained in a February 1971 speech at the National Congress of the Copper Workers Confederation (CTC), was "an essential and vital necessity for Chile and its destiny. And we have the right to do it, because the future of our country depends on it."⁷

Nationalization was not free of contradictions. It did not alter the country's historical dependence on copper and the international copper market, as copper production was critical to the success of the revolutionary government. This dependence became especially problematic as the government faced enormous obstacles to increase or maintain production. On the eve of nationalization, U.S. copper companies were exploiting the mines to the maximum extent, seeking to extract as many resources as possible in the short time they had left. In the specific case of El Salvador, in 1969 Andes

---

4. Moran, *Multinational Corporations*.
5. Salvador Allende, *Chile's Road to Socialism* (Harmondsworth, U.K.: Penguin Books, 1973), 38.
6. Allende, *Chile's Road to Socialism*, 79.
7. Allende, *Su pensamiento político*, 86.

Table 13 Copper production, 1970–1972 (metric tons)

Company	1970	1971	1972
Chuquicamata	263,400	250,187	234,643
La Exótica	1,900	35,264	31,271
El Salvador	93,000	84,909	82,777
Andina		53,584	53,910
El Teniente	176.000	147,280	190,618
Total	685.000	571,224	593,219

SOURCES: Data for 1970 from "Nacionalización del Cobre," *Ahora*, 4 November 1971; data for 1971 and 1972 from "Baja la producción de cobre," *Boletín Minero* 702 (1972).

Copper worked only the richest veins of the mine, compromising its future exploitation.[8] Similarly, as the new authorities stated in 1971, Andes Copper had not renewed machinery in Barquito, the smelter, and the railway.[9] In addition, the U.S. companies' sabotage and their international campaign to undermine Chilean copper, a shortage of spare parts, continual labor conflicts in El Teniente and Chuquicamata, and difficulties in the international market seriously disrupted production from 1971 to 1973 (Table 13).

In the copper mines, nationalization was the most important aspect of the program devised by the UP. Nationalization was a long-standing demand of workers, articulated in the discourse of the Left and of national labor organizations such as the CTC and the Central Única de Trabajadores (CUT) and rooted in the living and working experience of copper workers and the policies of segregation enforced by U.S. management, described in previous chapters.[10] For two decades, the CTC had called for nationalization of the mines. As Héctor Olivares, president of the CTC during the 1950s and 1960s, remarked, the CTC, in alliance with the political Left, had supported every project of nationalization that was presented in the National Congress.[11] For copper leaders, the struggle for nationalization had been above all a political struggle fought at the national level.

Given the long battle for nationalization, mine workers celebrated its arrival with great fervor and patriotism. The few North Americans employers who were still in the country immediately left the mines after hearing about the Chilean decision, and many people believed that these individuals had

---

8. Novoa, *La batalla por el cobre*, 318–29.
9. *El Siglo* (Santiago), August 11, 1971.
10. Klubock, "Nationalism, Race, and the Politics of Imperialism."
11. Héctor Olivares, "Cuarenta y nueve años haciendo patria," *Cobre Chileno* 55 (2000).

mysteriously disappeared overnight. Only three foreign employees stayed in Chuquicamata, two in Andina, and none in El Salvador.[12] On July 16, 1971, minister of mining Orlando Cantuarias visited El Salvador and led the official ceremony that marked nationalization. A large crowd of workers met at the central plaza, singing and cheering the government, while a military band played the national anthem. The national flag waved in the main plaza, and the Chilean general manager of the mine, Arturo Feliú, received, on behalf of the Chilean government, the property of the mine. In the same ceremony, Esteban Sánchez, the *intendente* of Atacama, highlighted workers' great responsibility in guaranteeing production in this crucial national industry.[13] Similar ceremonies took place in El Teniente and Chuquicamata. The symbolism of copper nationalization would be reinforced in anniversaries to come, marking what came to be known as the Day of National Dignity.

The nationalization program required a complete reorganization of the mines, both in how they were situated within the structure of the Chilean state and in relation to the internal administration of the companies. During the first year, the government maintained the same administrative structure as during the Chileanization period but without the presence of foreign directors. The Corporación del Cobre (CODELCO) and local administrative boards ran the mines from July 1971 to July 1972, when by decree of the Ministry of Mining, five state companies were created (Table 14). The state owned the mines through two state corporations: CODELCO (95 percent of the companies' capital) and Empresa Nacional de Minería (ENAMI; 5 percent of the companies' capital).

Workers' Participation

The construction of a nationalized and socialized sector of the economy raised critical questions about the role, involvement, and participation of workers within the new public enterprises. Government officers, political leaders, and labor activists agreed that workers should become an integral part of their companies and the production process, but they disagreed on the

---

12. Novoa, *La batalla por el cobre*, 265.
13. *Atacama* (Copiapó), July 18, 1971.

Table 14 Nationalized companies, 1972

Company	Mine	Location (Province)	Former Owner	Production 1970 (Tons)
Compañía de Cobre Chuquicamata (Cobrechuqui)	Chuquicamata	El Loa	Anaconda Company	263,400
Compañía Minera Exótica	Exótica	El Loa	Anaconda Company	1,900
Compañía de Cobre Salvador (Cobresal)	El Salvador	Chañaral	Anaconda Company	93,000
Compañía Minera Andina	Andina	Los Andes	US Cerro Corporation	—
Sociedad Minera El Teniente	El Teniente	Rancagua	Kennecott Company	176,000

SOURCE: Eduardo Novoa Monreal, *La batalla por el cobre: Comentarios y documentos* (Santiago: Editorial Quimantú, 1972), 101, 468.

best way of accomplishing these goals.[14] From the government's perspective, in the new political climate worker participation was part of *concientización* (consciousness building); the construction of a socialist society; and a foundation for the social, political, economic, and cultural transformation of Chile. It was from the local committees of production that a new worker would rise to construct a socialist nation.

Worker participation was a project imposed and conceived not only by political leaders. As French historian Frank Gaudichaud explains in his study of industrial belts in UP Chile, it was a response to Chilean workers' persistent fight to overcome abusive labor-management relations and improve economic conditions. From a broader perspective, participation implied a change of attitude, a revalorization and respect for workers' contributions to the economy, and a challenge to traditional job hierarchies.[15] Whereas Allende had initially conceived of participation as existing within the boundaries of a well-defined nationalized sector of the economy, workers struggled to incorporate new plants into the socialized sector of the economy.[16] After the "paro patronal" (bourgeois strike) of October 1972, worker

14. Augusto Samaniego, "Los límites de la estrategia de la unidad y el Área de Propiedad Social," *Contribuciones Científicas y Tecnológicas* 109 (1995).
15. Gaudichaud, *Poder popular,* 29.
16. See, for instance, Winn, *Weavers of the Revolution.*

organizations expanded independently of the state, creating new entities, such as industrial belts, which were groups of factory workers from the same geographical areas, and "comandos comunales," communal organizations that integrated local popular and working organizations, the industrial belts among them; neighborhood councils; mothers' centers; student groups; and peasant unions.[17]

The bases of worker participation in the nationalized sector of the economy were the agreements between the CUT and the UP of December 1970 and February 1971. In December 1970, the government and the CUT signed an agreement guaranteeing workers' direct participation in the workplace and at the national level.[18] In the socialized and mixed sector of the economy, workers would elect some of the members of the companies' board of directors and would participate in the workers assemblies and the production councils. The agreements set out general outlines for worker participation; each work center would organize a temporary participation committee (Comité Paritario de Participación) to discuss local regulations aimed at making participation a local reality. At the national and regional level, workers represented by CUT would participate in decisions regarding economic planning.[19]

In the copper mines, participation was a long-term demand that had its origin in the union struggle to improve relationships between workers, supervisors, and management; to fight against arbitrary firings; to have a voice in copper policies; and to share the benefits of copper production. Throughout the 1950s and 1960s, workers' vulnerability to changes in the international market and management's arbitrary employment decisions had convinced many that workers needed to be involved in the administration of the companies. Further, copper workers had pushed to participate in negotiations between foreign copper companies and the state, portraying themselves as defenders of the interests of Chile and accusing the state of

17. Gaudichaud, *Poder popular*, 27–28.
18. On CUT and the UP, see Franck Gaudichaud, "La Central Única de Trabajadores, las luchas obreras y los cordones industriales en el período de la Unidad Popular en Chile (1970–1973)," *Revista Rebelión* (May 2003), revista www.rebelion.org; Juan Andrés Medina, "La Central Única de Trabajadores y el gobierno de la Unidad Popular: Auge y desaparición," *Revista de Historia* (Universidad de Concepción) 1 (1991); Augusto Samaniego, "Les stratégies syndicales de la 'Central Unica de Trabajadores de Chile' et l'action socio-politique des salares (1952–1973)" (Ph.D. diss., Université de Paris VIII, 1998).
19. Central Única de Trabajadores de Chile y Gobierno, *Normas básicas de participación de los trabajadores en la dirección de las empresas de las áreas social y mixta* (Santiago: ODEPLAN, 1971).

surrendering to the needs of foreign capital. The CTC, through seasonal union training, had made special efforts to teach workers and leaders about the different economic and political aspects of copper production.

In 1964, during the CTC's third national congress, leaders called for the incorporation of workers in the industry and in discussions on copper policy. Workers should participate in discussions on general policies in the industry, in production policies, and in all decisions affecting workers and their families in the mining camps. They then "would be part not only of some or all production processes, but they would also understand the relationship between their work and economic development, markets, prices, commerce, and controls." On the eve of the presidential election of 1970, the CTC restated its demand for worker participation "in all stages of planning." Not only was participation inseparable from nationalization of the industry, but also the success of nationalization required the "creative participation of workers."[20]

With pressure from workers, and given the government's agenda and the importance of copper for the national economy, the authorities endeavored to guarantee the participation of workers in, and their commitment to, the copper industry. As Jaime Estévez, director of CODELCO, explained in November 1971, "If workers do not assume total control of the nationalized industries, socialization will not take place." Only when workers and the state shared responsibility for and management of the industry would large-scale mining "belong to the socialized sector of the economy; in other words, at that moment the mines would truly be collective property."[21] From a more pragmatic perspective, the government saw worker participation as key to increasing output and winning the Battle for Production.[22]

In July–October 1971 in Potrerillos and El Salvador, representatives of labor and management integrated a Comité Paritario de Participación (Participation Board) to discuss the terms and goals of worker participation in the industry. In October 1971, they submitted a document, "Reglamento Interno de Participación" (Internal Regulations for Participation), to the general workers assembly. Finally approved in January 1972, the regulations guaranteed the participation of workers on the board of directors, in the General Workers Assembly, and in several production councils.[23] At

20. *Cobre* (Santiago), October 1964, July 1970.
21. *Atacama* (Copiapó), November 19, 1971.
22. Gaudichaud, *Poder popular*, 30.
23. For a discussion of the participation experience in Chuquicamata, see Zapata, *Los mineros de Chuquicamata*, 54–58.

the sectional and departmental levels, workers elected representatives to the local production councils, which were charged with solving production problems and, more important, determining the production plan for each section and department. At the sectional level, they gave advice on how to increase production, studied measures to prevent accidents, looked after the machines and supplies, and trained workers. They also promoted commitment and solidarity, thus preventing sabotage, and involved people in efforts toward a common goal—the battle for production.[24]

The new board of directors of Cobresal was representative of the efforts of incorporating workers into the administration of a company. The board comprised eleven members (Table 15): six representatives of the state who were appointed by the president, one acting as general manager and another as president of the administration council, and five representatives who were elected by the General Workers Assembly.[25] Of the state representatives, two were former union leaders, Pablo Samuel Gutiérrez and Oscar González Galleguillos. Gutiérrez was a militant of the Socialist Party, a former union leader in Barquito, and a member of the CTC's board of directors in the early 1960s. In 1966, Andes Copper had fired Gutiérrez for supporting the controversial illegal strike in El Salvador. González had been a leader of the plant union in Potrerillos throughout the 1950s and 1960s, a militant of the Communist Party, and *regidor* (member of the local government) of Chañaral in the early 1960s. Of the five workers' representatives, one represented professional-technical workers (those who worked in jobs that required college degrees), one represented administrative workers, and three represented production workers. Representatives served a two-year term and could serve a maximum of two terms. The administrative board met twice a month and visited the shop floor at least once a month.

The General Workers Assembly played a key role in the process of participation. It had the responsibility of discussing the company's general policy and electing the workers' representatives to the board of directors. The Coordinating Workers' Committee was composed of the five workers' representatives at the board of directors, members of the union boards, and one additional worker from each sector of the company (Mining, Production, and Social Services). Headed by a labor leader, it coordinated and

---

24. *Andino* (Potrerillos), January 19, 1972.
25. Ministerio de Minería, Decreto "Crea el Consejo de Administración de la Compañía de Cobre Salvador," ARNAD, MM, Providencias, 1972, vol. 546-839.

Table 15   Board of directors of Cobresal, 1972

Representative of Workers	Representative of the State
Nicolás Acuña Acuña	Ricardo García Posada (general manager), Socialist Party
Mario Elgueta Elgueta	Pedro Aguirre Charlín (president), Radical Party
Maguindo Castillo Andrade	Oscar González Galleguillos, Communist Party
Enrique Rodríguez Saldaño	Pablo Samuel Gutiérrez Gutiérrez, Socialist Party
Hernán Breyer Ibarra	Horacio Justiniano Aguirre, navy officer Francisco Lira Bianchi, MAPU

SOURCE: Ministerio de Minería, decreto "Crea el Consejo de Administración de la Compañía de Cobre Salvador," Archivo Nacional de la Administración Central del Estado, Ministerio de Minería, Providencias, 1972 (546–839).

advised workers. Labor unions had an important role to play in making participation a successful process. By organizing workers and guaranteeing their participation, unions would help to "win the Battle for Production and assure the revolutionary transformations that would lead toward the implementation of socialism in Chile."[26]

To incorporate workers effectively into its administration, the company implemented a massive training program. A trained workforce was especially important to the success of the workers' assemblies and councils, particularly the latter, since councils not only discussed but also had to solve immediate problems. Training had long been a demand of workers, included in their list of 1971. For this purpose, the administration organized a Training Department (Departamento de Adiestramiento y Capacitación), directed by Hugo Yáñez, a lawyer and labor specialist from the Chilean state university.[27] The subsequent training programs gave workers the necessary knowledge to become effective agents in the process of production and decision making. They also were an effort to increase workers' awareness of copper's importance for Chilean economic development and for the success of the revolutionary program of the UP. Workers not only started receiving better training in their jobs, but also learned about the complete process of production and their role in the company. Understanding

26. *Andino* (Potrerillos), January 19, 1972.
27. Hugo Yáñez, conversation with the author, July 8, 2000.

the place of each section in the company's structure was vital in determining production quotas and implementing plans.

The Training Department brought in technicians and scholars and signed an agreement with the Instituto Nacional de Capacitación (INACAP) to organize regular and after-hours classes in the camps. Most courses provided by the company were directly related to production and the effort to develop a skilled labor force that could find solutions to local problems. The department also set up a scholarship fund. In 1972–73, Cobresal awarded nineteen scholarships to workers and employees for pursuing a college education in the fields of geology, electrical engineering, economics, math, language, medicine, commerce, medical technology, law, chemical engineering, nursing, electricity, mechanics, and medical assistance. Unlike previous scholarship schemes, the new programs benefited workers and not only high school students.[28]

Implementation of the participation project created discord between the company and the labor unions. Unions interpreted the workers' assemblies as the company's attempt to diminish unions' historical power. Workers participated in the assemblies as workers and not as union members, and it was the assembly and not the unions that were part of the company. The unions, according to the program, exclusively focused on the defense of workers' rights and, therefore, any involvement in the company would have implied that the necessary differentiation between employers and unions would have vanished. However, participation did not mean that the unions were left out of the process. In fact, they were constantly consulted about the best ways to maintain and improve working and living conditions. Regulations governing the process of participation clearly established the role of the labor unions: "The labor organizations and the unions of the company have the responsibility to direct, control, and guide, in an effective and creative way, the participation of company workers. It is a crucial condition for winning the battle for production and guaranteeing the revolutionary transformations that will open the road to the implementation of socialism in Chile."[29] Tensions increased during times of collective bargaining, causing conflict between union economic demands and the workers assembly's commitment to the government agenda and increase in production.

28. Cobresal, "Primer encuentro de producción y participación de los trabajadores de Cobresal," Museo El Salvador, El Salvador, Chile, chap. 4, pp. 42–45, chap. 4, annex 2, pp. 4–7.
29. "Reglamento de Participación de los Trabajadores en la Dirección de Cobresal."

The success of the Programa de Participación is still open to debate.[30] According to James Petras, copper workers in Chuquicamata had the lowest levels of participation in Chile. Poor participation among copper workers was a consequence of a labor movement that had historically focused almost exclusively on economic demands and only a little on political participation. Labor leaders, according to Petras, used participation more to increase economic benefits than to improve *productivity*.[31] In contrast, Francisco Zapata argues that internal political divisions were a major obstacle to participation in Chuquicamata.[32] In El Salvador and Potrerillos, although *participación* was an incomplete process, it was quite successful. Workers actively participated in the different assemblies and committees, joined volunteer projects, and maintained production. Similarly, participation broke down the traditional hierarchies embedded in the employer-employee relationship, opening new opportunities for workers.[33]

A New Community

Nationalization under socialism implied an attempt to construct a different society in the camps, respond to workers' demands, and solve old problems such as discrimination, segregation, isolation, and abusive labor practices. The new administration sought to enhance the social and urban infrastructure and thereby benefit common unskilled or semiskilled workers, through building schools and social and recreational centers. It focused on workers and their families and on ways of improving the lives of women and children in the isolated and sometimes very masculine communities. To solve the traditional problem of isolation, new authorities strove to integrate the mines into the rest of the country, improve transportation, create new opportunities for recreation in and outside the camps, and solve the immediate problems of the community. From a social perspective, nationalization and socialism implied a complete reform of the old company's welfare agenda.

---

30. For a general discussion of the success and limitations of *participación* in the country, see Manuel Barrera, *Worker Participation in Company Management in Chile: A Historical Experience* (Geneva: United Nations Research Institute for Social Development, 1981).

31. James Petras, "Chile: Nacionalización, transformaciones socioeconómicas y participación popular," *Cuadernos de la Realidad Nacional* 11 (1972).

32. Zapata, *Los mineros de Chuquicamata*, 57–58.

33. Manuel Trigo, conversation with the author, July 20, 2000.

A first priority of the new administration was the desegregation of housing and social services. From 1917 to 1971, Andes Copper had distributed housing and provided social and recreational services according to workers' positions in the company. Similarly, it had established strict segregation between the foreign staff and the native labor force. In contrast, the UP nationalization program questioned the basis of the company town model; for one thing, the foreign system was discriminatory and abusive and thus contrary to the ideals of the UP nationalization project, but above all, labor unions encouraged such questioning.

The dismantling of the company town model had a symbolic dimension for the local community, representing the end of foreign domination. When the new administration moved to the camp, they did not occupy the old houses of the American camp but moved into new houses in El Salvador. The general manager's house in Potrerillos became a guesthouse and the biggest houses in the old American camp were used as kindergarten and nursery schools and community institutions.[34] In Chuquicamata, Salvador Allende symbolically gave the board of directors' house to the unions.[35] While in the past the Welfare Department had assigned housing by marital status and job classification, during the UP, the main criteria were workers' needs, family size, and seniority. The decisions about housing became the joint responsibility of the workers' representatives and the company's administrators.[36] Facilities and services were also desegregated. The *ranchos*, the restaurants where single workers received their meals, had been segregated according to job classification. In January 1973, the administration opened the *rancho* that had served the administrative personnel to all unmarried workers and those who were living in the camps without their families, regardless of the job status of these groups.[37]

In a context of economic restrictions, the company did not carry out big programs of housing development. In August 1971, Cobresal had planned to build 380 houses in El Salvador, 16 in Llanta, 68 in Barquito and Chañaral, and 304 in Potrerillos.[38] However, it only built 110 houses between 1971 and 1972, and finished only 10, while 30 others were under construction during

34. Francisco Lira, conversation with the author, July 1, 2000.
35. Zapata, *Los mineros de Chuquicamata*, 4.
36. Cobresal, "Primer encuentro," chap. 4, pp. 6, 17–18.
37. Cobresal, "Primer encuentro," chap. 4, p. 6.
38. Gutiérrez to Cantuarias, August 12, 1971, ARNAD, MM, Providencias, 1971, vol. 777-0378.

the first six months of 1973.[39] Shortages of construction material and difficulties with the construction company in charge of the works (Viviendas Económicas del Norte, or VIENOR) slowed the process of construction. Despite these constraints, Cobresal was able to improve existing housing and advanced the eradication of collective bathrooms.

Education was a major concern of the company. The new administration expanded; desegregated; and, as general manager Ricardo García explained, democratized the school system in the camps.[40] The company improved elementary education by increasing the number of teachers, created high schools and kindergartens in Potrerillos and El Salvador, and organized programs of adult education and technical training. By 1973, there were two high schools, one in El Salvador and one in Potrerillos, with a total enrollment of 227 students.[41] The kindergartens were a new initiative, one that recognized the needs of working women. By August 1973, there were forty children between forty-five days and six years old enrolled in the preschool in Potrerillos, and sixty-six in El Salvador.[42] In addition, the Training Department (Departamento de Adiestramiento y Capacitación) organized a massive literacy campaign under the slogan "If you know, teach. If you don't know, learn." The Training Department trained brigades composed of three people, each of whom taught a group of about ten students.[43] The teachers, who were volunteers from the community, started working in July 1972. By 1973, they had taught sixty students, but then the program was suspended.[44]

In an attempt to break the traditional barriers of isolation, the company made special efforts to bring artists, theater companies, and orchestras to town. Sports competitions were encouraged, and television arrived in the camps for the first time.[45] Similarly, the company decided to build recreational facilities next to the coast, in Flamenco. The construction of Flamenco was part of the UP national initiative of building *balnearios populares* (popular vacation sites) and creating recreational opportunities for working people. Provisional facilities were opened for the summer of 1973, and 173

---

39. Cobresal, "Primer encuentro," chap. 4, p. 16.
40. Cobresal, "Primer encuentro," chap. 4, p. 30.
41. Cobresal, "Primer encuentro," chap. 4, p. 30.
42. Cobresal, "Primer encuentro," chap. 4, pp. 5–6.
43. Departamento de Capacitación Cobresal, "Campaña de Alfabetización," Museo El Salvador, El Salvador, Chile, n.d.
44. Cobresal, "Primer encuentro," chap. 4, annex 2, p. 8.
45. Cobresal, "Primer encuentro," chap. 4, pp. 6–7, 36.

workers and their families spent their weekends at the beach, sleeping in tents. The company provided free transportation and lodging and subsidized food, and workers paid only part of the food expenses. By mid-1973, the company and workers discussed the possibility of building permanent facilities at Flamenco.[46]

In an effort to solve immediate problems at the local level, to involve the community in its own affairs, and to create opportunities for participation, the administration encouraged volunteer work.[47] As the director of the Welfare Department, Raúl Vásquez, explained, volunteer works would "make the community more integrated, so that [the community] could solve its own problems."[48] Similarly, Vásquez viewed volunteer work as an alternative to the traditional paternalism of the company. Workers and their families joined the administrative staff in the construction of new schools and roads and in a wide range of social campaigns. Similarly, the need to encourage the community to solve its own problems, thus decreasing people's dependency on the company, led the administration to promote grassroots organizations. The community also benefited from national volunteer programs. During the summer of 1972, for example, male and female students from the Universidad Técnica del Estado arrived in El Salvador, Chuquicamata, and El Teniente as volunteer workers.[49]

Despite the government's efforts to supply the mines with necessary food and raw materials, by the end of 1972 the national problems of supply began to hit the camps. In October 1972, truck owners organized a national strike (the October *paro*) that disrupted transportation and aggravated the national economic crisis. The strike of 1972 isolated the mine, leading to a shortage of canned food. In November, management was forced to implement strict rationing at the company stores. Throughout 1973, a national shortage of foreign currency and an increase in prices in the international market restricted traditional imports such as beef, dry milk, tea, butter, and oils. Despite these problems, the company store had a normal supply of fresh produce provided by local producers.[50] The shortage caused internal conflicts and discontent in the mines. As a worker explained

---

46. Cobresal, "Primer encuentro," chap. 4, annex 3, pp. 10–12.
47. Cobresal, "Primer encuentro," chap. 4, annex 3, pp. 10–12.
48. *Andino* (Potrerillos), June 5, 1971.
49. *Cobre* (Santiago), February 1972.
50. Cobresal, "Primer encuentro," chap. 4, pp. 12–14.

to a newspaper in February 1973, "If you ask someone how we were before and how are we today, he will tell you that we were better in the past."[51] In Chuquicamata, rationing at the company store unleashed protests from housewives and a forty-eight-hour strike in January 1973.[52]

Labor Relations

For Allende, copper workers posed the most serious labor conflicts in the country. The long strike in El Teniente (April–June 1973) is considered one of the elements responsible for his downfall. Labor conflicts in the copper mines were a result of wage policies, internal political strife, and a traditional pattern of conflicts in an industry that had always had high rates of absenteeism, labor turnover, and illegal work stoppages. Labor tensions were also representative of the internal work, class, and political divisions within the mining camps. The majority of labor conflicts occurring during these years were led by white-collar workers, professionals, and supervisors. Similarly, the union leaders most vocal against the government and conditions in the mines were members of Christian Democracy and, in the case of Chuquicamata, the Unión Socialista Popular (USOPO), a small political party in the opposition. Given the historical centrality of copper and copper workers, the copper mines became a political battleground, and the political opposition rapidly manipulated local conflicts to challenge the legitimacy of the popular government.

In Cobresal, the strike of August 1971 was the first sign of trouble in the industry and an indication of how the political opposition would use labor conflicts to undermine the image of the government. The rapid resolution of the strike, however, also revealed a new attitude from the labor community, union leaders, and management. On August 3, only twenty-two days after nationalization of the copper industry, about forty-five hundred workers from Cobresal organized a legal strike. On the eve of the action, negotiations were deadlocked with the workers' petition for a 36 percent wage increase and the company's counteroffer of 33 percent. Both proposals were above the increase in the costs of living, which had reached 28 percent.[53]

---

51. *Atacama* (Copiapó), February 15, 1973.
52. Zapata, *Los mineros de Chuquicamata*, 5.
53. *El Siglo* (Santiago), August 11, 1971.

Labor unions also demanded an increase in bonuses and improvement of social and living conditions such as housing modernization and the installation of television in the camps. The list of demands was presented in the first week of July, before nationalization. Shortly after that, union leaders traveled to Santiago to meet with President Allende, with whom they discussed not only their demands but also "the role that workers would have when the mines are nationalized."[54] The new state company accepted all workers' demands but the 36 percent wage increase. On July 30, workers rejected the company's last wage offer and voted to strike. The count was lopsided: while 2,471 workers voted to strike, 1,605 favored the idea of accepting the last offer from the company. The strike started on August 1, with workers returning, after accepting the government's initial wage offer, on August 12.[55]

Although a relatively short stoppage compared with previous copper workers' legal strikes, the action had a negative impact on the national economy and meant a loss of 240 tons of copper a day. During that week, Allende and the UP intelligentsia asked workers to give up their demands, show "class consciousness," and realize "that other workers had lower income than they [did]."[56] Although the reasons for the strike had less to do with copper workers' commitment to the program of the UP than with an old pattern of labor relations, the new political environment made workers' attitudes the focus of enormous critiques. A furious Allende declared that "the behavior of the miners is not that of the *hombre nuevo* [new man] that we want to create, and, then, we cannot expect the creation, as we hope, of a *nueva sociedad* [new society]."[57] As other presidents had in the past when confronted with strikes, Allende highlighted economic costs: "Each ton of copper that is not produced is bread carried away from children, a piece of building material taken from our compatriots who lost their houses and for whom it is necessary to build better and new housing, and fewer schools for young people. It kills the hope of thousands of unemployed workers whom we need to employ in public works or in other industries that are created with the foreign currency that copper gives."[58] Similarly, journalist Víctor Alvarado from *Indoamérica* described workers

---

54. *Las Noticias de Chañaral* (Chañaral), July 3, 1971.
55. *El Siglo* (Santiago), August 12, 1971.
56. *Atacama* (Copiapó), August 5, 1971.
57. *Atacama* (Copiapó), August 5, 1971.
58. *Atacama* (Copiapó), August 5, 1971.

from Potrerillos and El Salvador as "a labor aristocracy, nursed and raised by the venal and corrupted morality of the old capitalist system."[59]

Political loyalties would shape the development of the strike. The most vocal leader against a compromise with the government was Guillermo Santana, labor leader from the professional union and a Christian Democracy militant. In a context of intense national confrontation, the political Right used the opportunity to blame "Marxism" for the strike. According to the right-wing newspaper *El Mercurio*, before the victory of the UP the Left had carried on an intensive campaign of destabilization in the mines, promoting strikes. This last strike was simply the outcome of that campaign. "Unfortunately, the country will have to suffer for a long time the consequences of the demagogic work that Marxism constantly developed when it was not in the government." As usual, the Right viewed strikes and labor problems as the result of manipulation by the Left, instead of recognizing the sources of grievances and the relative autonomy of the movement. Similarly, this newspaper accused the government of using a double standard, in that the government was encouraging strikes in the private sector while discouraging conflict and demands in the public sector. "While private businesses have to accept a list of demands with 40 percent or more of wage settlement and profit sharing, the Government wants the ones who work in the country's richest industry to accept compensation slightly higher than the increase in the cost of living."[60]

As in the rest of the country, the biggest challenges to the new administration did not come from workers but from the professional and supervisory sectors. Since 1969, copper supervisors were organized in a nationwide institution called Asociación Nacional de Supervisores del Cobre (National Association of Copper Supervisors, or ANSCO). Although a good number of professionals left the companies and even the country after nationalization in 1971, many others remained, working in the new state-owned sector.[61] The UP nationalization project challenged traditional hierarchies, eliminating social and monetary privileges. Professional employees were also anxious about the arrival of the new administrators, whom they considered too young, inexperienced, and politicized. The strongest argument of the professional employees was that technicians and not political nominees should administer the mines. The arrival of new staff also limited their possibilities

---

59. *Indoamérica*, October 1971.
60. Editorial, *El Mercurio* (Santiago), August 3, 1971.
61. *Reverbero* (Santiago), November 4, 1976.

of mobility within the company. Hugo Yáñez, a lawyer who worked at the Training Department, noted that nationalization "destroyed their expectations. Thus, they were a little bit disoriented about their social status. And that disorientation created a very tense relationship between supervisors and the company administration."[62] In the following two years, supervisors complained about the political criteria in administering the mines, the decrease of labor discipline, and the hostility against them. Framing their concerns within a very nationalistic discourse, they reacted against their loss of power and economic privileges.

The first serious conflict between ANSCO and the copper companies occurred in February 1971, when the government announced a plan to abolish the gold roll, or dollar roll (whereby employees were paid with foreign currency). The gold roll had been a great privilege of professional employees from the time when North Americans controlled the copper industry. After the election of Allende, supervisors were concerned about keeping their benefits. In December 1970, ANSCO leaders met with Jaime Faivovich, temporary vice president of the Corporación del Cobre (CODELCO). Faivovich agreed: "Severance pay will be paid in foreign currency until salaries start being paid in this currency. It is an acquired right."[63] However, he also declared that salaries that previously had been paid in foreign currency would now be paid in the national currency. In January 1971, ANSCO addressed a letter to the Orlando Cantuarias, minister of mining, asking for special legislation regulating labor and employment conditions for copper supervisors. Among the items he requested were a clear system of seniority and promotion, the recognition of health risks for supervisors working underground, and participation—when the companies were nationalized—in the planning and production councils.[64]

This problem inspired the first strike of supervisors in August 1971, a month after nationalization. A twenty-four-hour strike, called a *"paro de advertencia"* (warning strike) took place in the mines of Chuquicamata and La Exótica on August 10, a week after the end of the workers' strike in Cobresal. About 405 professionals from Chuquicamata and 80 employees from La Exótica struck that day. The strike continued over the following

---

62. Hugo Yáñez, conversation with the author, July 8, 2000.
63. *Reverbero* (Santiago), no. 1 (1971).
64. Alvarado and Cuadra to Cantuarias, Sewell, 21 January 1971, ARNAD, MM, Providencias, 1971, vol. 337-766.

several days and spread to El Teniente and Río Blanco, but the situation in Cobresal remained unaltered. The government repressed the illegal movement by decreeing a resumption of production and firing about fifty-five supervisors. This harsh repression pushed supervisors immediately into the opposition camp; Aníbal Rodríguez, national president of ANSCO, declared: "Now, we will have to nationalize the copper industry from the control of the Communists and give it back to Chile."[65]

The right-wing press defended ANSCO's position, arguing that the government had demonstrated its political and sectarian attitude. *El Mercurio* went so far as to accuse the government of discrimination against supervisors, contrasting the government's stance now to the attitude it had taken toward Cobresal workers in early August. While the government had negotiated with workers in Cobresal, it treated supervisors as "a bourgeoisie that is placing obstacles in the path of the Popular Unity." "This discrimination" would "damage production and increase discouragement and the exodus of the technical personnel from the copper mines."[66] *El Mercurio* failed to recognize, however, that the workers' strike in Cobresal had been a legal one, while supervisors had stepped outside the law, thereby inviting repression.

The new administration also faced problems associated with embedded practices of informal protests such as wildcat strikes, labor turnover, and absenteeism. While many local strikes were similar to those of the past, during the years of the UP the political opposition used strikes to reveal cracks in the socialist government. For instance, on February 1, 1972, two hundred workers from the Electrical Department began an illegal strike. They demanded a production bonus in accordance with their contribution to the company. On March 21, 1973, about fifty workers from the warehouse in Potrerillos started a strike motivated by problems of classification and the insufficient number of workers in that section. Over the following few days, thirty-five warehouse workers from El Salvador, who complained about similar issues, joined them.

In 1973, in the context of a deteriorating economic and political environment, local protests and wildcat strikes increased. Not only did blue-collar workers demand better salaries, but also, as in the rest of the country, professional employees such as doctors and schoolteachers and white-collar employees such as phone operators began to organize. Doctors from Potrerillos and

65. "Cobre: Nacionalizando el sueldo de Chile," *Qué Pasa* (Santiago), September 1971.
66. Editorial, *El Mercurio* (Santiago), August 13, 1971.

El Salvador struck at the beginning of June 1973. They asked for economic improvements and a wage settlement. Their strike lasted only twenty-four hours and involved about twenty doctors from the hospitals of El Salvador and Potrerillos. Simultaneously, twenty-nine teachers from the night school started an illegal strike to demand a wage settlement. That same week, the five phone operators in Barquito stopped working for one hour, interrupting communications between the port and the mine.[67]

The most serious conflict took place in El Teniente, where workers maintained a legal strike from April 18 to June 29, undermining the stability of the government. The strike of El Teniente would demonstrate the divisions within the copper labor movement and the limitations of UP economic and salary policies. The origin of the conflict was the government's wage law approved in 1972 (law 17.713) and the efforts of the government to control inflation. According to the new law, Chilean workers were entitled to a wage settlement equivalent to the increase in the cost of living between the approval of their last collective contract and September 1972. Unlike the great majority of Chilean workers, workers in the copper mines were already entitled to periodical wage increases tied to hikes in the price of basic consumer products, the so-called *escala móvil*. Copper workers in El Teniente and the government disagreed on how to calculate the wage increase. While copper workers argued that they were entitled to the benefits of law 17.713, the government explained that wage increases had to be calculated taking into account the periodical wage increase that workers had received since their last union contract.

The strike started on April 18, supported by all white-collar labor unions and one of the four blue-collar unions of El Teniente. It rapidly became a political conflict as the political opposition used the movement to question the legitimacy of the government. The two months of strikes seriously hurt production and the government's finances. Similarly, images of confrontations between workers and the police, the march of El Teniente miners and their families from Rancagua to Santiago, a twenty-four-hour solidarity strike in Chuquicamata, and violence between miners loyal to the government and those on strike degraded the reputation of the government and were carefully used by the political opposition. By June, about 75 percent of blue-collar workers were working, but only 2 percent

---

67. *Atacama* (Copiapó), June 6, 1972.

of white-collar workers were. On July 1, workers accepted the government's initial offer and returned to work.[68]

Conclusions

The years of the UP were a time of experimentation and great expectation. When the North Americans left the copper mines, the Chilean administrators were challenged by the need to maintain and increase production, satisfy workers' demands, and change the relationship between the company and the working community. They faced enormous obstacles, from shortages of raw materials and spare parts to embedded labor conflicts. The state's dependency on copper and the economic crisis made things even more complicated. The new administration made some progress in incorporating workers in the administration of the company and dismantling a company town. Nevertheless, many of the goals were only beginning to be realized when the military seized power on September 11, 1973.

68. Sergio Bitar and Crisóstomo Pizarro, *La caída de Allende y la huelga de El Teniente* (Santiago: Ediciones del Ornitorrinco, 1986).

Epilogue: Repression, Economic
Transformations, and the Struggle for
Democracy, 1973–1990s

The military coup of 1973 had a drastic effect on workers' activism and union power in the copper mines. An authoritarian state company reestablished many of the old labor practices and replaced the socialist project of nationalization that had sought to empower workers through production committees and people's participation. The traditional argument that workers' economic and social benefits were a heavy load for an industry trying to be competitive in the international market was the basis for an attack on workers' economic and social gains. As in the rest of the country, the brutal repression launched against the union movement and the Left rapidly demobilized workers, facilitating the imposition of economic policies and laws that destroyed union guarantees. In the 1980s, copper workers reorganized in a mass movement and participated in national labor organizations. Their movement had national repercussions, as they became one of the most visible actors in the struggle for democracy. In the 1990s, neoliberalism and globalization introduced new challenges such as the dismantling of mining towns, the flexibilization of employment conditions, and the general restructuring of the copper industry. In this chapter I explain how this thirty-year cycle of repression, grassroots and political activism, and production restructuring transformed copper labor unions between 1973 and the present.

The Military Coup and the Dismantling of the Labor Movement, 1973–1982

In September 1973, a military coup led by General Augusto Pinochet ended the socialist and democratic experiment of the Popular Unity (UP). General Pinochet, supported by the political Right and the United States, imposed an authoritarian, repressive, and violent regime. For the following seventeen years, the military suspended civil and political rights, massively and systematically violated human rights, and imposed a neoliberal economic agenda. The dictatorship was especially harsh on working people and the labor movement, who suffered the consequences of repression and the impact of economic reforms. While the dictatorship's economic reforms have been celebrated as the basis of the Chilean economic miracle, they had enormous costs for the great majority of Chileans. By the late 1980s, the economy was growing, but a third of the population was living below the poverty line and the gap between rich and poor was increasing.[1]

In the aftermath of the coup, the military repressed and attempted to co-opt the union movement and labor activists throughout the country.[2] In the copper mines, repression was very selective, targeting the pro-UP union leadership and the company management. In the days following the coup, the camps' police officers arrested union leaders, management, and political activists. In the specific case of Potrerillos and El Salvador, prisoners were sent to Copiapó, the provincial capital, to be tried by a military court. In Copiapó and other provincial cities, repression was initially less severe and arbitrary executions were less common than in Santiago. In October 1973, the military junta decided to extend its brutality from Santiago to the rest of Chile, giving this mission to General Sergio Arellano Stark. General Arellano organized the "Caravan of Death," a special military

---

1. For a history of the military dictatorship, see Ascanio Cavallo et al., *La historia oculta del régimen militar. Memoria de una época, 1973–1988* (Santiago: Grupo Grijalbo Mondadori, 1997); Pamela Constable and Arturo Valenzuela, *A Nation of Enemies: Chile Under Pinochet* (New York: Norton, 1991).

2. For a discussion of the labor movement under dictatorship, see Alan Angell, "Union and Workers in Chile During the 1980s," in *The Struggle for Democracy in Chile, 1982–1990*, ed. Paul W. Drake and Iván Jaksic; (Lincoln: University of Nebraska Press, 1991); Manuel Barrera and Gonzalo Falabella, *Sindicatos bajo regímenes militares: Argentina, Brasil, Chile* (Santiago: Centro de Estudios Sociales (CES) Ediciones, 1990); Manuel Barrera and J. Samuel Valenzuela, "The Development of the Labor Movement Opposition to the Military Regime," in *Military Rule in Chile: Dictatorship and Oppositions*, ed. J. Samuel Valenzuela and Arturo Valenzuela (Baltimore: Johns Hopkins University Press, 1986); Guillermo Campero and José Valenzuela, *El movimiento sindical chileno en el capitalismo autoritario* (Santiago: Instituto Latinoamericano de Estudios Transnacionales [ILET], 1981); Paul W. Drake, *Labor Movements and Dictatorships: The Southern Cone in Comparative Perspective* (Baltimore: Johns Hopkins University Press, 1996); Jaime Ruiz-Tagle, *El sindicalismo chileno después del Plan Laboral* (Santiago: Programa de Estudios del Trabajo [PET], 1985); Peter Winn, ed., *Victims of the Chilean Miracle: Workers and Neoliberalism in the Pinochet Era, 1973–2002* (Durham: Duke University Press, 2004); Francisco Zapata, "Las relaciones entre la Junta Militar y los trabajadores chilenos: 1973–1978," *Foro Internacional* 20, no. 2 (1979).

squad that traveled throughout the country to accelerate military trials and execute prisoners.³ Arellano arrived in Copiapó on October 16 and executed thirteen people, including two copper labor leaders, Benito Tapia and Maguindo Castillo, and the general manager of Cobresal, Ricardo García. Tapia was a young blue-collar worker at El Salvador, a leader of the Copper Workers Confederation (CTC), and a Communist Party militant. Maguindo Castillo, a militant from the Socialist Party, was an office worker and a leader of the white-collar union. Ricardo García was also a Socialist Party militant and had been general manager in 1971–73.

In the following months, a series of governmental decrees dismantled the national labor movement. In November 1973, the military government dissolved the national labor confederation, Central Única de Trabajadores (CUT), and in December, it suppressed all union elections.⁴ In 1973–76, a period defined by Paul Drake as one of "devastation and hibernation" for the Chilean union movement, workers refrained from overt action and union membership dropped. While leftist union leaders were persecuted, arrested, or assassinated or went into exile, nonleftist union leaders such as Tucapel Jiménez from the National Association of Government Employees, Gilberto García from the Teachers Federation, and Hernán Morales from the National Petroleum Workers Union tried to adapt to the military rules and negotiated some space for participation.⁵ Although some of these leaders were pessimistic about the impact of the military's repression on the union movement, they expressed "relief" that the coup had taken place and were sympathetic to the military. For example, Jiménez believed that the "junta will permit legitimate unions to pursue normal activities in the near future" and thanked the "Labor Attaché's government [the United States] for helping to bring about the change."⁶

In the copper mines, as in the rest of the country, the process of collective bargaining was interrupted, and workers sympathetic to the military government filled the vacancies of what remained of their labor organizations. Aware of copper workers' controversial attitudes during the years of the UP; the economic importance of the copper industry; and especially, the role of the El Teniente strike in the downfall of Allende, the military government

---

3. For an account of the actions of the Caravan of Death, see Patricia Verdugo, *Caso Arellano: Los zarpazos del puma* (Santiago: CESOC, 1989).
4. The two decrees were Decreto Ley 133 and Decreto Ley 198.
5. Drake, *Labor Movements*, 123.
6. Davis, October 1973, 12. NARA, GR, Chile 1970–73, box 2194.

treated the copper workers' labor movement with some deference, hoping to gain its support. The attempt by some copper union leaders to accommodate the military regime was the result of visible divisions within the copper unions and between white- and blue-collar workers on the eve of the coup and the influence of Christian Democracy, especially in El Teniente, since the late 1960s.

The military did not dissolve the CTC, as it did the CUT. Yet the new CTC bore little resemblance to its predecessor, as seven of its thirteen leaders were replaced and its new president, Guillermo Santana, worked closely with the government. Santana, a militant Christian Democrat and a leader of the white-collar union of Potrerillos, had been especially vocal against Allende and the UP, playing a key role during the legal strike of August 1971. Another central actor in the copper workers' labor movement was Guillermo Medina, a leader from El Teniente who had participated in the strike of April–June 1973.[7] Medina remained a close collaborator of the military government, joining the Council of State (Consejo de Estado), a national body created by the military in 1976 that represented the different groups of society.

In the aftermath of the coup, in an effort to adapt to the repressive environment, copper workers' leaders reinforced their relationship with the U.S. labor movement, specifically with the American Institute for Free Labor Development (AIFLD). Organized in 1962 by the American Federation of Labor and Congress of Industrial Organizations (AFL-CIO), the AIFLD included representatives of the U.S. business sector and received funding from the U.S. government through the U.S. Agency for International Development (USAID). By 1970, the AIFLD had representatives in nineteen cities in Latin America and the Caribbean and sponsored programs of union education and socioeconomic development. Strongly anti-Communist and close to the U.S. Department of State, the AIFLD had little success in Chile before 1973, only attracting some Christian Democrat and anti-Communist union leaders such as the president of the Confederation of Maritime Workers, Wenceslao Moreno. Despite its controversial past, after the coup

---

7. Thomas M. Klubock, "Class, Community, and Neoliberalism in Chile: Copper Workers and the Labor Movement During the Military Dictatorship and Restoration of Democracy," in Peter Winn, ed. *Victims of the Chilean Miracle: Workers and Neoliberalism in the Pinochet Era, 1973–2002* (Durham: Duke University Press, 2004), 217–18.

the AIFLD provided, as Art Nixon from the AIFLD put it in 1975, "a safe excuse for the leadership to get together."[8]

Beginning in 1975, the harsh social impact of government economic policies, the consolidation and institutionalization of Pinochet's dictatorship, and the government's opposition to reestablishing the most basic of workers' rights such as union elections and collective bargaining severed the fragile "alliance" between nonleftist labor leaders and the military. In 1975, the junta incorporated into the government the so-called Chicago Boys, a new generation of economists trained in the University of Chicago by Milton Friedman, who sought to consolidate a free-market, neoliberal, export-oriented economy in Chile. To do so, they implemented a series of drastic economic stabilization measures. In 1976, the appointment of Sergio Fernández as minister of labor (1976–78), to coordinate labor policies according to the new economic directions, ended any possibility of an understanding between labor and the government.

In this context, nonleftist labor leaders, increasingly dissatisfied with political and economic conditions, started articulating a more critical discourse against the government. Maintaining their distance from the Left, especially the Communist Party, they formed the Group of Ten in December 1975. The Group of Ten included important and influential labor leaders such as Manuel Bustos (textile workers), Tucapel Jiménez (public employees), and Guillermo Santana (copper workers).[9] In May 1976, they addressed a public letter to the military junta protesting the current situation. The government launched a public campaign against the group. Guillermo Medina especially attacked Santana, accusing him of putting the CTC outside the law and siding with Communist labor leaders.[10] As a result, the government forced Santana out of the CTC and appointed Bernardino

---

8. From Art Nixon to McLellan, April 11, 1975, GMMA, CF (1969–81), box 5, folder 19.

9. The Group of Ten was integrated by Manuel Bustos (textile workers union), Pedro Cifuentes (sugar workers union), Andrés del Campo (bank workers union), E. Díaz (maritime workers union), Tucapel Jiménez (public employees union), Enrique Mellado (peasant federation), Antonio Minimiza (oil workers union), Francisco Mujica (private employees union), Eduardo Ríos (maritime workers union), Guillermo Santana (Copper Workers Confederation), and Ernesto Vogel (railway workers). There were all members of the Christian Democracy but Jiménez, who was a member of the Radical Party. The Group of Ten evolved over time, in 1981 it became the Democratic Union of Workers (UDT) and in 1984 the Confederation of Democratic Workers (1984). Campero and Valenzuela, *El movimiento sindical chileno*, 389.

10. Campero and Valenzuela, *El movimiento sindical*, 389.

Castillo as its new president. The Group of Ten and its criticism of the government's labor policies illustrate the divisions between nonleftist labor leaders and the government and are representative of the final rupture between Christian Democracy and the military regime.

Critical voices also started coming from international organizations. In April 1975, for example, the CTC invited George Meany, the president of the AFL-CIO, to visit Chile and attend the forty-ninth anniversary of the confederation. A couple of months before, Meany had also received an invitation from General Pinochet to visit the country. Turning down both invitations, Meany declared that leaders from the AFL-CIO would not visit Chile until there was "a complete restauration [sic] of trade union rights and a return to the old system, as it existed in Chile before the regime of Allende."[11] Although copper workers feared the government's reaction, they sympathized with Meany's decision, joking that "el viejo tiene huevos."[12] In the following years, the AFL-CIO and the ORIT continually threatened the Chilean government that they would organize an international boycott against the country and maintained a close relationship with Christian Democrat union leaders and the Group of Ten.[13]

In 1977, Chilean workers became more active and organized in response to deteriorating economic conditions and the new labor policies of the government, which threatened workers' few remaining rights. In the copper mines, a series of protests took place in 1977 and 1978. Copper workers addressed public letters to the government, criticized the CTC and its lack of independence, and organized absenteeism strikes and *movimientos de viandas* (lunch actions) or *loncheras vacías* (empty lunchboxes) that consisted of workers' refusal to eat at company cafeterias. In El Teniente, workers organized a *movimiento de viandas* in September 1977 and an absentee strike in November. In the following months, similar movements took place in El Salvador and Chuquicamata, where workers led absentee strikes, openly criticized the lack of independence of the CTC, and protested against the economic conditions. New *movimientos de viandas* took place in Chuquicamata and in El Salvador in August–September 1978.[14] The Corporación del Cobre (CODELCO) and the government severely repressed these mobilizations, firing, arresting, and deporting workers. In

11. From Meany to Valencia, April 8, 1975, GMMA, CF (1969–81), box 5, folder 19.
12. From Art Nixon to McLellan, April 11, 1975, GMMA, CF (1969–81), box 5, folder 19.
13. Barrera and Valenzuela, "Development of the Labor Movement Opposition," 249.
14. Klubock, "Class, Community, and Neoliberalism"; Zapata, "Las relaciones."

1978 in the mine of El Salvador, Bernardino Castillo, president of the CTC, declared that management was "systematically persecuting copper workers, humiliating them, doing arbitrary dismissals, violating legal dispositions and refusing to accept fair labor demands."[15]

These protests laid the foundations for the reconstruction of the labor movement in the copper mines. Given the political and legal context, workers developed new forms of activism to confront management and the government. Moving away from traditional union actions such as collective bargaining, labor courts, and strikes when, as noted in a 1986 newsletter for Potrerillos workers, they explained that "the old methods of solving problems with employers were not useful anymore," they organized innovative protests such as *cuchareos* (bumping of spoons) in company cafeterias, *movimientos de viandas*, and hunger strikes.[16]

By 1978, the military's labor and economic policies had driven the majority of union leaders toward the opposition and in doing so made possible an understanding between Christian Democrat and Leftists union leaders. A broad coalition of union leaders from the opposition organized the National Union Coordinator (Coordinadora Nacional Sindical, or CNS) in 1978. Led by Manuel Bustos, who abandoned the Group of Ten, the CNS played a critical role in the reactivation of the workers' movement from 1978 to 1983.[17]

New Labor Laws and the Struggle for Democracy, 1982–1989

The new labor laws enacted in 1979–82 (known as the Labor Plan) and the economic crisis that started in 1982 motivated new protests and activism among copper and other Chilean workers. For copper workers, the new legislation implied the abolition of the Statute of Copper Workers, the special legislation that had regulated labor relations in the copper mines since 1956, and the loss of their traditional benefits. The Labor Plan, conceived by the new minister of labor José Piñera, completely transformed labor relations in Chile.[18] First, it eliminated the classic distinction between plant,

---

15. *La Tercera* (Santiago), July 17, 1978.
16. Juán Luan, "Ayuno por el derecho al trabajo," October 1986, Potrerillos, Sindicato 1.
17. Angell, "Union and Workers," 209.
18. For the regime perspective, see José Piñera, *La revolución laboral en Chile* (Santiago: Zig-Zag, 1990).

professional, and rural unions and created four new categories: company unions (workers from one company), intercompany unions (workers from at least three different companies), independent workers, and construction workers. Only company unions had the right to bargain collectively. Collective bargaining topics were limited to salaries and working conditions, excluding, according to article 12, those issues that could limit the employer's decision to "organize, rule, and administer the company." The right to strike was especially restricted. Strikes were limited to sixty days, striking workers had the right to break the strike after thirty days, and employers had the right both to declare a lockout and to hire temporary personnel during the strike.

In August–September 1981, a series of repressive laws left workers in an even more vulnerable position. Law 18.018 modified labor contracts and working conditions, abolished workers' protections against unfair firing and massive layoffs, and homogenized working conditions by eliminating special guarantees granted to specific groups of workers; this law particularly affected copper workers, intimating negation of the Statute of Copper Workers. Law 18.020 eliminated unemployment insurance, creating emergency employment programs; law 18.044 affected collective bargaining and union finances, limiting wage settlements to once a year; and in 1982, law 18.134 restricted automatic wage increases and severance payments.[19]

In addition, the economic crisis of 1981–83, a result of failed monetarist and neoconservative policies, had a terrible effect on the Chilean working people.[20] In 1982, GDP fell by one-seventh; the financial and industrial sectors collapsed; and national unemployment reached 23.7 percent, compared with 12.3 percent in 1980.[21] The industrial sector was most affected, with an unemployment rate of about 29.5 percent; in construction, the figure was 54.2 percent. The government devaluated the peso twice in 1982, and in 1983, it took control of several banks. In February 1983, about 463,000 people were working in one of the two emergency employment programs (Programa de Empleo Mínimo [Basic Work Program, or PEM] and Programa de Ocupación para Jefes de Hogar [Work Program for Heads of Households, or POHJ]), and wages continued to decline. With the enactment of the Labor Plan and the decrease in social investment, workers were left in

---

19. Barrera and Valenzuela, "Development of the Labor Movement Opposition," 258–59.
20. For an economic history of the period, see Patricio Meller, *The Unidad Popular and the Pinochet Dictatorship: A Political Economy Analysis* (New York: St. Martin's Press, 2000).
21. Cavallo et al., *La historia oculta*, 396.

an extremely precarious condition. Living conditions deteriorated for the great majority of Chilean working people, including copper workers, and the level of poverty grew.

In the copper mines, workers faced corporate efforts to restructure and rationalize production. While these endeavors were not new, the existing political and economic context reduced union power and workers' capacity to resist these changes. In an attempt to improve efficiency and competitiveness, CODELCO increased mechanization and outsourcing, and externalized services such as health care and education. The labor force became smaller and more skilled, and the proportion of contract workers higher. As a result, between 1974 and 1986, total employment in the large-scale copper industry fell from 32,800 to 24,886.[22] These changes, as exemplified in the case of El Teniente, threatened workers' skills, salaries, and job security.[23] For many, the increase in the number of contract workers was a sign of the military's hidden agenda to privatize the copper industry; copper union leaders warned in 1986 that contract workers were a "permanent threat to job stability" and would eventually lead to the "privatization of CODELCO."[24]

The economic crisis, the new Labor Plan, and the restructuring of CODELCO motivated copper workers to organize. In the early 1980s, El Teniente workers complained about the company's efforts to restructure shifts, reduce salaries, and fire people. In Chuquicamata, a workers' assembly in 1982 protested against CODELCO and its plan to eliminate profit sharing and increase the number of contract workers.[25] In the process, they became critical not only of the military government, but also of those union leaders who had favored a policy of accommodation. In April 1982, the CTC officially sanctioned Guillermo Medina, who now represented El Teniente within the CTC and worked for the government as a labor advisor, for his "having anti-union attitudes and helping to reduce union freedom in Chile."[26]

Throughout 1983, the lack of response from CODELCO or the government provoked new waves of protests in the copper mines. The copper workers' movement had both a strong political and economic content, as the demand for economic and labor reforms entailed criticism of the military dictatorship and, eventually, a call for the restoration of democracy. How these elements

22. Angell, "Union and Workers," 194.
23. Klubock, "Class, Community, and Neoliberalism."
24. "Empresas contratistas: Escandalosa privatización," *Cauce*, March 10–16, 1986.
25. *Dialogando: Informes SIAL* 7 (1982).
26. *Dialogando: Informes SIAL* 8 (1982).

intertwined became clear at the CTC's national congress in April 1983. At that meeting, the leaders of the CTC declared that the problem was not "one law more or less . . . but a complete economic, social, cultural, and political system that has us smothered and bound." Concluding that it was the time "to stand up and say ENOUGH," they called for a national strike.[27]

This decision took most Chilean political parties by surprise. Skeptical of the possibilities of a successful national strike and aware of the degree of state repression, political Christian Democracy leaders persuaded copper workers to call a day of "national protest" instead.[28] On May 11, 1983, responding to the call of copper unions and political parties, Chileans expressed their opposition to the government through several peaceful strategies. They worked slowly, did not send their children to school, and abstained from shopping. Copper workers in El Salvador, Andina, and El Teniente struck; students protested in the main universities; and that night a loud *cacerolazo* (banging of empty pots) was heard in middle-class neighborhoods and shantytowns throughout the country.

New leaders, many of whom held union positions as a result of the government's call for regular union elections in 1979–80, and organizations emerged in the conjuncture of 1983. Despite the government's expectations of controlling the 1979–80 union elections, they had opened a legitimate space for union leaders who opposed the regime. For instance, in the Chuquicamata union election of 1980, 100 percent of blue-collar workers supported union leaders from the opposition.[29] In addition, national labor organizations increased efforts to create alliances. In 1983, the CTC joined other Chilean unions in the Comando Nacional de Trabajadores (CNT). The CNT played a prominent role in the organization of mass protests against the Pinochet regime and was emblematic of the involvement and leadership of copper workers in a national labor movement.[30] The CNT's first president was Rodolfo Seguel, a twenty-nine-year-old white-collar worker from El Teniente, who became one of the most influential labor figures of the 1980s. Seguel had started working in El Teniente in 1974

---

27. "Resoluciones del Congreso de Punta de Tralca, abril 1983," quoted in Oscar Mac-Clure and Iván Valenzuela, *Conflictos de la Gran Minería del Cobre, 1973–1983* (Santiago: CEDAL, 1985), 69.

28. Patricio Aylwin, *El reencuentro de los demócratas: Del golpe al triunfo del no* (Santiago: Ediciones B, 1998), 276–77.

29. Campero and Valenzuela, *El movimiento sindical*, 517.

30. Marcelo Castillo and Magaly Chamorro, "Movimiento sindical: En busca de un nuevo rostro," *Cauce*, August 7–20, 1984.

and was elected to the union board of the Professional Union of Caletones in 1982. In 1982, he also joined the Christian Democratic Party. An unknown leader outside El Teniente, he was elected president of the CTC in 1983. Although he was fired from El Teniente in 1983, he continued, despite the government's opposition, as CTC president until 1987.

National protests continued in the following years. From May 1983 to October 1984, the CNT and political parties called eleven successful mass protests. Chileans, and especially workers and *pobladores* (residents of working-class neighborhoods and shantytowns), paid a high price for their participation. In the copper mines, for example, workers were systematically fired for participating in national protests. In June 1983, CODELCO fired eighty-three workers for participating in a national protest, and union leaders were incarcerated, including Seguel. In the following months, five hundred workers were dismissed from El Salvador for political reasons, leading to a hunger strike.[31] During the eleventh protest, in October 1984, nine people were shot and 265 people were deported to Pisagua. In November, the government decreed a state of siege and censored several magazines and newspapers. The state of siege lasted until August 1985, and in September, the CNT called a national protest that was massively supported but brutally repressed. In September–December 1985, the CNT leadership was imprisoned. Protests continued throughout 1986, led by a broad coalition of political parties and social organizations.

Despite the role of the labor movement in the first national protests, the CNT was unable to lead a national movement, and the political parties assumed leadership of the protest after 1985. Divisions within the union movement, systematic repression against the union leadership, the impact of the economic crisis, the increasing importance of other social groups, and the reorganization of political parties explained this loss of a protagonist role. Unionized workers were more vulnerable to repression on the shop floor, and they were more isolated than community organizers in shantytowns and students in universities. As Arturo Medina, secretary of the CNT, explained in 1987: "The union movement is alive, although not as we want it. But considering that under dictatorship, workers risk their jobs, it is not the same as for students, who, for instance, can generally go back to their activities."[32]

---

31. Mac-Clure and Valenzuela, *Conflictos*, 69.
32. Hernán Dinamarca, "Movilización: Trabajadores retoman el comando," *Cauce*, March 23, 1987.

While popular mobilization was instrumental in opening new political spaces, it did not overthrow the regime. By 1986, the military government did not show signs of weakness and repression increased, especially after the failed attempt to assassinate Pinochet in September 1986. That year, with its constantly escalating levels of violence, was a turning point for many political sectors, and as Patricio Aylwin, a Christian Democrat and the first democratic president after the fall of the dictatorship in 1990, remarked: "What happened made clear—and I think we all understood it in this way—that since then, social mobilization—because it was exposed to violent actions or consequences—was not the way to achieve democracy."[33] While many union leaders called the decision to stop social mobilization a political compromise, in reality they did not have the power to sustain a massive movement. On May 1, 1987, Seguel restated the crucial importance of social mobilization: "Social mobilization has opened new avenues of expression for political parties and social organizations. Today, when some people question mobilization, it is good to remember that the mere opportunity to have and negotiate proposals is a result of that mobilization that they would like to bury."[34]

In 1987, the political opposition began working toward politically defeating the dictatorial regime of Pinochet. They used the national constitution enacted in 1980, which established a national plebiscite for 1988. The victory against General Pinochet in the plebiscite of October 1988 and the first presidential election in December 1989 began the transition to democracy. Workers, among them copper workers, joined political campaigns, participating in political demonstrations, registering in the electoral service to vote, voting no (against Pinochet) in the plebiscite, and supporting the candidates of the Concertación de Partidos por la Democracia (Coalition of Parties for Democracy) in the following elections. Nevertheless, on the eve of democracy copper unions were not the powerful agents that they were in the 1960s.

Copper Workers and the Dream of Democracy, 1990–2000

The return of democracy in 1990 did not bring an immediate restoration of workers' traditional rights and power. In the 1990s, as historian Peter Winn acknowledges, "despite the restoration of democracy and a decade of

---

33. Aylwin, *El reencuentro*, 315.
34. "CNT ratifica movilización," *Cauce*, May 4–10, 1987.

center-left governments, there was more continuity than changes in economic policy and labor relations."[35] While the Concertación governments have increased social expenditure and made efforts to decrease poverty levels in the country and to consolidate (or construct) democratic institutions, they have also attempted to consolidate an export-oriented economy and create a comfortable environment for private investors, both national and foreign. In their efforts to build a more socially oriented market economy and a more democratic country, labor has been a very difficult issue. Overall, the Concertación has concentrated on two tasks in regard to workers and labor rights: restoration of traditional labor rights abolished during the dictatorship and modernization of labor relations.[36] But these efforts have been especially slow and controversial, shaped by the governments' effort to reach a balance of power between employers and employees, maintain high levels of economic growth and investment, and consolidate Chile's integration into the global market through bilateral free trade agreements. On the one hand, employers have demanded reforms that can guarantee maximum flexibility in the labor market (especially in terms of contract, hiring, firing, and length of workday). On the other hand, workers and union organizations have pressed for protection and guarantees for the union movement.

The history of copper workers under democracy has been conditioned by the shortcomings of labor reforms and the efforts of CODELCO to modernize the copper industry and successfully compete against smaller and more efficient private companies. In 1994, CODELCO launched a project to modernize the company through the introduction of technological innovations, rationalization of the administration, expansion of investment, and improvement of commercialization. Acknowledging the historical importance of the labor movement in the copper mines, the new project of modernization considered by CODELCO entailed an alliance with labor unions, represented through the Copper Workers Federation (FTC).[37] The agreement, called the Strategic Alliance, guaranteed the unions' participation in some level of decision

35. Peter Winn, "The Pinochet Era," in *Victims of the Chilean Miracle: Workers and Neoliberalism in the Pinochet Era, 1973–2002* (Durham: Duke University Press, 2004), 51.
36. Ministerio del Trabajo y Previsión Social, "Un nuevo marco normativo para el mundo del trabajo." *Observatorio Laboral*, no. 19.
37. In 1992, the Copper Workers Confederation (CTC) became the Copper Workers Federation (FTC) because the Labor Code requires confederations to have at least twenty affiliated labor unions.

making within the company and, in return, had assured unions' support for the modernization of the industry. In the year 2000, representatives of workers, supervisors, and CODELCO renewed their alliance, in an agreement called the Common Project.

The Strategic Alliance has implied that labor unions have not been critical of the restructuring of CODELCO. For example, the FTC has been less critical than in the past regarding flexibilization and subcontracting and has focused exclusively on defending the rights and economic gains of permanent workers. As a result, it has been successful in maintaining a relatively low number of contract workers and high salaries and benefits. In 1995, for example, 21.9 percent of the labor force employed in CODELCO's mines were contract workers, compared with more than 52 percent in private companies.

The reorganization of CODELCO has transformed the lives of copper workers and their families. Continuing with a process that started in the late 1960s, CODELCO has closed mining camps and begun housing workers in nearby cities, creating systems of commuting and building modern shelters and dormitory cities next to the work site. It closed the Sewell camp next to El Teniente mine in 1986 and the Potrerillos camp in 1999 and started closing the Chuquicamata camp in 2002. Economic and environmental circumstances have influenced CODELCO's decisions. Today, mining companies such as CODELCO questioned the need to provide workers and their families with shelter, food, and recreation, regarding these services as unnecessary costs. In addition, environmental organizations have judged mining camps located next to plants to be unsuitable for human beings, forcing CODELCO to find alternative solutions.

The changes in Potrerillos and El Salvador illuminate the recent economic and environmental trends of the copper industry. In 1997, CODELCO announced the Potrerillos Plan, a program to make viable the operation of the smelter and refinery in Potrerillos without maintaining a mining camp. The company's decision was a response to a resolution of the Corporación Nacional del Medio Ambiente (National Commission on the Environment, or CONAMA). Based on the extremely toxic emissions of the Potrerillos smelter, CONAMA pronounced Potrerillos unsuitable for human habitation. In September 1997, during negotiations between the unions and the company, the latter gave workers in Potrerillos three choices. First, they could move to company houses in the mining camp of El Salvador, about twenty-eight miles northwest of Potrerillos, and commute every day to the plants. Second, they could purchase houses in another city through state housing programs (*subsidio habitacional*) and live in the Centro de Alojamiento (a workers' lodge) in Potrerillos during the workweek.[38] Under this second plan, they would work shifts of twelve hours for five consecutive days, followed by five days off. Third, they could take part in an early retirement plan.

The construction of the Centro de Alojamiento symbolized the new policies of the company. Initially, 120–230 people were to be housed, but in following years capacity would expand to 260–325. The building has bedrooms with one or two beds, one bathroom for every two bedrooms, recreational areas (TV room, library, gym, multipurpose court), and a dining area. Workers take their meals in the dining area, where their food is healthfully prepared. Alcohol is strictly prohibited in the Centro de Alojamiento, and visitors are only allowed during the daytime.

The reorganization of work and life has had enormous consequences for workers, their families, and the company. It is still too soon to evaluate the dramatic impact of these changes, but labor union leaders and even the company itself have begun to notice the consequences that twelve-hour shifts and disruptions in family life are having on the pace of work, the frequency of accidents, and labor turnover. However, many of the changes have also had positive consequences, decreasing copper workers' isolation and dependence. Mining families now have access to a wide range of economic, social, and cultural opportunities in regional cities. The opportunities have been especially important for women and have transformed traditional gender roles and household economies. Similarly, CODELCO has promised to invest in regional cities as a way to improve the urban and social infrastructure and convince workers of the advantages of moving out of the camps.

Conclusions

Dictatorship and the economic changes in the copper industry have transformed the labor movement. Before 1973, the strength of the copper workers' labor movement was in the workers' success in collective bargaining and in enforcing rights through labor courts, illegal strikes, trade solidarity, and political connections. The overlap of living and working

---

38. *Andino* (Potrerillos), November 13–26, 1999.

spaces and the close relationship between the union movement and the community had also been crucial. Dictatorship seriously undermined these elements. Throughout the 1980s, to confront political repression and changes in the workplace, copper workers organized a mass movement. The return of democracy, however, did not imply a return to the predictatorship labor scenario. Changes in legislation, the structure of the copper industry, the country's political culture, and the community have remade the role of the labor union. Labor unions have lost the militancy of the past and have played a minor role in workers' daily life. Copper labor unions have joined CODELCO in its efforts to modernize the company and to confront the threat of privatization, an alliance that for many has been a negative compromise. In addition, the FTC has strongly supported Ricardo Lagos's administration in its effort to create a special tax for mining industries. Today, when union halls are usually empty, labor leaders face new challenges: incorporating the increasing number of contract workers; overcoming the traditional division between large- and medium-scale mines; protecting workers' rights in an increasingly unregulated sector; and above all, legitimating unions as institutions that represent workers' demands despite political divisions.

Conclusion

In July 2006, Juan Villarzú, president of CODELCO, announced the closure of the El Salvador mine by 2011. The announcement was far from a surprise. As the mine's production costs increased throughout the 1990s, rumors about closure spread. Efforts to find other ore bodies in the area failed, leaving CODELCO without other choices. Salvadoreños contested the decision of CODELCO. On August 9, local residents raised black flags in their houses and, despite the cold Andean winter night, organized a massive demonstration throughout the town. In the process, they not only defended their right to continue living near and working in the mine, but also linked their local struggle to the importance of the mine for the regional economy and, as a state-owned company, for the entire country. The imminent closure of the mine has critical raised questions about the history of this community, its historical dependence on—and vulnerability to—nature and the international copper market, and the role of copper in Chile.

In this book I have explored the history of copper and copper workers and their families in Potrerillos and El Salvador from the 1940s to the 1990s. Local, national, and transnational forces shaped the history of copper, first as a foreign-owned commodity (1917–71) and then as a state-owned enterprise (1971–present). Until the nationalization of copper in July 1971, workers, foreign capital, and the state debated conditions in the production of Chile's most important commodity. Workers' salaries, safety, and living conditions intertwined with discussions about taxation, investment, organization of production, and the commercialization of Chilean copper in the international market. In the long run, the copper debate raised critical questions about workers' social, economic, and political rights; the country's model of economic development and its dependency on the export market;

the role of the national state; and the rights of foreign capital to own natural resources in Chile. Thus the role of copper workers and their families in modern Chile went beyond producing what President Salvador Allende called the *sueldo de Chile,* or the wage of Chile. Their struggle also exposed the contradictions and limitations of Chile's democracy and development.

The characteristics of copper production and its role in the national economy created a distinctive and powerful union movement in the copper mines. In the early twentieth century, U.S. capital, incorporating new technology, labor and welfare policies, and production strategies, transformed the Chilean copper industry into a large-scale, modern, dynamic business. Given the isolation of the mines and a need to control the labor force, foreign companies such as Andes Copper built company towns to house their employees. Despite a discourse that emphasized the modernity and good conditions of mining camps, the urban segregation and strict internal regulations of company towns and the limitations of material conditions such as lack of private bathrooms created tension between management and labor organizations. At the workplace, harsh working conditions, accidents and disease, and abusive and authoritarian work relations created a very conflictive environment. The foreign ownership of the industry, the power of multinational companies, and the vagaries of the export market helped to consolidate a discourse in which the struggle for labor rights was interwoven with calls for economic nationalism and anti-imperialism.

The inability of the Chilean state to protect and incorporate workers' rights and the instability of the domestic economy influenced workers' lives and politics throughout the twentieth century and consolidated their alliance with the political Left, both the Communist and the Socialist Parties. In the 1930s and 1940s, the pro-labor discourse and legislation of the Popular Front provided the legal basis for the organization of a labor movement. An important component of the copper workers' labor movement was the use of labor laws, institutions, and authorities on behalf of its members. In the following years, the labor agenda of the state fell short. Anti-Communism, authoritarianism, and economic instability inspired antilabor policies and stabilization programs that threatened working people's income. In addition, the state's dependence on copper and foreign capital restrained its freedom in the copper mines.

From the 1950s up to the military coup of 1973, labor unions were powerful and legitimate institutions in the copper camps. They represented workers' living and working demands, provided a unique space of politicization and sociability, and became a link between the local community and the nation as a whole. Their history reveals the critical importance of the union movement as a labor, political, and cultural institution in predictatorship Chile.

BIBLIOGRAPHY

Archives and Public Records, with Abbreviations

American Heritage Center (AHC), University of Wyoming
   Anaconda Geological Document Collection (AGDC)
   Blair Stewart Papers
   Philip Wilson Papers
Archivo Nacional, Santiago
   Records of the Intendencia de Antofagasta
Archivo Nacional de la Administración Central del Estado (ARNAD), Santiago
   Records of the Dirección General del Trabajo (DT)
   Records of the Ministerio de Minería (MM)
   Records of the Ministerio de Salubridad, Previsión y Asistencia Social
   Records of the Ministerio del Trabajo (MT)
Corporación Justicia y Democracia, Santiago
   Archivo Radomiro Tomic
Archivo de la Dirección del Trabajo (ADT), Santiago
   Records of Labor Unions
The George Meany Memorial Archives (GMMA), Silver Spring, Md
   International Affairs Department, Country Files, 1945–71 (CF)
   International Affairs Department, Jay Lovestone Files, 1939–74 (JLF)
Hoover Institutional Archives, Stanford, Calif
   Chilean Subject Collection, 1933–97
   Jay Lovestone Papers
Kheel Center for Labor-Management Documentation and Archives, Cornell University (KC)
   Serafino Romualdi Papers (SRP)
Montana Historical Society Archives (MHSA), Helena
   Anaconda Company Records (ACR)
Museo División El Salvador, El Salvador, Chile
Robert J. Alexander Papers: Interview Collection, 1947–94, microfilm, IDC
Servicio Electoral, Centro de Documentación, Santiago
   Records of National Elections, 1930–73
U.S. National Archives and Records Administration (NARA)
   Department of State, General Records, Chile (GR)

Newspapers

Andino (Potrerillos), 1956–73
Atacama (Copiapó), 1971–73
Avance (Chañaral), 1939–41
Diario Ilustrado (Santiago), 1955, 1965
El Día (Copiapó), 1950–72
El Mercurio (Santiago), 1955, 1959, 1965, 1971
El Popular (Antofagasta), 1955, 1965
El Progreso (Chañaral), 1916–53
El Siglo (Santiago), 1940–48, 1952–73
La Nación (Santiago) 1955, 1959, 1965, 1971
La Usina (Potrerillos), 1942–48
La Verdad (Chañaral), 1918–21, 1925–26
La Voz de Potrerillos (Potrerillos), 1942–43
La Voz de la Victoria (Potrerillos), 1943
Las Noticias de Chañaral (Chañaral), 1966–72
Las Noticias de Copiapó (Copiapó), 1967–69
Observer (Potrerillos), 1967–70
Orientación (Potrerillos), 1948
Rumbos (Potrerillos), 1947–48

Other Periodicals

Ahora
Anales del Instituto de Ingenieros
Annual Report (Anaconda Copper Company)
Anuario de la Minería de Chile, 1962–75
Arauco
Boletín Minero (Sociedad Nacional de Minería)
Causa Marxista-Lenilista (ML)
Cauce
Cobre (Confederación de Trabajadores del Cobre, Santiago)
Chiflón (Federación Industrial Minera)
Dialogando: Informes SIAL (Vicaría de la Pastoral Obrera de Santiago)
Economic Survey of Latin America (United Nations)
Engineering and Mining Journal
International Labour Review (International Labour Organization, or ILO), 1921–2004
Inter-American Labor Bulletin (ORIT)
Minerales
Punto Final
Reverbero

Unpublished Sources

Andes Copper Mining Company. "Reglamento Interno de la Andes Copper Mining Co. y Potrerillos Railway Co." c. 1933, Biblioteca Nacional de Chile.

Butelmann, Aurelio. "Productivity and Wage Determination: A Microeconomic Model for the Gran Minería of Copper in Chile." Master's thesis, Cornell University, 1969.
Consejería Nacional de Promoción Popular. "Valores y actitudes en los obreros de la Gran Minería en Chile." Santiago: Universidad Católica de Chile, Instituto de Economía, 1968.
De Viado, Manuel. "Informe sobre la Comisión Oficial al Mineral de Cobre de Potrerillos." Archivo Nacional de la Administración Central del Estado (ARNAD), Ministerio de Salubridad, Previsión, y Asistencia Social, Providencias, August–September 1941.
Figueroa, Tirso. "Los conflictos colectivos en la Gran Minería del Cobre." Undergraduate thesis, Universidad de Chile, 1963.
Galaz, Eliana, and María Angélica Alvear. "Factores de trabajo en Chuquicamata." Undergraduate thesis, Universidad Católica de Chile, 1957.
Galves, Emilio. "La fuerza de trabajo en la Gran Minería del Cobre." Undergraduate thesis, Universidad de Chile, 1966.
Marín, Clorinda, and Sonia Trivick. "Servicio Social en la Gran Minería del Cobre: Chuquicamata." Undergraduate thesis, Universidad de Chile de Antofagasta, 1970.
Olivares, Jaime R. "The Creation of a Labor Aristocracy: The History of the Oil Workers in Maracaibo, Venezuela, 1925–1948." Ph.D. diss., University of Houston, 2003.
Pavilack, Joann C. "Black Gold in the Red Zone: Repression and Contention in Chilean Coal Mining Communities from the Popular Front to the Advent of the Cold War" Ph.D. diss., Duke University, 2003.
Porzio, Huguette. "El capital humano en la industria del cobre y particularmente en Chuquicamata." Undergraduate thesis, Universidad de Chile, 1961.
Samaniego, Augusto. "Les stratégies syndicales de la 'Central Unica de Trabajadores de Chile' et l'action socio-politique des salaries (1952–1973)." Ph.D. diss., Université de Paris VIII, 1998.
Silva, J. Pablo. "White-Collar Revolutionaries: Middle-Class Unions and the Rise of the Chilean Left, 1918–1938." Ph.D. diss., University of Chicago, 2000.
Stillerman, Joel. "From Solidarity to Survival: Transformations in the Culture and Style of Mobilization of Chilean Metalworkers Under Democratic and Authoritarian Regimes, 1945–1995." Ph.D. diss., New School for Social Research, 1998.
Toole, K. Ross. "A History of the Anaconda Copper Mining Company: A Study in the Relationships Between a State and Its People and a Corporation, 1880–1950." Ph.D. diss., University of California Los Angeles, 1954.

Oral Histories

Corbett, Robert. "Oral History, 1940–1978." Montana Historical Society, Oral History Collection.
Henshaw, Helen. "Recollections of Life with Paul C. Henshaw: Latin American, Hometake Mining Company." An oral history conducted by Eleanor Swent in 1987. Regional Oral History Office, Bancroft Library, University of California, Berkeley, 1988.
Humphrey, William. "Mining Operations and Engineering Executive for Anaconda, Newmont, Homestake, 1950 to 1995." An oral history conducted by Eleanor

Swent in 1994 and 1995. Regional Oral History Office, Bankroft Library, University of California, Berkeley, 1996.
Perry, Vincent. "A Half Century as Mining and Exploration Geologist with the Anaconda Company." An oral history conducted by Eleanor Swent in 1990. Regional Oral History Office, Bancroft Library, University of California, Berkeley, 1991

Published Sources

Agacino, Rafael, Cristián González, and Jorge Rojas. *Capital transnacional y trabajo: El desarrollo minero en Chile.* Santiago: LOM Ediciones, 1998.
Ahumada, Jorge. *En vez de la miseria.* Santiago: Editorial del Pacífico, 1965.
Alexander, Robert J. *Labor Relations in Argentina, Brazil, and Chile.* New York: McGraw-Hill, 1962.
Allende, Salvador. *Chile's Road to Socialism.* Harmondsworth, U.K.: Penguin Books, 1973.
———. *Su pensamiento político.* Santiago: Quimantú, 1972.
Anaconda Company. *This Is Anaconda.* New York: Anaconda, 1960.
Angell, Alan. *Politics and the Labour Movement in Chile.* London: Oxford University Press, 1972.
Arrate, Jorge, and Eduardo Rojas. *Memoria de la Izquierda Chilena: Tomo I (1850–1970).* Santiago: Javier Vergara Editor, 2003.
———. *Memoria de la Izquierda Chilena: Tomo II (1970–2000).* Santiago: Javier Vergara Editor, 2003.
Aylwin, Patricio. *El reencuentro de los demócratas: Del golpe al triunfo del no.* Santiago: Ediciones B, 1998.
Baros, María Celia. *El Teniente: Los hombres del mineral, 1905–1945.* Rancagua, Chile: CODELCO-Chile, Mineral El Teniente, 1995.
Barr-Melej, Patrick. *Reforming Chile: Cultural Politics, Nationalism, and the Rise of the Middle Class.* Chapel Hill: University of North Carolina Press, 2001.
Barrera, Manuel. *El conflicto obrero en el enclave cuprífero.* Santiago: Universidad de Chile, 1973.
———. *El sindicato industrial como instrumento de lucha de la clase obrera chilena.* Santiago: Universidad de Chile, 1971.
———. *Worker Participation in Company Management in Chile: A Historical Experience.* Geneva: United Nations Research Institute for Social Development, 1981.
Barrera, Manuel, and Gonzalo Falabella. *Sindicatos bajo regímenes militares: Argentina, Brazil, Chile.* Santiago: Centro de Estudios Sociales (CES) Ediciones, 1990.
Barría, Jorge. *Historia de la CUT.* Santiago: Ediciones Pla, 1971.
———. *El movimiento obrero en Chile.* Santiago: Universidad Técnica del Estado, 1971.
———. *Los sindicatos de la Gran Minería del Cobre.* Santiago: Instituto de Administración de la Universidad de Chile (INSORA), 1970.
Bergquist, Charles. *Labor in Latin America: Comparative Essays on Chile, Argentina, Venezuela, and Colombia.* Stanford: Stanford University Press, 1986.

Bethel, Leslie, and Ian Roxborough. "Latin America Between the Second World War and the Cold War: Some Reflections on the 1945–8 Conjuncture." *Journal of Latin American Studies* 1 (1988): 167–89.
Bitar, Sergio, and Crisóstomo Pizarro. *La caída de Allende y la huelga de El Teniente*. Santiago: Ediciones del Ornitorrinco, 1986.
Bonilla, Heraclio. *El minero de los Andes: Una aproximación a su estudio*. Lima: Instituto de Estudios Peruanos, 1974.
Brennan, James P. *The Labor Wars in Córdoba, 1955–1976: Ideology, Work, and Labor Politics in an Argentine Industrial City*. Cambridge: Harvard University Press, 1994.
Brown, Jonathan C., ed. *Workers' Control in Latin America, 1930–1979*. Chapel Hill: University of North Carolina Press, 1997.
Bulmer, M. I. A. "Sociological Models of the Mining Community." *Sociological Review* 1 (1975): 61–92.
Bulmer-Thomas, Victor. *The Economic History of Latin America Since Independence*. New York: Cambridge University Press, 1994.
Campero, Guillermo, and José Valenzuela. *El movimiento sindical en el régimen militar chileno, 1973–1981*. Santiago: Instituto Latinoamericano de Estudios Transnacionales (ILET), 1984.
Cárdenas, Nicolás. *Empresas y trabajadores en la gran minería mexicana, 1900–1929*. Mexico City: Instituto Nacional de Estudios Históricos de la Revolución Mexicana, 1998.
Cavallo, Ascanio, et al. *La historia oculta del régimen militar: Memoria de una época; Chile, 1973–1988*. Santiago: Grupo Grijalbo-Mondadori, 1997.
Central Única de Trabajadores de Chile y Gobierno. *Normas básicas de participación de los trabajadores en la dirección de las empresas de las áreas social y mixta* Santiago: ODEPLAN, 1971.
Collier, Ruth Berins, and David Collier. *Shaping the Political Arena: Critical Junctures, the Labor Movement, and Regime Dynamics in Latin America*. Princeton: Princeton University Press, 1991.
Collier, Simon, and William F. Sater. *A History of Chile, 1808–1994*. Cambridge: Cambridge University Press, 1996.
Constable, Pamela, and Arturo Valenzuela, *A Nation of Enemies: Chile Under Pinochet*. New York: Norton, 1991.
Contreras, Carlos. *Mineros y campesinos en los Andes*. Lima: Instituto de Estudios Peruanos, 1987.
Corporación Nacional del Cobre. *El cobre chileno*. Santiago: Editorial Universitaria, 1974.
Corporación Nacional del Cobre, División Salvador. *Monografía centros productivos división Salvador*. El Salvador: Corporación del Cobre (CODELCO), 1978.
Correa, Sofía, et al. *Historia del siglo XX chileno: Balance paradojal*. Santiago: Editorial Sudamericana, 2001.
Crawford, Margaret. *Building the Workingman's Paradise: The Design of American Company Towns*. New York: Verso, 1995.
De la Maza, Gonzalo, and Mario Garcés. *La explosión de las mayorías: Protesta nacional, 1983–1984*. Santiago: Educación y Comunicaciones (ECO), 1985.
De Ramón, Armando, et al. *Biografía de Chilenos*. Vols. 1–3. Santiago: Ediciones Universidad Católica, 1999–2003.

De Shazo, Peter. *Urban Workers and Labor Unions in Chile, 1902–1927*. Madison: University of Wisconsin Press, 1984.
De Viado, Manuel. "Morfología social de Potrerillos," *Previsión Social*, May–June 1941.
Deustua, José. *The Bewitchment of Silver: The Social Economy of Mining in Nineteenth-Century Peru*. Athens: Ohio University Press, 2000.
DeWind, Adrian. *Peasants Become Miners: The Evolution of Industrial Mining Systems in Peru, 1902–1974*. New York: Garland, 1987.
Di Tella, Torcuato, et al. *Sindicato y comunidad: Dos tipos de estructura sindical latinoamericana*. Buenos Aires: Editorial del Instituto, 1967.
Drake, Paul W. "International Crises and Popular Movements in Latin America: Chile and Peru from the Great Depression to the Cold War." In *Latin America in the 1940s: War and Postwar Transitions*, edited by David Rock. Berkeley and Los Angeles: University of California Press, 1994.
———. *Labor Movements and Dictatorships: The Southern Cone in Comparative Perspective*. Baltimore: Johns Hopkins University Press, 1996.
———, ed. *Money Doctors, Foreign Debts, and Economic Reforms in Latin America: From the 1890s to the Present*. Wilmington: SR Books, 1994.
———. *Socialism and Populism in Chile, 1932–1952*. Urbana: University of Illinois Press, 1978.
Drake, Paul W., and Iván Jaksic. *The Struggle for Democracy in Chile, 1982–1990*. Lincoln: University of Nebraska Press, 1991.
———. *El modelo chileno: Democracia y desarrollo en los noventa*. Santiago: LOM, 1999.
"El Salvador, ciudad minera proyectada como tal," *AURA* 5 (1996).
Emmons, David M. *The Butte Irish: Class and Ethnicity in an American Mining Town, 1875–1925*. Urbana: University of Illinois Press, 1989.
Farnsworth-Alvear, Ann. *Dulcinea in the Factory: Myths, Morals, Men, and Women in Colombia's Industrial Experiment, 1905–1960*. Durham: Duke University Press, 2000.
Fermandois, Joaquín. "Guerra fría y economía política internacional: El cobre en Chile, 1945–1952." *Ciclos* 8 (1998): 143–62.
———. "La larga marcha de la nacionalización: El cobre en Chile, 1945–1971," *Jahrbuch für Geschichte Lateinamerikas* 38 (2001): 287–312.
Ffrench-Davis, Ricardo. *Políticas económicas en Chile, 1952–1970*. Santiago: Ediciones Nueva Universidad, 1973.
Ffrench-Davis, Ricardo, and Ernesto Tironi, eds. *El cobre en el desarrollo nacional*. Santiago: Ediciones Nueva Universidad, 1974.
Finn, Janet L. *Tracing the Veins: Of Copper, Culture, and Community from Butte to Chuquicamata*. Berkeley and Los Angeles: University of California Press, 1998.
Fleet, Michael. *The Rise and Fall of Chilean Christian Democracy*. Princeton: Princeton University Press, 1985.
Flores Galindo, Alberto. *Los mineros de la Cerro de Pasco, 1900–1930: Un intento de caracterización social*. Lima: Universidad Católica de Lima, 1974.
French, John D. *The Brazilian Workers' ABC: Class Conflict and Alliances in Modern São Paulo*. Chapel Hill: University of North Carolina Press, 1992.
———. *Drowning in Laws: Labor Law and Brazilian Political Culture*. Chapel Hill: University of North Carolina Press, 2004.

French, William E. *A Peaceful and Working People: Manners, Morals, and Class Formation in Northern Mexico*. Albuquerque: University of New Mexico Press, 1996.
Gaete, Alfredo. *Código del Trabajo (concordado y anotado)*. Santiago: Ediciones Ercilla, 1945.
Gall, Norman. "Chile: The Struggle in the Copper Mines." *Dissent* (Winter 1973): 99–109.
Garcés, Eugenio. "Las ciudades del cobre: Del campamento de montaña al hotel minero como variaciones de la company town." *Revista de Estudios Urbanos Regionales* (EURE) 88 (2003): 131–48.
——— . *Las ciudades del salitre: Un estudio de las oficinas salitreras en la región de Antofagasta*. Santiago: Editorial Universitaria, 1988.
Gaudichaud, Franck. "La Central Única de Trabajadores, las luchas obreras y los cordones industriales en el período de la Unidad Popular en Chile (1970–1973)." *Revista Rebelión* (May 2003), www.rebelion.org.
——— . *Poder popular y cordones industriales: Testimonios sobre el movimiento popular urbano, 1970–1973*. Santiago: LOM, 2004.
Gedicks, Al. "The Nationalization of Copper in Chile: Antecedents and Consequences." *Review of Radical Political Economics* 5 (1973): 1–25.
Girvan, Norman. *Copper in Chile: A Study in Conflict Between Corporate and National Economy*. Kingston: Institute of Social and Economic Research, University of West Indies, 1972.
Glendenning, Miles. "The New Town 'Tradition': Past, Present—and Future?" In *Back from the Utopia: The Challenge of the Modern Movement*, edited by Hubert-Jan Henket and Hilde Henyen. Rotterdam: 010 Publishers, 2002.
González, Rodrigo, and Alonso Daire. *Los paros nacionales en Chile (1919–1973)*. Santiago: Centro de Estudios Democráticos de América Latina (CEDAL), 1984.
González, Sergio. *Hombres y mujeres de la pampa: Tarapacá en el ciclo del salitre*. Santiago: LOM, 2002.
Greaves, Thomas, and William Culver, eds. *Miners and Mining in the Americas*. London: Manchester University Press, 1985.
Gregory, Peter. *Industrial Wages in Chile*. Ithaca: Cornell University Press, 1967.
Gutiérrez, Eulogio, and Marcial Figueroa. *Chuquicamata: Su grandeza y sus dolores*. Santiago: Imprenta Cervantes, 1920.
Gutman, Herbert G. *Work, Culture, and Society in Industrializing America: Essays in American Working-Class and Social History*. New York: Knopf, 1976.
Hiriart, Luis. *Braden: Historia de una mina*. Santiago: Editorial Andes, 1964.
Holston, James. *The Modernist City: An Anthropological Critique of Brasilia*. Chicago: University of Chicago Press, 1990.
Huneeus, Pablo. *Estructura y dinámica social en los trabajadores del cobre*. Santiago: Instituto de Sociología Universidad Católica de Chile, 1974.
Hutchison, Elizabeth Q. *Labors Appropriate to Their Sex: Gender, Labor, and Politics in Urban Chile, 1900–1930*. Durham: Duke University Press, 2001.
Illanes, María Angélica. *La dominación silenciosa: Productores y prestamistas en la minería de Atacama, Chile, 1830–1860*. Santiago: Instituto Profesional Superior Blas Cañas, 1992.
Instituto Nacional de Estadísticas. *Población de los centro poblados de Chile, 1875–1992*. Santiago: Instituto Nacional de Estadística, n.d.

James, Daniel J. *Resistance and Integration: Peronism and the Argentine Working Class, 1946–1976.* New York: Cambridge University Press, 1993.
Jelin, Elizabeth, and Juan Carlos Torres. "Los nuevos trabajadores en América Latina: Una reflexión sobre la tesis de la aristocracia obrera." *Desarrollo Económico* 85 (1982): 3–23.
Jobet, Julio César. *Historia del Partido Socialista de Chile.* 2d ed. Santiago: Ediciones Documentas, 1987.
Kerr, Clark, and Abraham Siegel. "The Inter-industry Propensity to Strike: An International Comparison." In *Industrial Conflict,* edited by Arthur Kornhauser. New York: McGraw-Hill, 1954.
Klubock, Thomas M. *Contested Communities: Class, Gender, and Politics in El Teniente's Copper Mine, 1904–1951.* Durham: Duke University Press, 1998.
———. "Nationalism, Race, and the Politics of Imperialism: Workers and North American Capital in the Chilean Copper Industry." In *Reclaiming the Political in Latin American History: Essays from the North,* edited by Gilbert M. Joseph. Durham: Duke University Press, 2001.
Kuntz, Julio. *Informe sobre un viaje a los principales centros mineros del Departamento de Chañaral.* Santiago: Imprenta y Litografía Universo, 1923.
Labrianidis, L. "Flexibility in Production Through Subcontracting: The Case of the Poultry Meat Industry in Greece." *Environmental and Planning A* 27 (1995): 193–209.
Latcham, Ricardo. *Chuquicamata: Estado Yankee.* Santiago: Editorial Nascimento, 1926.
Lobato, Mirta Z. *La vida en las fábricas: Trabajo, protesta y política en una comunidad obrera, Berisso (1904–1970).* Buenos Aires: Prometeo, 2001.
Loveman, Brian. *Chile: The Legacy of Hispanic Capitalism.* New York: Oxford University Press, 2001.
———. *Struggle in the Countryside: Politics and Rural Labor in Chile, 1919–1973.* Bloomington: Indiana University Press, 1976.
Loveman, Brian, and Elizabeth Lira. *Las ardientes cenizas del olvido: Vía chilena de reconciliación política, 1932–1994.* Santiago: LOM, 2000.
Macchiavello, Santiago. *El problema de la industria del cobre en Chile y sus proyecciones económicas y sociales.* Santiago: Imprenta Fiscal de la Peninteciaría, 1923.
Mac-Clure, Oscar, and Iván Valenzuela Rabi. *Conflictos de la Gran Minería del Cobre 1973–1983.* Santiago: Centro de Estudios Democráticos de América Latina (CEDAL), 1985.
Maldonado, Héctor. *Albores de el mineral El Salvador.* Potrerillos, Chile: Imprenta Cobresal, 1989.
———. *El alegre y legendario Potrerillos del ayer.* Copiapó, Chile: Talleres Gráficos de la Universidad de Atacama, 1983.
Mallon, Florencia. *The Defense of Community in Peru's Central Highlands: Peasant Struggles and Capitalist Transition, 1860–1940.* Princeton: Princeton University Press, 1983.
Mamalakis, Markos. *The Growth and Structure of the Chilean Economy: From Independence to Allende.* New Haven: Yale University Press, 1976.
———. *Historical Statistics of Chile: Demography and Labor Force.* Wesport, Conn.: Greenwood, 1980.

Mamalakis, Markos, and Clark W. Reynolds,eds. *Essays on the Chilean Economy.* Homewood, Ill.: Richard D. Irwin, 1965.
Manns, Patricio. *Las grandes masacres.* Santiago: Quimantú, 1972.
Marcosson, Isaac. *Anaconda.* New York: Dodd, Mead, 1976.
Matus, Raúl. *Régimen jurídico del trabajo en las minas.* Santiago: Editorial Universitaria, 1962.
McBride, James. *The Mission, Means, and Memories of Arizona Miners: A History of Mining in Arizona from Pre-history to Present.* Phoenix: Arizona Mining Association, n.d.
Medina, Juan Andrés. "La Central Única de Trabajadores y el gobierno de la Unidad Popular: Auge y desaparición." *Revista de Historia* (Universidad de Concepción) 1 (1991): 63–86.
Meller, Patricio, ed. *Dilemas y debates en torno al cobre.* Santiago: Dolmen Ediciones, 2002.
———. *The Unidad Popular and the Pinochet Dictatorship: A Political Economy Analysis.* New York: St. Martin's Press, 2000.
———. *Un siglo de economía política chilena (1890–1990).* Santiago: Editorial Andrés Bello, 1996.
Mercier, Laurie. *Anaconda: Labor, Community, and Culture in Montana's Smelter City.* Urbana: University of Illinois Press, 2001.
Mikesell, Raymond F. *The World Copper Industry: Structure and Economic Analysis.* Baltimore: Johns Hopkins University Press, 1979.
Ministerio de Vivienda y Urbanismo. *Chañaral: Estudio pre-inversional.* Santiago: n.p., n.d.
Monteon, Michael. *Chile and the Great Depression: The Politics of Underdevelopment, 1927–1948.* Tempe: Arizona State University, 1998.
———. "The Enganche in the Chilean Nitrate Sector," *Latin American Perspectives* 3 (1979): 66–79.
Moran, Theodore H. *Multinational Corporations and the Politics of Dependence: Copper in Chile.* Princeton: Princeton University Press, 1977.
Moreno, Julio. *Yankee Don't Go Home! Mexican Nationalism, American Business Culture, and the Shaping of Modern Mexico, 1920–1950.* Chapel Hill: University of North Carolina Press, 2003.
Morris, James, and Roberto Oyaneda. *Afiliación y finanzas sindicales en Chile, 1932–1959.* Santiago: Instituto de Administración de la Universidad de Chile (INSORA), 1962.
Muñoz, Liliana. *Estudio ocupacional de la minería del cobre.* Santiago: Servicio Nacional del Empleo, 1971.
Muñoz, Oscar. *Chile y su industrialización. Pasado, crisis y opciones.* Santiago: CIEPLAN (Corporación de Estudios para Latinoamérica), 1986.
Murphy, Mary. *Mining Cultures: Men, Women, and Leisure in Butte, 1914–41.* Urbana: University of Illinois Press, 1997.
Nash, June. *We Eat the Mines and the Mines Eat Us: Dependency and Exploitation in Bolivian Tin Mines.* New York: Columbia University Press, 1979.
Názer, Ricardo. *José Tomás Urmeneta: Un empresario del siglo XIX.* Santiago: Centro de Investigaciones Diego Barros Arana, 1994.
Novoa, Eduardo. *La batalla por el cobre: La nacionalización chilena del cobre; Comentarios y documentos.* Santiago: Quimantú, 1972.

O'Brien, Thomas. *The Century of U.S. Capitalism in Latin America.* Albuquerque: University of New Mexico Press, 1999.
———. *The Revolutionary Mission: American Enterprise in Latin America, 1900–1945.* Cambridge: Cambridge University Press, 1999.
———. "'Rich Beyond the Dreams of Avarice': The Guggenheims in Chile." *Business History Review* 63 (1989): 122–59.
Oppenheim, Lois H. *Politics in Chile: Democracy, Authoritarianism, and the Search for Development.* Boulder, Colo.: Westview Press, 1999.
Ortiz, Fernando. *El movimiento obrero en Chile (1891–1919).* Madrid: Michay, 1985.
Palma, J. Gabriel. "Chile, 1914–1935: De economía exportadora a sustitutiva de importaciones," *Estudios CIEPLAN* 12 (1984): 61–88.
Parker, David S. *The Idea of the Middle Class: White-Collar Workers and Peruvian Society, 1900–1950.* University Park: Pennsylvania State University Press, 1998.
Parpart, Jane L. *Labor and Capital on the African Copperbelt.* Philadelphia: Temple University Press, 1983.
Peppe, Patrick V. *The Frei Government and the Chilean Labor Movement.* New York: New York University Ibero-American Language and Area Center, 1974.
Petras, James. "Chile: Nacionalización, transformaciones socioeconómicas y participación popular." *Cuadernos de la Realidad Nacional* 11 (1972): 3–24.
Petras, James, and Maurice Zeitlin. "Miners and Agrarian Radicalism." *American Sociological Review* 4 (1967): 578–86.
———. *El radicalismo político de la clase trabajadora Chilena.* Buenos Aires: Centro Editor de América Latina, 1969.
Piñera, José. *La revolución laboral en Chile.* Santiago: Zig-Zag, 1990.
Pinto, Julio, ed. *Episodios de historia minera. Estudios de historia social y económica de la minería chilena, siglos XVIII–XIX.* Santiago: Universidad de Santiago, 1997.
———. *Trabajos y rebeldías en la pampa salitrera: El ciclo del salitre y la reconfiguración de las identidades populares (1850–1900).* Santiago: Universidad de Santiago, 1998.
Pinto, Julio, and Verónica Valdivia. *¿Revolución proletaria o querida chusma? Socialismo y Alessandrismo en la pugna de la politización pampina (1911–1932).* Santiago: LOM, 2001.
Pizarro, Crisóstomo. *La huelga obrera en Chile, 1890–1970.* Santiago: Ediciones SUR, 1986.
Poblete, Moisés. *El derecho del trabajo y la seguridad social en Chile: Sus realizaciones, panomara americano XXV años de legislación social.* Santiago: Editorial Jurídica, 1949.
Porteous, Douglas. "The Company State: A Chilean Case-Study." *Canadian Geographer* 2 (1973): 113–26.
———. "Social Class in Atacama Company-Towns." *Annals of the Association of American Geographers* 3 (1974): 409–17.
Porzio, Huguette. *El capital humano en la industria del cobre y particularmente en Chuquicamata.* Santiago: Editorial Universitaria, 1961.
Power, Margaret. *Right-Wing Women in Chile: Feminine Power and the Struggle Against Allende, 1964–1973.* University Park: Pennsylvania State University Press, 2002.

Przeworski, Joanne F. *The Decline of the Copper Industry in Chile and the Entrance of North American Capital, 1870–1916*. New York: Arno Press, 1980.
Ramírez Necochea, Hernán. *Historia del movimiento obrero en Chile, siglo XIX*. Santiago: Ediciones LAR, 1956.
Comisión Nacional para la Verdad y Reconciliación. *Report of the Chilean National Commission on Truth and Reconciliation*. Translated by Phillip E. Berryman. Notre Dame: University of Notre Dame Press, 1993.
Reynolds, Clark W. "Development Problems of an Export Economy: The Case of Chile and Copper." In *Essays on the Chilean Economy*, edited by Markos Mamalakis and Clark W. Reynolds. Homewood, Ill.: Richard D. Irwin, 1965.
Rimingler, Gaston V. "International Differences in the Strike Propensity of Coal Miners: Experience in Four Countries." *Industrial and Labor Relations Review* (1959): 389–405.
Rock, David. *Latin America in the 1940s: War and Postwar Transitions*. Berkeley and Los Angeles: University of California Press, 1994.
Rojas, Jorge. *La dictadura de Ibáñez y los sindicatos (1927–1931)*. Santiago: Centro de Investigaciones Barros Arana, 1993.
Romualdi, Serafino. *Presidents and Peons: Recollections of a Labor Ambassador in Latin America*. New York: Funk and Wagnalls, 1967.
Rosemblatt, Karin A. *Gendered Compromises: Political Cultures and the State in Chile, 1920–1950*. Chapel Hill: University of North Carolina Press, 2000.
Ruiz-Tagle, Jaime. *El sindicalismo chileno después del Plan Laboral*. Santiago: Programa de Estudios del Trabajo (PET), 1985.
Salazar, Gabriel. *Labradores, peones y proletarios: Formación y crisis de la sociedad popular chilena del siglo XIX*. Santiago: Ediciones SUR, 1985.
Salzinger, Leslie. *Genders in Production: Making Workers in Mexico's Global Factories*. Berkeley and Los Angeles: University of California Press, 2003.
Samaniego, Augusto. "Los límites de la estrategia de la unidad y el Área de Propiedad Social." *Contribuciones Científicas y Tecnológicas* 109 (1995): 21–35.
Sariego, Juan Luis. *Enclaves y minerales en el norte de México: Historia social de los mineros de Cananea y Nueva Rosita, 1900–1970*. Mexico City: Centro de Investigaciones y Estudios Superiores en Antropologia Social (CIESAS), 1988.
———. "Los mineros de la Real del Monte: Un proletariado en formación y transición." *Revista Mexicana de Sociología* 4 (1980): 1379–404.
Saunders, William B. "The Construction of La Ola Pipe Line in Chile." *Transactions* (American Society of Civil Engineers) 1795 (1930).
Schatz, Ronald W. *The Electrical Workers: A History of Labor at General Electric and Westinghouse, 1923–60*. Urbana: University of Illinois Press, 1983.
Scott, James C. *Seeing Like a State: How Certain Schemes to Improve the Human Conditions Have Failed*. New Haven: Yale University Press, 1999.
Seminario de problemas regionales de Atacama organizado por la Universidad de Chile. Santiago: Universidad de Chile, 1957.
Silva, J. Pablo. "The Origins of White-Collar Privilege in Chile: Arturo Alessandri, Law 6,020, and the Pursuit of a Corporatist Consensus, 1933–1938." *Labor* 3 (2006): 87–112.
Spalding, Hobart. "U.S. and Latin American Labor: The Dynamics of Imperialist Control." *Latin American Perspectives* 3 (1976): 45–69.

Stabili, María Rosaria. "Relaciones de producción capitalista: Los empresarios norteamericanos en la minería del cobre de Chile (1905–1918)." *Revista Latinoamericana de Historia Económica y Social* (HISLA) 6 (1985): 43–57.
Striffler, Steve, ed. *Banana Wars: Power, Production, and History in the Americas.* Durham: Duke University Press, 2003.
———. *In the Shadows of State and Capital: The United Fruit Company, Popular Struggle, and Agrarian Restructuring in Ecuador, 1900–1995.* Durham: Duke University Press, 2002.
Tanzer, Michael. *The Race for Resources: Continuing Struggles over Minerals and Fuels.* New York: Monthly Review Press, 1980.
Tidball, Eugene C. "What Ever Happened to the Anaconda Company?" *Montana* 47, no. 2 (1997): 60–68.
Tinsman, Heidi. *Partners in Conflict: The Politics of Gender, Sexuality, and Labor in the Chilean Agrarian Reform, 1950–1973.* Durham: Duke University Press, 2002.
Topik, Steven, Carlos Marichal, and Zephyr Frank eds. *From Silver to Cocaine: Latin American Commodity Chains and the Building of the World Economy.* Durham: Duke University Press, 2006.
United States Department of Labor, Bureau of Labor Statistics. *Foreign Labor Information: Labor in Chile.* n.p.: U.S. Department of Labor, 1956.
———. *Labor in Chile.* n.p.: U.S. Department of Labor, 1962.
———. *Labor Law and Practice in Chile.* n.p: U.S. Department of Labor, 1969.
Urzúa Valenzuela, Germán. *Historia política de Chile y evolución electoral (desde 1810 a 1992).* Santiago: Editorial Jurídica, 1992.
Valdés, Víctor, and Aurelio Butelman. *Aspectos económicos y laborales de la Gran Minería del Cobre, 1955–66.* Santiago, Chile: n.p., 1969.
Valenzuela, Arturo. *Political Brokers in Chile: Local Government in a Centralized Polity.* Durham: Duke University Press, 1977.
Valenzuela, Arturo, and Samuel Valenzuela eds. *Military Rule in Chile: Dictatorship and Opposition.* Baltimore: Johns Hopkins University Press, 1986.
Valenzuela, Luis. "The Chilean Copper Smelting Industry in the Mid-nineteenth Century: Phases of Expansion and Stagnation, 1834–1858," *Journal of Latin American Studies* 3 (1992): 507–50.
———. "The Copper Smelting Company 'Urmeneta y Errázuriz' of Chile: An Economic Profile, 1860–1880." *The Americas* 2 (1996): 235–71.
Valenzuela, J. Samuel. "Labor Formation and Politics: The Chilean and French Cases in Comparative Perspective, 1850–1950." Ph.D. diss., Columbia University, 1979.
Vargas, Zaragosa. *Proletarians of the North: A History of Mexican Industrial Workers in Detroit and the Midwest, 1917–1933.* Berkeley and Los Angeles: University of California Press, 1993.
Vayssière, Pierre. *Un siècle de capitalisme minier au Chili, 1830–1930.* Paris: Editions du Centre National de la Recherche Scientifique (C.N.R.S.), 1980.
Vera, Mario. *El cobre en el centro de la política.* Santiago: Centro de Estudios Sociales (CESOC), 1994.
———. *La política económica del cobre en Chile.* Santiago: Ediciones de la Universidad de Chile, 1961.

Vera, Mario, and Elmo Catalán. *La encrucijada del cobre.* Santiago: Editorial Prensa Latinoamérica, 1965.
Winn, Peter, ed. *Victims of the Chilean Miracle: Workers and Neoliberalism in the Pinochet Era, 1973–2002.* Durham: Duke University Press, 2004.
———. *Weavers of the Revolution: The Yarur Workers and Chile's Road to Socialism.* New York: Oxford University Press, 1986.
Alejandro Witker, ed. *Archivo Salvador Allende: Historia documental del PSCH, 1933–1993; Forjadores y signos de renovación.* Mexico City: IELCO, 1993.
Zapata, Francisco, ed. *¿Flexibles y productivos?Estudios sobre flexibilidad laboral en México.* Mexico City: El Colegio de México, 1998.
———. *Los mineros de Chuquicamata ¿Productores o proletarios?* Mexico City: Centro de Estudios Sociológicos, Colegio de México, 1975.
———. "Mineros y militares en la coyuntura actual de Bolivia, Chile, Perú (1976–1978)." *Revista Mexicana de Sociología* 39 (1977): 719–31.
———. "Las relaciones entre la Junta Militar y los trabajadores chilenos: 1973–1978." *Foro Internacional* 2 (1979): 191–219.
———. "Towards a Latin American Sociology of Labour." *Journal of Latin American Studies* 2 (1990): 375–502.

INDEX

absenteeism in copper mines, 114–19
African copper industry, impact in Chile of, 75, 88
agricultural crisis in Chile, 49
Aguirre Cerda, Pedro, 59–61, 145
Ahumada, Jorge, 2
Alessandri, Arturo, 25
Alessandri, Jorge, 116, 126
Alexander, Robert, 73, 77–78, 83, 102, 105
Alfaro, Walter, 149
Allende, Salvador: copper workers and, 2, 61, 86–87, 171–77; Frei and, 145–54; nationalization of copper industry and, 1, 5–6, 126, 149, 155–60, 168, 196; Nuevo Trato criticized by, 98, 100
Alliance for Progress, 137
Alvarado, Víctor, 172
American Brass Company, 15
American Federation of Labor-Congress of Industrial Organizations (AFL-CIO), 82–87, 182–84
American Institute for Free Labor Development (AIFLD), 182–83
American School (Andes Copper Company), 34–35
Ampuero, Raúl, 61, 72–73, 77, 100
Anaconda Copper Company, 3; Atlantic Richfield purchase of, 14; Chilean government relations with, 93; Copper Workers Confederation denunciation of, 127–28; economic strategies of, 74–76; El Salvador project and, 107–19; Greater Butte Project of, 108–9; hiring process at, 28–29; historical background, 13–18; investment in Chile by, 11; joint ventures proposals with, 149; labor laws and influence of, 102–7; layoffs in Chile by, 133–37; management structure at, 26–32; nationalization of copper industry and, 152–54, 158–60; Nuevo Trato and, 96–100; political power of, 35; Potrerillos mine development by, 19–25; production and company restructuring trends, 137–44; strikes against, 68–70, 89–90; transformation of Chilean copper mining by, 13–14; U.S. labor leaders' criticism of, 85–86
Anaconda-Jurden Associates, 112
Andes Copper Company, 3–4; Chileanization and, 153; Chilean refineries of, 142–43; company towns constructed by, 38–48; contract workers for, 140–44; copper depletion and decline of, 75–76; El Salvador project and, 108, 110–19; employment and recruiting policies at, 48–56; foreign employees' community at, 32–35; general managers' roster for, 28; hiring process at, 28–29; history of, 16–17; Indio Muerto project and, 93; labor policies of, 8–12, 15–16, 37, 42–45; labor turnover at, 39, 50–51; layoffs by, 133–37; management structure at, 26–32; modernization efforts of, 11–12, 123–25; nationalization of copper industry and, 158–60; police and security guards at, 43, 46–47; Potrerillos mine development by, 19–25; productivity and restructuring of, 138–44; strikes against, 67–70, 129–33, 147; unions in, 59; Welfare Department of, 39–48; women employees in, 54–56
Andino newspaper, 97, 114, 123
Angell, Alan, 60
Araya, Bernardo, 90
Arellano Stark, Sergio, 180–81
Areo Survey Company, 109–10
Arizona Mining Company, 19–20
Association of Copper Supervisors (Asociación Nacional de Supervisores del Cobre) (ANSCO), 173–75
Atlantic Richfield Company (ARCO), Anaconda Copper Company purchased by, 14

214   INDEX

Avance newspaper, 61
Aylwin, Patricio, 190

balnearios populares (vacation sites), 169–71
Bancroft copper mine, 75
Barquito mining camp, 39, 41–43, 159; telephone operators strike at, 176; wartime restrictions in, 68; working conditions in, 134–35
Barrera, Manuel, 6–7
Barría, Jorge, 6, 59, 131
Bart, Manuel, 88
base production statistics, Nuevo Trato and, 94, 99–100
Bates, Ruth, 34
Bennett, William J., 27, 129, 133, 136
Bergquist, Charles, 9
Blest, Clotario, 86–87
blister copper production, at Potrerillos mine, 24–25
blue-collar workers, 49–53; Copper Workers Federation and, 77–82; family allowances for, 79n.56; impact of modernization on, 139–44; Labor Code provisions for, 50, 52–53, 57–63; layoffs of, 134–37; military coup of 1973 and, 182–85; modernization of El Salvador and, 122–25; strikes by, 176–77
Bowers, Claude, 85
Braden, William, 16–17, 25
Braden Copper, 147
Brazil, geological exploration in, 109
Brilladeros, Benigno, 134–35
Brinckerhoff, Charles, 27, 110–11, 117–18
British Guiana, geological exploration in, 109
Bustos, Manuel, 183, 185

Calcument mining, 19
Callaway, L. A., 29
Cantuarias, Orlando, 160, 174
"Caravan of Death," 180–81
Carey, Guillermo, 26
Carmona, Juan de Dios, 61, 104
Carpenter, Stewart, 111
Castillo, Bernardino, 183–85
Castillo, Jorge, 148
Castillo, Maguindo, 181
Castillo Cerda, Alamiro, 119
Castro, Baltazar, 76, 88
Central Joint Salaries Board (Comisión Mixta de Sueldos), 41
Central Única de Trabajadores (CUT), 78, 86–87, 89, 101, 104; government relations with, 146; military coup and repression of, 181–85; nationalization of copper industry and, 159–60, 162–67; political activism of, 147–54
Centro de Alojamiento, at Potrerillos, 192–93
Cerro de Pasco Corporation, 148–49
Chañaral (city): El Salvador project and, 118–19; housing for miners in, 42–43, 45; impact of Potrerillos mine on, 20–25, 44–48; political activism in, 61–63; refinery construction project in, 143
Chelén, Alejandro, 61, 76, 100, 124, 140
Chibuluma copper mine, 75
Chicago Boys, 183
Chilean Central Bank, control of copper industry, 95
Chileanization policy, 148–54
Chilean Workers Confederation (Confederación de Trabajadores de Chile) (CTCH), 60, 90
Chile Exploration Company, 17, 111; as Anaconda shareholder, 153; strikes against, 68–70; technological innovations of, 138
Christian Democratic Party, 53, 61, 144, 156; Chileanization proposal and, 150–51; military coup of 1973 and, 182–85; nationalization proposals and, 153–54; union relations with, 145–46, 148, 171–77, 184–85
Christian Left Party, 156n.1
Chuquicamata mine: Anaconda purchase of, 17; base production at, 94; Chileanization project at, 149–50; collective bargaining at, 147; company store at, 46–48; labor history at, 7; layoffs at, 133; local government operations in, 141–42; management and hiring structure at, 26, 29, 31; modernization and restructuring of, 138; nationalization of copper industry and, 159–60, 168–71; Programa de Participación at, 167; refinery construction at, 143; Strategic Alliance reforms and, 192–93; strike activity at, 67–70, 87–90, 105, 150, 155, 174–75, 184–85; sulphide plant at, 112; volunteer programs at, 170; Women's Committee at, 104; worker resettlement at, 142
Claro, Jaime, 142–43
class issues: Chilean professionals in mining management and, 144; company town communities and, 38–48; Copper Workers Federation interclass alliances and, 77–82; copper workers' labor history and, 7–12;

INDEX 215

democratic transition and Labor Plan and, 185–90; foreign employees in Chilean mining and, 35; Labor Code impact on, 58–63; modernization of El Salvador mining camp and, 122–25; nationalization of copper and, 168–71; for white- and blue-collar mine workers, 49–53. *See also* blue-collar workers; white-collar workers
Clements, Ted, 32
Cobresal mine, 163–72, 174–75
Cold War politics: copper industry and, 94–95, 108; impact in Chile of, 65, 72, 74, 82–87; international labor solidarity and, 82–87
collective bargaining: copper workers' system for, 59–60; military coup and interruption of, 181–85; political agendas and, 129–33
Comando Nacional de Trabajadores (CNT), 188–90
Comité Paritario de Participación, 162–67
Communist Party of Chile: economic nationalism and, 65–66; government criticism of, 106; international labor solidarity against, 83–87; miners' involvement in, 53; political repression of, 11, 65–66, 70–74, 90; Popular Unity movement and, 156n.1; Socialists' alliance with, 86–87; union coalition with, 60–63. *See also* Partido Obrero Socialista
community organization: company town construction and, 38–48; labor movement bond with, 7, 62–63; modernization of mining and, 120–25; nationalization of copper industry and, 167–71; strike support and, 66–67
Compañía Exploradora Cordillera, 149
Compañía Minera Andina (Andina Mining Company), 149, 160
Compañía Minera Potrerillos, 16
Compañía Sudamericana de Minas, 110
company store: impact of modernization on, 139; modernization of, El Salvador mining camp, 120–25; social and political functions of, 45–48; as strike issue, 87
company town: declining importance of, 141–44; nationalization and dismantling of, 168–71; Potrerillos mine as example of, 37–48
compensation system *(compensaciones)* at Chilean mines, 47–48
Concertación de Partidos por la Democracia (Coalition of Parties for Democracy), 190–93

conciliation board *(juntas de conciliación)*, 57
Con-Con oil refinery, 95
Confederation of Maritime Workers, 182
consumer price index (CPI), mine workers' salaries and, 89–90
contract workers, introduction of, 139–44
Coordinating Workers' Committee, 164–65
Coordinator of Inter-American Affairs (CIAA), 83
Copper Club (Andes Copper Company), 33
Copper Corporation, 152
copper industry in Chile: African competition with, 75; Anaconda's transformation of, 13–18; economic conditions and, 1–2, 74–76, 90–93; historical background, 13; layoffs and, 133–37; modernization of, 93–94; nationalization of, 1, 5; Nuevo Trato impact on, 94–100; production and company restructuring trends in, 137–44
copper mine workers: Allende and, 156–60; class issues among, 49–53; collective identity of, 9–12; demobilization of, in 1970s, 6; democratic ideology and, 190–93; *enganche* system and, 48–56; Frei supported by, 145–54; government conflicts with, 146–54; labor history of, 6–12; migratory patterns of, 48–56; nationalization of copper industry and, 5–6; organization at Potrerillos by, 22–25; political repression of, 93–94, 181–85; segregation from foreign supervisors, 4; unionization and political activism of, 2, 37; working conditions for, 3
Copper Workers Confederation (Confederación de Trabajadores del Cobre) (CTC): Allende and, 2; Chileanization project opposed by, 150151; contract workers denounced by, 140–41; foreign investors and, 3–4; international solidarity with, 82–87, 104–5; labor demands of, 103–7; layoffs protested by, 136–37; military coup and repression of, 181–85; nationalist ideology of, 100; nationalization of copper industry and, 158–60, 163–67; national strike initiative of, 188–90; political activities of, 76–82, 91; strike activities of, 74, 129–33; union movement and, 127–28
Copper Workers Federation (FTC), Strategic Alliance and, 191–93
Corbalán, Salomón, 100
Corporación del Cobre (CODELCO), 3, 160, 174, 184–85., 187–93

Corporación Nacional de l Medio Ambiente (National Commission on the Environment) (CONAMA), 192–93
Council of State (Consejo de Estado), 182
cuchareos protests, 185
cultural programs in mining camps, nationalization of copper and, 169–71

Daire, Alonso, 131
Delfín, Eduardo, 104–5
Democratic Party of Chile, 22
democratic transition in Chile: copper workers and, 190–93; economic transformation and, 179–97; impact on copper mining of, 5; labor history and, 9–12; labor reforms and, 185–90
Development Corporation (Corporación de Fomento Fabril) (CORFO), 95
de Viado, Manuel, 45, 55
Díaz Iturrieta, José, 67
Drake, Paul, 181
Dutton, Adam, 26-27, 30, 143–44

economic conditions: Allende's socialist reforms and, 156–60; Chilean mining and, 17–18; collapse of labor movement and, 186–90; copper industry deterioration and, 74–76, 90–91; Copper Workers' Federation nationalization demands and, 78–82; democratic transition in Chile and, 179–97; labor history and, 11–12; military coup of 1973 and, 179–85; mining layoffs and, 133–37; nationalist ideology and, 65–66; nationalization of copper and, 170–71; Nuevo Trato and, 94–100; political repression and, 65–91; productivity and restructuring of copper industry and, 137–44; strike demands tied to, 69–70, 87–90. *See also* inflationary pressures in Chile
Educación Primaria Obligatoria (Compulsory Elementary Education) law (1920), 44–45
education programs in mining camps, 33–35, 44–45, 169
El Cobre newspaper, 132, 136, 140
El Día newspaper, 48, 97, 140
El Diario Ilustrado newspaper, 106
electrolytic refining process, copper production and, 24
El Mercurio newspaper, 173, 175
El Progreso newspaper, 41
El Salvador mine, 3–4; Chilean professionals at, 144; construction of, 11–12, 32; contract workers at, 140–44; expansion and development project at, 107–19; government takeover of responsibilities in, 141–44; impact of modernization on, 139; Indio Muerto project at, 93; joint ventures proposals involving, 149; labor history at, 8–12; layoffs at, 133–37; military coup of 1973 and repression at, 180–85; mining camp and housing at, 39, 41–43, 119–25; nationalization of copper industry and, 158–60, 163–71; Nuevo Trato and, 100; Programa de Participación at, 167; proposed closing of, 6, 195–97; salaries and bonuses at, 56; Strategic Alliance reforms and, 192–93; strike activity at, 147, 150, 175–76, 184–85; violence against workers at, 147–48; volunteer programs at, 170
El Siglo newspaper, 69, 71–72, 87, 102–4, 136
El Teniente mine: Allende's speech at, 1; base production at, 94; Chileanization agreement involving, 148–49; Communist Party influence in, 61; democratic transition and Labor Plan reforms and, 187–90; foreign staff at, 144; history of, 16–17; layoffs at, 136; local government operations in, 141–42; military coup of 1973 and, 182–85; nationalization of copper industry and, 159–60; "Operación Valle," 142; Strategic Alliance reforms and, 192–93; strike activity at, 2, 67–70, 101, 147, 150, 155, 176–77; volunteer programs at, 170
employment practices in Chilean copper mines, 26–32; emergency employment programs and, 186–90; impact of modernization on, 139–44; job segregation in mines, 50–56; Labor Code regulation of, 58–63; layoffs and job insecurity and, 133–37
Empresa Nacional de Minería, 161
enganche system: Labor Code abolishment of, 58; mine worker recruitment through, 48–56
Engineering and Mining Journal, 113
escala móvil, 176
Espinoza, Edmundo, 133
Estévez, Jaime, 163

Faivovich, Jaime, 174
Falange Nacional, 61, 104
family allowances: Copper Workers' Federation demands for, 79; government support for, 89–90

Federation of Chilean Workers (Federación Obrera de Chile, FOCH): activism of, 39; evolution of, 22–23
Feeney, James, 34
Feliú, Arturo, 160
Fernández, Sergio, 183
fichas (tokens), Labor Code abolishment of, 58
Finn, Janet, 7–8, 67
Flores, Roberto, 61, 104
foreign employees in Chilean mines: Chilean professionals as replacement for, 143–44; community relations among, 32–35; government takeover of responsibilities from, 141–44; modernization efforts at El Salvador and segregation of, 124–25; nationalization campaign and exodus of, 159–60; salary comparisons with Chilean miners, 131–33; skilled workforce in mining as, 26–32
foreign ownership of Chilean copper mines: Chilean economic conditions and, 137; Copper Workers' Federation nationalization demands and, 78–82; government relations with, 103–7; impact on copper workers of, 3–4, 11–12, 53; joint ventures agreements and, 148; nationalization efforts and, 148–54; Nuevo Trato and, 94–100, 103–4
Forsyth, H. F., 30
Frei Montalva, Eduardo, 105, 144–54
French, William, 45
Frente de Acción Popular (FRAP), 151
Frente del Nacional Pueblo (People's National Front), 86
Friedman, Milton, 183

Galleguillos, Víctor, 61
Gálvez, Cristián, 55
Gálvez, Hugo, 137
García, Gilberto, 181
García, Ricardo, 181
Gaudichaud, Frank, 161
gender issues: for blue- and white-collar mine workers, 54–56; copper workers' labor history and, 7; for foreign employees in Chilean copper mining, 34–35; hiring practices at Chilean mining companies and, 29; Labor Code impact on, 58–63; strike support and, 67–70
General Workers Assembly, 163–67
geological exploration, El Salvador project and, 109
Glover, Roy, 93, 107

gold roll, abolishment of, 174–77
González, Félix, 74
González, Rodrigo, 131
González Galleguillos, Oscar, 164
González Videla, Gabriel, 65–66, 70–74, 102, 145; Copper Workers Federation and, 77–82; state capitalism ideology of, 95; U.S. labor leaders and, 85
Great Depression, impact on copper mining of, 24–25
Greater Butte Project (Anaconda Copper Company), 108–9
Greninger, Irl, 66
Group of Ten, 183–85
Guggenheim brothers, 17
Gurupi mine (Brazil), 109
Gutiérrez, Pedro Samuel, 147, 164

Hales, Alejandro, 153
Henshaw, Helen, 34
Herrera, Oscar, 89
Hilsinger, John, 30
historiography, copper workers' labor history and, 6–12
Hoffman, Alvin, 38
housing in Chilean mining camps: for Chilean mine workers, 39–48; for foreign workers, 31–35, 40; modernization of, 120–25; nationalization of copper mining, 167–71; Potrerillos Plan and, 192–93; for women mine employees, 55–56
Huachipato steel plant, 55, 84, 95
Humphrey, Thomas Z., 29, 33
Humphrey, William, 33–34
Huneeus, Pablo, 27, 42

Ibañez, Bernardo, 72, 83–84, 90
Ibañez del Campo, Carlos, 11, 25, 83, 89; Anaconda Copper Company and, 93; copper workers and, 94, 100–107, 145, 151
import substitutions, Nuevo Trato and, 94–100
Independent Popular Action (API), 156n.1
Indio Muerto project, 93, 110–19
Indoamérica newspaper, 172
Industrial Mining Federation (Federación Industrial Minera) (FIM), 67, 104
inflationary pressures in Chile: collective bargaining agreements and, 129–33; national political crises and, 101–7; Nuevo Trato and, 96–100; politicalization and radicalization as response to, 145–54. *See also* economic conditions

Instituto Nacional de Capacitación (INACAP), 166
Inter-American Confederation of Workers (Confederaciónon Interamericana del Trabajo) (CIT), 83
Inter-American Labor Organization (Organización Interamericana del Trabajo) (ORIT), 73, 184; Copper Workers' Confederation and, 82–87, 91, 105
"Internal Security" law of 1937 (Ley de Seguridad Interior del Estado), 69
International Confederation of Free Trade Unions (ICFTU), 83
international copper market, Chilean mining practices and, 3–5
International Labor Organization (ILO), 68
International Petroleum Company, 153
International Union of Mine, Mill and Smelter Workers, 84

James, Daniel, 66
Jaramillo, Rodolfo, 41
Jiménez, Tucapel, 181, 183
Jobet, Julio César, 72–73
job segregation in mines, 50–56
joint ventures agreements, Chilean copper mining and, 148–49
Junta de Conciliación para la Gran Minería del Cobre, 106
Jurden, Wilbur, 20, 26, 112–13

Kennecott mining company, 13, 16–18, 35; base production at, 94; Chileanization agreement with, 148–49; labor laws and influence of, 102–7; nationalization of copper industry and, 158–60
Klein-Sacks mission, 101–2
Klubock, Thomas, 7–8, 67
Koepel, Norbert, 27, 111
Korean War, impact on Chilean copper industry of, 80–82
Kuchs, Oscar M., 21

La Africana mine, 17; management and hiring structure at, 29
Labor Code, 37; blue- and white-collar distinctions in, 50, 52–53; *enganche* system abolished by, 48; family allowances provisions of, 79n.56; government production decrees in, 69; layoff obligations in, 133–37; political and social impact of, 56–63; reform proposals for, 102–7; union organization and, 57–63, 65–66; workplace transformation requirements under, 76
labor force: anti-Communist legislation and divisions in, 72–74; Chileanization proposal opposed by, 150–54; contract workers in, 139–44; El Salvador project and role of, 111–19; history of copper workers in, 6–12; impact of unionization on, 56–63; instability in Chile of, 38–48; migratory patterns of mine workers, 48–56; military coup and repression of, 179–85; mining employment and recruiting patterns, 48–56; nationalization of copper industry and, 160–67, 171–77; national politics and role of, 100–107, 128–29; political repression of, 44–48, 65–91, 103–7; at Potrerillos mine, 21–25; size changes in mining industry of, 50–51; strike activities and, 66–70; unemployment threats and activism of, 76; urban resettlement of, 141–44; violence against, 147
Labor Plan, democratic transition and, 185–90
La Exótica mine, 149, 174–75
Lafertte, Elías, 80
Laist, Frederick, 27, 29
La Mina mining camp, 39; women employees at, 55–56
La Nación newspaper, 106, 151
La Ola Dam, 22
La Ola pipeline, 21, 23
Las Vegas mining camp, 39, 42
Latin America: Communism in, 65; export sector and labor history in, 8–12
La Usina newspaper, 53, 68, 70–74
Law for the Permanent Defense of Democracy, 72–73, 102, 105; labor challenges to, 77–82, 87
layoffs in Chilean copper industry, labor prevention efforts concerning, 133–37
Ley de Estabilizaciín de Precios, Remuneraciones y Pensiones, 102
literacy campaigns, nationalization of copper and, 169–71
Llanta mining camp, 39, 43
Lo Aguirre mine, 17
loncheras vacías, 184
London Metal Exchange, copper trading on, 94
López, Luis, 134–35

López, Víctor, 31–32
López Aliaga, Luis, 73, 84

Magalhaes, Manuel, 61–62, 76, 104, 117
Magallanes oil industry, 55
Magna Copper Corporation, 113n.74
Mamalakis, Markos, 55
management structure in Chilean copper mining: Chilean professionals in, 143–44; foreign nationals predominance in, 26–32
mano dura policy, 147–48
Manufactura de Cobre (Copper Manufacturers) (MADECO), 95
Manufactura de Metales (Metal Manufacturers) (MADEMSA), 95
March, Walter, 24, 29–32, 110
Marcosson, Isaac, 93
Maritime Confederation of Workers (COMACH), 86
Martin, Martin, 29
Martínez, Osvaldo, 66
Meany, George, 184
Medina, Arturo, 189–90
Medina, Guillermo, 182–83, 187
Melej, Carlos, 62
Mercier, Laurie, 62–63
Mexican copper miners, 113
Mexican maquiladoras, local management of, 143n.58
Michels, Rodolfo, 26
migratory labor patterns, Chilean mining and, 48–56
military coup of 1973: copper mining in aftermath of, 12; dismantling of labor movement and, 179–85; impact on copper industry of, 6; political repression following, 179–97
mining camps: Andes Copper construction of, 39–48; CODELCO closing of, 192–93; demographic changes in, 75–76; El Salvador project, 119–25; gender issues in, 54–56; government operation of, 141–44; social benefits and company regulations in, 43–48
mixed economic sectors, Allende's socialist reforms and, 156–60
modernization of Chilean copper mining: El Salvador project, 108–19; mining camp improvements, 119–25; production and company restructuring trends, 137–44
molybdenum plants, development of, 138

Monge, Luis Alberto, 75
Morales, Hernán, 181
Moran, Theodore, 74, 94, 98, 144
Moreno, Wenceslao, 182
Movimiento de Acción Popular Unitaria (Unitary People's Action Movement) (MAPU), 154, 156n.1
movimientos de viandas, 184–85
Munchemeyer, Carlos, 144
Muñoz Herrera, F., 37–38

National Federation of Bakers, 86
National Federation of Chemical and Pharmaceutical Workers, 87
nationalist ideology: labor political activism and, 100–107; political polarization concerning, 148–54
nationalization of copper mining, 2, 5; Allende regime and, 1, 5–6, 126, 155–60; community restructuring and, 167–71; Copper Workers' Federation demands for, 78–82; economic conditions and, 65–66, 88–89; labor force demands for, 88–90, 128–29, 151–54; Nuevo Trato and, 94–100; politicization and radicalization and, 144–45; workers' participation in, 160–67
National Union Coordinator (Coordinadora Nacional Sindical) (CNS), 185
neoliberal policies, copper mining and, 6
nitrate industry in Chile, 49
Nixon, Art, 183
Nuevo Trato of 1954, 74, 93–100, 108; labor opposition to, 100–107, 149; legacy of, 125–26; modernization of Chilean copper mining and, 118

Oasis newspaper, 97
Ocampo, Salvador, 80
Olivares, Héctor, 77–78, 152, 159
Olson, Raymond, 120
Ovalle, Manuel: imprisonment of, 152; layoffs protested by, 136–37; mine workers' salaries supported by, 89–90; mining strikes and, 84, 105, 147; Socialist Party and, 72–73, 77–78

Palacios, Galvarino, 100
Pan-Americanism, international labor solidarity and, 83–87
Parker, David, 52
Parliamentary Republic of Chile (1891–1924), Anaconda and, 15–18

Pearson, Norman, 132, 137
Perry, Vincent, 30, 109
Peru: geological exploration in, 109; nationalization of industry in, 153
Petras, James, 167
Phelps Dodge Company, 13
Piñera, José, 185
Pinochet, Augusto, 179–85, 190
Pinto, Aníbal, 74, 101
Poblete, Moisés, 67–70, 72
police and security operations: at Andes Copper Company, 43, 46–47; anti-strike activities of, 147; local control over, 141–44
political activism: of Chilean labor force, 39–48; class divisions and, 53; of copper workers, 2, 5, 25–26, 44–48; economic demands of labor and, 87–90; labor-state relations and, 100–107; military coup and repression of, 181–85; nationalist ideology and, 144–54; polarization among miners and, 145–54; strike support and, 66–70; union organization and, 57–63
political repression in Chile: of Communist Party, 11, 65–66, 70–74, 90; economic conditions and, 65–91; military coup and, 179–97; of mining labor force, 44–48, 65–91, 103–7, 146–54, 181–85; strike activity and, 71–74
Popular Front of 1936, 59–61, 70; state capitalism ideology and, 95, 97–98
Popular Socialist Party (PSP), 72–73, 77, 89
Popular Unity (Unidad Popular) (UP) coalition: labor relations with, 172–77; nationalization of copper and, 5–6, 12, 136, 155–60, 162–67
Porteous, J. Douglas, 123
Potrerillos mine, 3–4; anti-Communist legislation and conditions at, 72–73; base production at, 94; Chileanization proposals protested at, 150; Communist Party influence in, 61; community unionism in, 62–63; company store at, 46–48; company town structure at, 37–48; depletion and decline of, 75–76; development of, 11–12, 16–25; *enganche* system in, 48–56; foreign employees at, 26–35, 143–44; González Videla supported by, 70–74; government takeover of responsibilities in, 141–44; housing facilities at, 41–48; Labor Code's impact on, 59–63; labor history at, 5, 8–12; layoffs at, 133–37; management structure at, 26–32, 37; military coup of 1973 and repression at, 180–85; mining camp at, 39,

41; nationalization of copper industry and, 163–71; political activism at, 61–63, 65–66; Programa de Participación Popular at, 167; refinery construction at, 142–44; salaries and bonuses at, 55–56; Strategic Alliance reforms and, 192–93; strike activity at, 66–70, 73–74, 87–91, 101, 105, 129–33, 147, 150, 175–76; women employees at, 55–56
Potrerillos Plan, 192–93
Potrerillos Railway Company, 20–21; unions in, 59
price controls, Nuevo Trato elimination of, 94
Principios magazine, 72
private contracting, modernization of Chilean copper mines and, 139–44
private sector, Allende's socialist reforms and, 156–60
productivity, technological innovations and, 137–44
Professional Union of Caletones, 189
Programa de Empleo Mínimo, 186
Programa de Ocupación para Jefes de Hogar, 186
Program of Popular Participation (Participación Popular), 155, 163–67
Promoción Popular, 146
public sector workers: Allende's socialist reforms and, 156–60; Labor Code restrictions on, 58
Pueblo Hundido, 42–43, 48, 111, 119
Puentes, Juan Eduardo, 88
Puerto Montt, 147–48
Punto Final newspaper, 136, 152

Quinteros, Luis Alberto, 100

racial issues, foreign employees in Chilean mining and, 35
radicalization of politics, nationalist ideology and, 144–54
Radical Party, 41, 53, 60; Chileanization opposed by, 154; political reforms of, 65, 70–75; Popular Unity movement and, 156n.1; strikes supported by, 88–90, 104; union coalition with, 60–63
railway construction by mining companies, 20–21, 42–43
Raritan Copper Works, 24
Recabarren, Luis Emilio, 22–23
Reed, Paul, 82, 84, 105
Reglamento Interno de Participación, 163
Reinosismo ideology, 71–74
Reinoso, Luis, 71–74

"Revolution in Liberty" movement, 154
Ricketts, Louis D., 19
Robbins, H. E., 111
Roberts, J. T., 32
Rockefeller, Nelson, 83
Rodríguez, Anibal, 175
Rodríguez, Aniceto, 100
Rodríguez, Manuel, 134–35
Romualdi, Serafino, 82–84, 86
Rossetti, Juan, 72

salaries and bonuses for copper mine workers, 55–56; collective bargaining negotiations for, 129–33; Copper Workers' Federation demands for, 81–82; democratic transition and Labor Plan reforms and, 186–90; impact of modernization on, 139–44; stabilization programs and reduction of, 102–7; as strike issue, 87–90
Sales, Reno, 31
Salzinger, Leslie, 143n.58
Sánchez, Carlos, 139
Sánchez, Estaban, 160
San Manuel mine (Arizona), 113n.74
Santana, Guillermo, 173, 182–83
Santiago Mining Company, 16–17
Sariego, Juan Luis, 113
Saunders, William B., 21–22
school construction in mining camps, 44–45
Seguel, Rodolfo, 188–90
seniority, lack of, for Chilean mine workers, 135–37
Sepúlveda, José Luis, 41
silicosis, copper miners' risk of, 50–51
Silva, Ramón, 61, 88, 104
sindicato industrial (plant/industrial union), 57
sindicato professional (professional/craft union), 57
Social Democratic Party (PSD) 156n.1
socialism, nationalization of copper industry and, 155–60
Socialist Party of Chile (PSCh), 72–73
Socialist Party (Partido Obrera Socialista [POS]), 22; activism of, 39; Allende and, 156–60; Chileanization opposed by, 154; class issues in support for, 53; Copper Workers Federation and, 77–78; Frei administration and, 149–50; labor movement tensions with, 72–74; military coup and repression of, 181–85; Popular Unity movement and, 156n.1; strikes supported by, 88–90; union alliance with, 60–63

Socialist Republic (Chile), failure of, 25
Sociedad Nacional de Minería (National Mining Society) (SONAMI), 143
sovereignty issues, nationalization of copper industry and, 158–60
Soviet Union, Chile's relations with, 71
state capitalism ideology, 95
state government structure: El Salvador project and, 118–19; joint ventures with foreign mining and, 148–49; labor force activism and, 127–29; military coup and economic policies of, 183–18; nationalist ideology and, 100–107; refinery construction and industrialization initiatives, 142–44
Statute of Copper Workers (1956), 11, 106–7, 474; labor reforms and, 185; legacy of, 125–26; negation of, 186; reform proposals for, 151, 152
Strategic Alliance, 191–93
strike activity: Chileanization project protests, 150–54; in copper mines, 66–70; Copper Workers' Federation and, 81–82; democratic transition and Labor Plan limits on, 186–90; economic demands and, 87–90; economic impact of, 129–33; government opposition to, 147–54; nationalization of copper and, 171–77; national political crises and, 101–7; national strike initiative of CTF, 188–90; *paro patronal* (bourgeois strike) of 1972, 161–62; political repression and, 71–74; by supervisors, 174–77
subcontracting, modernization of copper mining and, 139–44
Swayne, William, 110, 112, 118

Tapia, Benito, 181
Tapia, Luis, 76–77
taxes on copper industry: job layoffs and, 137; Nuevo Trato and, 94–100
technological innovation in copper mining, production and company restructuring trends, 137–44
Thayer, William, 105, 146, 151
Toole, K. Ross, 14–15
Toro, Luis, 133
Torres, Isauro, 62
trade union immunity *(fuero sindical)*, 57–58, 81–82
transnational capitalism, Anaconda in Chile and, 14–18
Trask, Frank, 112

Treaty of Washington (1951), 80, 95, 149
Trench, Edwin, 153

unemployment: copper mining industry deterioration and, 75–76; layoff patterns at mines and, 133–37
union organizations: Allende regime and, 171–77; contract workers denounced by, 140–41; copper mining and history of, 6–12; democratic transition and Labor Plan and, 185–90; economic nationalism and, 65–66; electoral politics and, 188–90; government repression of, 101–7, 146–54, 179–97; layoffs protested by, 133–37; military coup and repression of, 179–85; political and social impact of, 2, 5, 37, 43, 56–63; political polarization among, 145–54; Strategic Alliance and, 191–93; strikes in copper mining and, 66–70; unemployment threats and, 76
Unión para la Victoria, 68
Unión Socialista Popular (USOPO), 171
United Mine Workers Journal, 86
United Mine Workers (UMW), 82, 84, 105
United States copper companies: anti-labor rhetoric of, 132–33; Chilean conflicts with, 80–82; Chileanization policy and, 153–54; dominance in Chilean mining management of, 27–32; nationalization of copper mines and, 157–60; Nuevo Trato of 1954 and, 93–100, 103–4
United States labor organizations: military coup protested by, 184; solidarity with Chilean miners, 82–87, 104–5
University of Chicago, 183
U.S. Agency for International Development (USAID), 182

Vásquez, Raúl, 170
Velasco Alvarado, Juan, 153
Venezuela, oil industry in, 50
Vera, Mario, 98
Verdu, Angelo, 84
Vergara, Arturo, 73–74
Vergara, Roberto, 117
Villarzú, Juan, 195

Viviendas Económicas del Norte (VIENOR), 169
volunteer programs in mining camps, nationalization initiatives for, 170–71

wage policies in Chilean copper mines, for foreign nationals, 30–32
Wallace, Louis R., 19–20, 22
Weed, Clyde, 117–18
white-collar mine workers *(empleados)*, 49–53; Allende regime and, 171–77; Copper Workers Federation and, 77–82; family allowances for, 79n.56; impact of modernization on, 139–44; Labor Code provisions for, 50, 52–53, 57–63; layoffs of, 134–37; military coup of 1973 and, 182–85; modernization of El Salvador and, 122–25; nationalization impact on, 173–77; strikes by, 174–77
Winn, Peter, 190–91
women in mining communities: conditions for, 55–56; Frei supported by, 145; Labor Code provisions for, 58–63; modernization efforts at El Salvador and, 123–25; strike support from, 67–70, 104
worker representation (participación popular), in mining management, 136–37
working conditions: for copper miners, 3, 50–51; on El Salvador mining project, 111–19; impact of modernization on, 139–44; Labor Code regulation of, 58–63; labor force demands concerning, 133–37; labor history and impact of, 10–12; nationalization of copper industry and, 161–67; at Potrerillos mine, 21–25
World War II, impact on copper mining of, 68
Wraith, William, 20, 23

Yáñez, Hugo, 165, 174
Yerington mine project (Anaconda Copper Company), 108–10, 112

Zambia, copper production in, 75
Zapata, Francisco, 6–7, 167

www.ingramcontent.com/pod-product-compliance
Lightning Source LLC
Chambersburg PA
CBHW021943290426

44108CB00012B/951